**BIVOCATIONAL MINISTRY FOR THE SAKE OF THE GOSPEL**
Copyright © 2021
College Press Publishing Co., Inc.
All rights reserved
ISBN: 9780899005478
www.collegepress.com

Unless otherwise noted, all Scripture quotations in this book are from the 1995 *New American Standard Bible* by the Lockman Foundation.

# TABLE OF CONTENTS

i

# FIGURES

# TABLES

# ACKNOWLEDGMENTS

This book grew out of the dissertation I wrote while I was a student at Western Seminary. I owe a debt of gratitude to the wonderful people who helped me with my research. During the spring of 2017, I undertook the massive project of sending out surveys to over 5,000 churches listed in the *2016 Directory of the Ministry*.[1] Later in the fall of 2017, I conducted a follow up survey of 432 Ministers. I want to thank the members of the Minnehaha Church of Christ and the students of Northwest College of the Bible who helped me stuff, label, and stamp over 5,000 envelopes. Jason and Karissa Parrish, Lois Dailey, Reilly Deaton, Jordan Devena, Sam Judd, Janelle Judd, Jessica Judd, Rachel Judd, Melissa Judd, Jimmy Kennedy, Stephanie Kennedy, Lauren Priest, Elliott Ryan, Joyce Ryan, Mark Williams and Rose Marie Williams, you guys are AWESOME!

I also want to thank the first readers of this project who gave me valuable insights and constructive criticism. Thank you, Cal Habig, Steve Mathewson, Adam Christian, Reid Kisling, and Jonathan Haukaas. Your unique perspectives helped me to see important concerns that I never would have considered. The time you generously gave to this project has helped me to transform my often clumsy and awkward writing into something God can use for His glory and the building up of His Kingdom.

Thanks to all my fellow workers in Christ,

**Mike Kennedy**

---

1. Judy Noll, *2016 Directory of the Ministry: A Yearbook of Christian Churches and Churches of Christ* *(Springfield, IL.)*, 2016.

# PREFACE

This book examines the effectiveness of bivocational ministry when it is focused on the gospel. The research for this project was a mixed methods approach based primarily on two surveys conducted in 2017. The first survey was a quantitative survey of over five thousand churches. The main purpose of the first survey was to find out how many of the ministers in the independent Christian Churches and instrumental Churches of Christ are bivocational. The second survey was a qualitative survey of the 432 bivocational ministers who responded to the first survey. The main purpose of the second survey was to gather information about how the gospel is helping bivocational ministers and how bivocational ministers are viewing the connection between the gospel and the effectiveness of their ministries. This book seeks to answer two questions: "What does it mean for a bivocational minister to be gospel-centered?" and "How can the gospel help the bivocational minister be more effective?"

The first part of the book (chapters 2-7) focuses on answering the first question. The second half of the book (chapters 8-13) focuses on answering the second question. From my research and personal experience, I hope to show how the gospel provides both the best motivation and the best model for effective and fulfilling bivocational ministry.

# CHAPTER 1

*"I do all things for the sake of the gospel,
so that I may become a fellow partaker of it."*
—1 Corinthians 9:23

*"Of this gospel I was made a minister
according to the gift of God's grace, which
was given me by the working of his power."*
—Ephesians 3:7 (ESV)

Have you ever had a crisis of purpose or calling in your life? Have you ever evaluated your ministry, your motives and your methods and wondered, "Am I doing what God wants me to do for the right reason and in the right way?" Have you ever looked at your struggles, sacrifices, and shortcomings and prayed, "God, why did You choose me for this? Are you sure You got the right person for this job?" I have wrestled with those questions many times in my life. One of those times was on a mission trip to Jamaica. Yes, people do go on mission trips to Jamaica. And no, this was not a call to share the gospel at luxurious resorts on the beach. Occasionally, I teach at the Jamaica Bible Seminary where Jamaican students from the rural mountain churches come and take classes. In 2015, I went a couple weeks early with a work team to help with medical clinics, vacation Bible school, and construction projects. Whenever I go on a mission trip, I always keep a prayer journal. This is the entry for Tuesday, July 28, 2015:

> Dear Father,
> Thank You for another great day serving in Jamaica. I really see Your hand moving and working in the lives and ministries of all the people on this trip… I think the group we have this week is working together really well. I have been giving devotions each night from the book of Exodus. And each night, several people have shared about how You are opening their eyes and helping them to grow as they serve. Today, I talked about Moses and how Moses asked, "Who am I?" Sometimes I wonder who I am that You would choose me to do what You have called me to do. But then I remember what You said to Paul, how Your power is perfected in my weakness. Thank You! Love, Mike.

In that prayer, the Holy Spirit reminded me of 2 Corinthians 12:9, and that was comforting. However, at that point, I had not allowed the dynamic principle of grace to saturate my soul. It was still just a theological doctrine stored somewhere on the hard drive of my brain. In my heart, my emotions were still wrestling with my purpose and calling in life. Exactly one week later, God answered my questions with a penetrating display of 2 Corinthians 12:9 in the life of a bivocational Jamaican preacher. We were working in a small mountain community called "Top Hill." This was my journal entry for Tuesday, August 4, 2015:

> Dear Father,
> Thank You for another great day in Jamaica… Today, most of the men in our group went up to Nathan's house to work on building him some steps into his house and pouring a concrete floor. Right now, Nathan, his wife, and two children have cinder blocks for steps and a dirt floor. They have no running water and very little food. God, help us to be a blessing to this family…

Nathan Stewart is a humble yet dedicated minister of the gospel. He is motivated to serve and sacrifice because his life was transformed by the gospel. Through the gospel, God rescued Nathan from a childhood of heartache and rejection. At the Top Hill Church of Christ, Nathan continued to grow in his faith, love, and knowledge. He began to lead the youth group and help out with the preaching. The main preacher at Top Hill drove in from out of town and was only there on Sundays. Nathan, however, lived in Top Hill. He has been a part of the community for over thirty years. He is known both in the church and in the community as a man of character with a good work ethic and a sincere faith. Soon after that mission trip in 2015, Nathan became the main preacher of the Top Hill congregation. He continued to work at the local hardware store for about $60 a week while the church gave him about $40 a week for his ministry.

On that mission trip, God used Nathan Stewart to open my eyes and give me a glimpse of what it means to be a bivocational minister for the sake of the gospel. As I was flying back home and thinking about my job and ministry in Vancouver Washington, I pulled out my prayer journal and wrote these words:

> Dear Father,
>      Thank You again for an amazing and life-shaping mission trip. I especially want to thank You for the powerful example and testimony I see in Nathan Stewart. God, please take care of him and his family. He is living out the message of the gospel in Mark 8:34-35 while he preaches the message of the gospel. Help me to have that same kind of faith and dedication in the ministries You have entrusted to me... I am reminded of the words on my ordination certificate and the weight of responsibility they carry. "The Church of Christ... sends greetings to all of like precious faith. This is to certify that our beloved brother Michael Kennedy was formally ordained to the Ministry of the Gospel on the 4th day of April 1993. And we commend him to our Brethren in all the world."

If you have been ordained into the ministry you probably have a similar document hanging on the wall in your office or packed up in a box somewhere. If you do, look at what it says. Read it out loud. What does it mean for you to be a minister of the gospel? If you are like most ministers, you are confident that God has called you to be a minister of the gospel. But if you are anything like me, you occasionally wonder if you are answering that call the way God wants you to.

I am a "bivocational" minister. That simply means I am a minister employed by the local church, but I also have a job outside the ministry of the church. As a bivocational minister, I often feel overwhelmed with responsibilities and time demands pulling me in different directions. As a minister of a small congregation in a "non-denominational" fellowship, I occasionally feel isolated and alone. But I am not alone. Thom Rainer notes that "50% of all churches in America average less than 100 in worship attendance."[2] In many cases, small churches are not able to support a full-time minister.

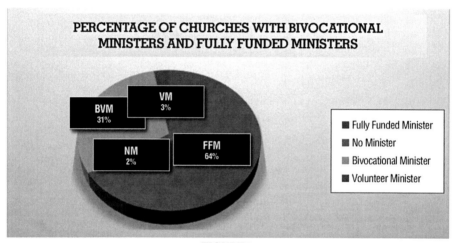

FIGURE 1

As part of my research for this book, I conducted a survey of all the churches listed in the *2016 Directory of the Ministry*.[3] This first survey revealed that 31 percent of the Churches of Christ and Christian Churches in the United States have bivocational ministers (BVM), 64 percent have fully funded ministers (FFM), 3 percent have volunteer ministers (VM) and 2 percent have no ministers (NM).[4]

---

2. Thom Rainer, "One Key Reason Most Churches Do Not Exceed 350 in Average Attendance," *ThomRainer. Com,* last modified March 25, 2015, accessed May 28, 2017, http://thomrainer.com/2015/03/one-key-reason-churches-exceed-350-average-attendance/.

3. Judy Noll, *2016 Directory of the Ministry: A Yearbook of Christian Churches and Churches of Christ* (Springfield, IL.), 2016.

4  Michael Kennedy, "Bivocational Ministry for the Sake of the Gospel: A Study of Effective Bivocational Ministry among the Churches of Christ and Christian Churches" (DMin. Dissertation, Western Seminary, 2018), 228.

Many bivocational ministers feel like they are trapped in a situation they can't get out of. Because of the demanding schedule of two jobs, they don't have the time or energy it takes to build up a congregation to where it can support a full-time minister. Many small congregations feel a similar frustration when they are struggling to meet their budget each year and desperately wanting to put their minister on full-time support. Few if any ministers began their preparation for ministry with the plans to be bivocational. Few if any Bible colleges have classes specifically designed to prepare students for bivocational ministry.[5]

While there are many struggles and difficulties that accompany bivocational ministry, there are also many opportunities for evangelism, discipleship, and service that are unique to bivocational ministry. Thom Rainer identified some of these opportunities in an article he wrote about a new kind of bivocational minister.[6] We typically think of a bivocational minister as a minister in a small congregation that cannot afford to pay their preacher a full-time wage. However, in this article, Rainer considers a growing trend of bivocational ministers in larger churches that *can* afford to pay them a full-time wage. These ministers are strategically *choosing* to be bivocational not out of necessity but for positive reasons that are helping the church and the community. Rainer calls these pastors "marketplace ministers" (Acts 17:17). He predicts that this trend will continue to gain momentum.

If large churches see bivocational ministry as more than just a financial benefit, shouldn't small churches also have a more positive view of bivocational ministry? Perhaps the small churches with bivocational ministers have a much greater potential for growth and effective service than they realize. Perhaps bivocational ministry should be a dynamic strategy rather than a fallback position. Perhaps Bible colleges and seminaries can intentionally and strategically prepare students for effective bivocational ministries. In this book, I will explore these possibilities and present bivocational ministry for the sake of the gospel as an effective and fulfilling method of ministry.

## THE PURPOSE

I have three driving motivations for writing this book. First, I have a heart for bivocational ministers. Having been bivocational for many years, I understand

---

5. Kennedy, 260.
6. Thom S. Rainer, "Eight Characteristics of the New Bivocational Pastor," *ThomRainer.Com,* January 18, 2016, accessed June 17, 2016, http://thomrainer.com/2016/01/eight-characteristics-of-the-new-bivocational-pastor/.

some of the frustrations, obstacles, and challenges commonly faced in this kind of ministry. It is my earnest desire to provide a resource for my fellow bivocational ministers that will help them find fulfillment and effectiveness in their ministries.

Second, I am also writing because of the personal investment I have made in students who are preparing for ministry. For the last twenty-five years, I have seen dozens of students giving their time, money, and effort to prepare for ministry, assuming that, when they graduate, they will easily find a full-time ministry position. Then when they graduate and realize that their dream job is highly unlikely, they quickly discover that they are not prepared for a bivocational ministry. I have written this book to serve as a ministry textbook. I hope and pray that Bible colleges and Christian universities will recognize the need to include training in this area for their ministry students.

Third, and most importantly, I am writing from a sincere passion for the gospel. I am convinced that regardless of whether we are full-time ministers, bivocational ministers, or ministry volunteers, all of us, as Christians, have a bivocational calling. We are all called to be ministers in the Lord's Church *and* missionaries in this fallen world. It is my goal to encourage all Christians to view their calling through the lens of the gospel. I will talk more about our callings in chapter three, but the Bible says that we have been called through the gospel (2 Thess. 2:14). The calling we have through the gospel certainly includes our own personal salvation, but it is much bigger than that. If you don't get anything else out of this book, please get this gospel principle. This is the main point of the book: the key to effectiveness and fulfillment in every Christian's ministry is found in the gospel.

## THE SCOPE

I am focusing my research on bivocational ministry among independent Christian Churches and instrumental Churches of Christ for four reasons. First, I am more familiar with this tradition than any other. This is the fellowship I have been a part of all my life. My father was a bivocational preacher in a small instrumental Church of Christ. And I know several other bivocational ministers in Christian churches and Churches of Christ. Second, there are certain aspects in our heritage and our theology that can have a significant impact on the effectiveness of bivocational ministry. Third, no one has done any research on bivocational ministry in the Restoration Movement. If our movement is going to be prepared for the future of this growing trend, we need to know where we stand and how to move forward. And fourth, most of the literature on bivocational ministry comes from a denominational perspective. The models and examples of bivocational ministry that I read about usually begin with the assumption of denominational structure and support. While isolation is often a problem among bivocational ministers in all denominations, it is much more pronounced in non-denominational churches. I want this book to be a helpful and practical resource for bivocational ministers in non-denominational congregations.

While my research will focus on bivocational ministers within the Restoration Movement, my hope is that most of the observations and insights gathered will be general enough to benefit bivocational ministries in any Christian tradition. I believe that this study will provide a much-needed resource both for ministers and students preparing for ministry.

## THE TERMINOLOGY

There are some terms that I will be using throughout this book that should be defined upfront. Many of these words have more than one meaning and you will have to consider the context to determine how each word is being used. A few of the words are terms I rarely use, but because the literature I quote uses them, you should probably know what they mean.

### VOCATION

Most people, when they hear the word, "vocation," think of a job or a career. In fact, that is the primary definition given for this word in modern dictionaries. However, in this book, I will be using this term to refer to more than just a person's career. I will explain in chapter three how this term originally referred to person's divine calling regardless of whether he or she was paid to fulfill that calling.

### BIVOCATIONAL

"Bivocational" refers to a person who has two different vocations. I will often use this term to refer to people who have two different callings regardless of whether they are being paid to fulfill those callings. However, I recognize that most of the current literature uses this word to refer to employment more so than calling.

## BIVOCATIONAL MINISTER

Most people see a bivocational minister as someone who has two or more jobs at the same time, one job being employed as a minister of a local congregation and the other job being employed by some other organization. Luther Dorr writes, "The term refers to a minister who earns his living through two vocations."[7] Doran McCarty says, "Bivocational ministers are persons who serve more than one vocation or institution and/or whose income is partly derived from some other source than the institutions of their primary religious employment."[8] Dennis Bickers chooses to define a bivocational minister as "anyone who serves in a paid ministry capacity in a church and has other personal sources of income."[9] While I generally accept these definitions as valid, I don't like the way they focus on time and money and fail to say anything about calling. Ray Gilder provides the missing element when he writes, "The root meaning of vocation is 'calling.' A bivocational pastor is called to pastor a church and also has another job or activity to which he gives part of his time and attention."[10] In this book, I will emphasize the importance of seeing both vocations as callings.

## PART-TIME MINISTER

This is another term used to refer to bivocational ministers. I prefer not to use this term for two reasons. First, it emphasizes the time of paid ministry rather than the call to ministry. The second problem with this description is that it implies that the minister is only doing ministry part of the time. As a result, some bivocational ministers see the phrase as demeaning. Bickers notes:

> Bivocational ministry is looked at by some as "second-class" ministry performed by people who don't have the gifts to serve a larger church. At times, those who don't understand the need for bivocational ministers question our commitment to ministry. Some continue to refer to us as "part-time" preachers.[11]

7. Luther M. Dorr, *The Bivocational Pastor* (Nashville, TN: B&H Publishing Group, 1988), 3.
8. Doran C. McCarty ed., *Meeting the Challenge of Bivocational Ministry* (Nashville, TN: Seminary Extension of the Southern Baptist Seminaries, 1996), 7.
9. Dennis W. Bickers, *The Work of the Bivocational Minister* (Valley Forge, PA: Judson Press, 2007), 2.
10. Ray Gilder, *Uniquely Bivocational-Understanding the Life of a Pastor Who Has a Second Job: For Bivocational Pastors and Their Churches* (Forest, VA: Salt & Light Publishing, 2013), 3.
11. Dennis Bickers, *The Bivocational Pastor: Two Jobs, One Ministry* (Kansas City, MO: Beacon Hill Press, 2004), 8.2004

## DUAL-ROLE MINISTER

The term "dual-role" minister is not used very often in the literature on bivocational ministry. Back in 1976, this term was given a rigid definition by the CODE (Clergy Occupational Development and Employment) project. In his book about the project, John Elliott says,

> The term "Dual Role minister" is defined as a fully trained, ordained clergyperson who is employed full time (thirty-five to forty hours a week) in a nonchurch job as well as twenty to twenty-five hours a week as a pastor or in a specialized church staff function.[12]

Even when the description is used in a general way, it still places the emphasis on the two different roles or types of work the minister is doing rather than on the calling.

## TENTMAKER

I like this description because it calls our attention to the New Testament examples of bivocational ministry that we see in the Apostle Paul and his coworkers, Priscilla and Aquila. However, a lot of people have no idea what I'm talking about when I say that "I am a tentmaker." In Christian circles, the word also has a broader range of meaning than the phrase "bivocational minister." Sometimes the word is used to refer to any Christian who uses his or her occupation to share the gospel. Sometimes the word is used to describe self-supporting church planters. And sometimes the word is used to describe a strategy for foreign missions. Patrick Lai observes:

> Tentmaking is often understood to refer to an economic factor: "a missionary being financially self-supporting." A handful of missiologists stubbornly stress this narrow point of view, relating Tentmaking to money. However, Tentmaking is not about money; it is about God. Tentmaking is about a way of revealing God's glory to the ends of the earth…Tentmakers know that Tentmaking is not about money, visas, entry strategies, or all the other issues missiologists love to debate.[13]

---

12. John Y. Elliott, *Our Pastor Has an Outside Job: New Strength for the Church Through Dual Role Ministry* (Valley Forge, PA: Judson Press, 1980), 7.

13 Patrick Lai, *Tentmaking: The Life and Work of Business as Missions* (Downers Grove, IL: IVP Books, 2006), 3.

## FULL-TIME MINISTER

"Full-time" ministry simply means that the minister is receiving all his income from his employment as a minister and he does not have another job on the side. The "full-time" aspect refers to the minister's wages more so than the amount of time he puts into ministry. Many ministers do more than forty hours of ministry each week and yet they are only being paid a "part-time" wage. I will occasionally use this term. However, I do recognize that it has the same drawbacks as the term "part-time." The idea of being "full-time" places the emphasis on the time and the money rather than the calling and purpose of ministry. The term also gives people the idea that ministers who are not "full-time" are not fully devoted to the ministry or that they are not ministers all the time.

## FULLY FUNDED MINISTER

This seems to be the preferred term to describe the minister who receives a full-time wage from the church. However, this word is not without problems. Dennis Bickers describes an objection he heard concerning this description. He writes:

> Not everyone appreciates the new terminology. One fully funded pastor took great offense at my use of the term fully funded. He feels that he and many other ministers he knows are not adequately compensated by their churches for the work they do.[14]

Again, this term places the emphasis on the money rather than the calling. However, we don't have a term for this role that draws our attention to the calling. We could invent a new word like "uni-vocational," but somehow, I don't think that's going to fly.

## RESTORATION MOVEMENT

While there have been many "restoration movements" throughout church history, I will be using this phrase to refer to the early nineteenth-century unity/restoration movement. At that time, there were several Christian leaders from different denominations in America who wanted to put away denominational divisions and restore New Testament Christianity. The more prominent early leaders of this movement included Thomas Campbell, Alexander Campbell, Barton Stone, and Walter Scott.

---

14. Bickers, *The Work of the Bivocational Minister*, 3.

## STONE/CAMPBELL MOVEMENT

In order to distinguish the Restoration Movement from other similar movements in church history, some of the literature uses the phrase "Stone/Campbell Movement" instead of "Restoration Movement." I prefer the latter simply because those early leaders would have been strongly opposed to naming the movement after themselves. I am convinced that all the early leaders of the movement would have rejected the label "Stone/Campbell Movement" as unbiblical and divisive. They did not claim to be the "only Christians" but they insisted on being known as "Christians only."[15]

## INSTRUMENTAL CHURCHES OF CHRIST

Ironically, this "unity/restoration" movement could not remain unified. Shortly after the Civil War, some churches began to change in ways that other churches saw as unauthorized and unbiblical. One of those changes was the use of musical instruments in the worship service. This eventually resulted in a division between the instrumental churches and the non-instrumental churches. Instrumental Churches of Christ believe that worship with musical instruments is a matter of Christian liberty.

## INDEPENDENT CHRISTIAN CHURCHES

Sadly, the movement split again in the twentieth century. One of the distinct characteristics of the movement was always a strong emphasis on local autonomy. Among the instrumental churches, there were many "Christian Churches" and "Disciples of Christ" churches that were more liberal in their view of Scripture. For various reasons many of these churches chose to form a denominational structure. When that happened, the denomination became known as the Christian Church (Disciples of Christ). Those Christian Churches that refused to join the denomination became known as "Independent" Christian Churches.

The research for this book includes surveys conducted among all the ministers of the churches listed in the *Directory of the Ministry*. In the 2016 edition, this directory is a list of 5,032 independent Christian Churches and instrumental Churches of Christ in the United States.

---

15. James D. Murch, *Christians Only: A History of the Restoration Movement* (Cincinnati, OH: Standard Publishing, 1962).

## THE FOCUS

I applaud the work the Southern Baptist Conference has done to support the bivocational pastors in their denomination. I also appreciate the authors from various denominations who have written books and articles about bivocational ministry. While these resources are usually directed at ministers within a denominational setting, they can be helpful to the ministers of non-denominational churches. However, most of these resources fail to focus on the most important aspect of bivocational ministry: the gospel.

Church leaders need to start thinking about the connection between bivocational ministry and the ministry of the gospel. A lot of people are writing about gospel-centered ministry and several authors have written about bivocational ministry. But no one seems to be connecting the dots. The gospel brings "good news" to the community it touches in more ways than one. When the gospel is proclaimed and lived out by Christians in a community, all the people of that community are blessed in practical ways. Bivocational ministry holds great potential for bringing these gospel blessings both to the Christians in the local congregation and to the people outside the walls of the church building. The focus of this book will be to show why and how a gospel-centered approach is essential for effective bivocational ministry.

# DISCUSSION QUESTIONS

1. If you have an ordination certificate, what does it say? If you don't have one, ask a pastor or minister who has one if you can see it and write down what it says. What are the implications of the words recorded on that certificate?

2. What do you think it means to be a minister of the gospel?

3. In your opinion, how important is it for a minister of a congregation to be ordained? Are ordination ceremonies and certificates just empty traditions, or do they serve a meaningful and practical purpose?

4. What does it mean to be a bivocational minister?

5. Why might a bivocational minister feel like he is trapped in a ministry that cannot grow or improve?

6. Why might a minister in a large church choose to be bivocational even if he doesn't need to be bivocational?

7. The author claims that "isolation is often a problem among bivocational ministers." What does he mean by "isolation"? Why would that be a common problem for bivocational ministers?

8. The author suggests that isolation is "more pronounced in non-denominational churches." Do you agree? Why or why not?

9. Why might someone think that a minister who is not working full-time for a church is not fully devoted to the ministry?

10. What does the author believe to be the most important thing to focus on in bivocational ministry? Do you agree? Why or why not?

# CHAPTER 2

THE BUS DRIVING PREACHER

"If others share the right over you, do we not more?
Nevertheless, we did not use this right, but we endure all things
so that we will cause no hindrance to the gospel of Christ."
—1 Corinthians 9:12

When I survey the wondrous cross
On which the Prince of glory died,
My richest gain I count but loss,
And pour contempt on all my pride.
—Isaac Watts

## THIS IS MY STORY

The small suburban church in Vancouver, Washington was facing a financial crisis. I had been their full-time minister for five years but in 2007 we had a difficult decision to make. Should I take a cut in pay and get a part-time "secular" job? Or should we just let the church struggle through the recession as missions and ministries continued to get cut out of the budget?

I remembered my father running a janitorial business and preaching in a small church. He had been a bivocational minister throughout my childhood. As a child, that kind of ministry seemed normal to me. However, as an adult, I had never thought of bivocational ministry as God's calling in my life until it seemed like I had no other choice. Even then, I saw it more as a trial God wanted me to endure rather than a ministry for the sake of the gospel.

There were some bus drivers in the congregation who told me that the local school district was looking for drivers. I also knew of several pastors who had been bus drivers at different times in their ministries, so I began to consider the possible blessings and struggles of bivocational ministry. There was the potential of being overworked. Would I be able to manage my time wisely, giving the necessary attention to my family and my ministry without getting burned out? However, there was also the potential to develop new contacts with people outside the church. I would be working with over a hundred fellow bus drivers in addition to school employees, students, and parents.

When I decided to take the job, I pictured myself as a baseball player stepping up to the plate with the bases loaded. I thought to myself, "This could turn out to be incredibly good…or this could turn into a nightmare. I could either hit a home run or I could strike out." Unfortunately, when I stepped up to the plate, my stance was all wrong. I was focused only on what I thought would be good for me and my ministry. I thought, "The only way I will be able to go back to full-time ministry is if the church gets out of this economic slump. And that's not going to happen unless the church grows."

Christians who work in the public-school system are limited in the ways they can share the gospel. But I kept looking for evangelistic opportunities at work that would somehow be acceptable. Three weeks into my new job, I invited all the students on my middle school route to be my friend on Myspace. I thought, "Perhaps if some of these students saw the church youth programs and activities on my social media, they might just show up without me actually inviting them." Oblivious to the concerns of others, I had no idea how my awkward invitation was making people feel. Catie Larimer, one of the students on the bus who was also a church member, talked to me about it at youth group. With a puzzled expression, she asked, "Mr. Mike, why did you do that?" I began to realize my blunder. I was selfishly thinking only from my own perspective and not from the perspective of the students and parents in the community that I was entrusted to serve. If a forty-year-old man invited my teenage daughter to be his friend on Myspace, I would have been outraged! That was strike one.

Later that week, I was called into my supervisor's office. Several parents had called the transportation office to voice their concerns about the creepy new bus driver. I was warned not to cross the line of separation between church and state. I knew I was out of line and I needed to change my perspective. So instead of aiming for an evangelistic home run, I swung the pendulum in the other direction. I started to see myself as the sacrificial martyr taking one for the team. I thought, "Maybe God just wants me to develop more humility, perseverance, and faith. I just need to trust Him as I endure this trial of having a secular job." I'm sure God was working on my heart to help me grow in those areas; however, the victim mentality did not help me develop any of those character traits. It did not help me to minister more effectively to the members of my congregation. It did not help me to produce an encouraging environment on my bus where students could flourish. That was strike two. I knew I was still missing something, but I didn't see what God wanted me to see. I wasn't evaluating my situation from a gospel perspective. I needed to stand with Isaac Watts at Calvary and "survey the wondrous cross." I needed to allow the gospel to motivate me to sacrifice "my richest gain" and empower me to "pour contempt on all my pride."

We will come back to my story later. For now, let's consider the reality that many ministers and churches are facing in our current culture.

## FACING THE FACTS

Whether we like it or not bivocational ministry is going to be the only reasonable option for many churches and ministers, especially after the events of 2020. Many churches today are struggling with financial difficulties. According to a report from the National Congregations Study, "the average congregation has only 75 regular participants and an annual budget of $90,000."[16] In his book, *The Tentmaking Pastor,* Dennis Bickers says that "Approximately 60 percent of all Protestant churches now average less than one hundred in attendance, and this percentage continues to grow as established churches continue to age. Few of these churches can afford a fully funded pastor."[17] The financial struggles of ministry will continue to compound as the older, more generous church members move on to their heavenly reward.

---

16. Mark Chaves, Shawna Anderson, and Jason Byassee, "American Congregations at the Beginning of the 21st Century," *National Congregations Study,* (2007) http://www.soc.duke.edu/natcong/Docs/NCSII_report_final.pdf, accessed 10/9/2018.
17. Dennis Bickers, *The Tentmaking Pastor: The Joy of Bivocational Ministry,* (Grand Rapids, MI: Baker Books, 2000), 29.

### THE PERCENTAGE OF U.S. ADULTS WHO REPORT
### DONATING 10% OR MORE OF INCOME, BY GENERATION

| | % Millennials (born 1984-2002) | % Gen-Xers (born 1965-1983) | % Boomers (born 1946-1964) | % Elders (born before 1946) |
|---|---|---|---|---|
| To a church | 1 | 2 | 3 | 7 |
| To a nonprofit | 3 | 4 | 4 | 8 |
| Did not tithe to a church or nonprofit | 95 | 93 | 92 | 85 |

TABLE 1

Table 1 is from a 2016 report showing the sobering generosity gap between the different generations.[18] This table shows that elders (those born before 1946) are by far, the most generous of all church attendees when it comes to giving to the local church. Who is going to pay the salary of our full-time ministers twenty years from now when all our generous givers are gone?

Research shows that bivocational ministry is a growing trend in American Churches. In 2009, Robert LaRochelle noted that "in some states, the majority of current openings for pastors fall under the aegis of part-time."[19] Nearly half of the Southern Baptist churches in the country rely on bivocational ministers.[20] Many of the recent articles that discuss bivocational ministry identify decreasing membership and financial struggles as the main reasons for this growing trend.

According to the last twelve *Directories of the Ministry,* the total number of independent Christian Churches and instrumental Churches of Christ has dropped from 5,330 to 4,287. In the last six years, the total church membership in these churches has dropped from 1,285,046 to 1,224,117. However, there are many new church plants that have not registered in the *Directory of the Ministry.* The number that appears to be growing is the total number of mega-churches (table 2). When smaller churches that are struggling to survive finally give up and close their doors the remaining members and resources are often absorbed by a larger church in the area.

---

18. David Kinnaman, *The Generosity Gap: How Christians' Perceptions and Practices of Giving Are Changing—and What It Means for the Church* (Ventura, CA: Barna Group, 2017), 9.
19. Robert LaRochelle, *Part-Time Pastor, Full-Time Church* (Cleveland, OH: The Pilgrim Press, 2010), 21.
20. Bob Smietana, "More preachers need a 'day job,' too," *USA Today,* (6/29/2010), http://usatoday30.usatoday.com/news/religion/2010-06-21-preachers20_ST_N.htm, accessed 10/9/2018.

## MEMBERSHIP STATISTICS FOR THE INDEPENDENT CHRISTIAN CHURCHES AND INSTRUMENTAL CHURCHES OF CHRIST

| | Total Number of Churches | Number of Churches Reporting a Membership of 1,000 or more | Number of Churches Reporting a Membership of less than 1,000 | Estimated Total Membership |
|------|------|------|------|------|
| 2009 | 5,330 | 152 | 4,653 | 1,242,235 |
| 2010 | 5,325 | 157 | 4,637 | 1,260,288 |
| 2011 | 5,346 | 158 | 4,640 | 1,272,174 |
| 2012 | 5,320 | 159 | 4,615 | 1,274,665 |
| 2013 | 5,283 | 161 | 4,548 | 1,264,131 |
| 2014 | 5,289 | 162 | 4,521 | 1,269,084 |
| 2015 | 5,087 | 170 | 4,352 | 1,285,046 |
| 2016 | 5,032 | 172 | 4,300 | 1,254,788 |
| 2017 | 4,973 | 171 | 4,260 | 1,230,595 |
| 2018 | 4,921 | 171 | 4,213 | 1,228,573 |
| 2019 | 4,867 | 173 | 4,167 | 1,216,204 |
| 2020 | 4,287 | 175 | 4,121 | 1,224,117 |

TABLE 2

## LOOKING AT THE BRIGHT SIDE

For a long time, I saw my bivocational ministry as a trial I had to endure until the church was able to put me back on full-time support. I grew discouraged because I was only considering the negative reasons for bivocational ministry. While declining church membership and decreases in financial giving are legitimate concerns, there is a bright side to bivocational ministry. After taking a course on "Cultural Creativity and the Church," I began to see my bivocational ministry as a remarkable opportunity not just for the local church but also for the common good of the community.

Just as the gospel is a message of good news for both the church and the community it reaches, so also bivocational ministry can and should be an effective blessing to both the church and the community. I am convinced that the key to an effective bivocational ministry is found in a gospel-centered approach to ministry. According to 1 Corinthians 15, the gospel is the death, burial, and resurrection of Jesus for our salvation. Paul also says that this message is of "first importance" and we must "stand" in it and "hold fast" to it. The message of the gospel is the good news of God's grace. It is a message of God's love that should be communicated

19

in the life of every Christian not just with words but also with actions, not just at church but also at work.

While pastors cannot ignore financial problems in the church, the decision to be a bivocational minister should be based on more than just convenience and economics. Bivocational ministry must be for the sake of the gospel. Bivocational ministry has the potential to demonstrate and communicate the gospel to the whole community at several levels. Appendix B includes multiple examples of bivocational ministers living out the gospel in many ways.

## QUESTIONS I HAD

While I was confident that God had called me to the ministry and I was certain that God had called me to the Minnehaha Church of Christ, I wasn't sure if God wanted me to be a full-funded minister, a bivocational minister, or a volunteer minister. I also considered the possibility that God might just want me to choose whichever option I wanted and just be faithful with the choice I made.

As I continued to pray and search for a better understanding of God's will for my life and ministry, I also continued to take classes in seminary. Every class I took had a strong emphasis on being "gospel-centered." I noticed a common theme popping up over and over of how the gospel was not just a message of salvation; it was also a message of transformation. A gospel perspective changes everything we do in life. The gospel empowers us to live a transformed life. I already knew that in a general way, but I had not specifically and intentionally applied a gospel perspective to my struggles as a bivocational minister. These thoughts and convictions soon developed into a topic for my dissertation. I knew I needed to study and write about bivocational ministry for the sake of the gospel. In my initial quest for information on this topic, I developed more questions than answers. The following chapters of this book will attempt to answer some of those questions.

Chapters 3-7 of this book will focus on the biblical, theological, and historical foundations of bivocational ministry and how it relates to the gospel. In these chapters, I will explore the following questions.

### Questions About Vocation
- What is a "vocation"?
- How does vocation relate to our calling?

**Questions About the Gospel**

- What is the "ministry of the gospel"?
- What does it mean to have a "gospel-centered" ministry?

**Questions about Bivocational Ministry in the Bible**

- What does the Old Testament teach us about bivocational ministry?
- What does the New Testament teach us about bivocational ministry?

**Questions about Bivocational Ministry in Church History**

- What does Church history teach us about bivocational ministry?
- What does Church history teach us about the "ministry of the gospel"?

**Questions about the Connection between the Gospel and Bivocational Ministry**

- What does it mean to be bivocational "for the sake of the gospel"?
- How did Paul connect the gospel to his bivocational ministry?

**Questions about Gospel Transformation**

- How can the gospel continue to improve a minister?
- How can the gospel continue to empower a minister?

Chapters 8-13 focus more on the practical applications of the principles discussed in the first half of the book. In these chapters, I will answer the following questions.

**Questions about Time Management**

- How can the gospel help us with time management?
- What are some practical time management strategies?

**Questions about the Challenges of Bivocational Ministry**

- How can we prevent isolation among bivocational ministers?
- How can we prevent burnout among bivocational ministers?

**Questions about Preparing for Bivocational Ministry**

- How can we know if a bivocational ministry is right for our congregation?
- How can we prepare a local congregation for bivocational ministry?

Both the process and the results of my search for answers to these questions has helped me apply the gospel to every aspect of ministry. This study has transformed my bivocational ministry into a rewarding, Christ-centered calling. It is my prayer that as you ponder these questions in the following chapters, that you will gain a deeper understanding of how the gospel can make your ministry more fulfilling and effective regardless of whether you are engaged in full-time, part-time, or volunteer ministry.

## DISCUSSION QUESTIONS

1. What would some of the struggles be for you if you were a bivocational minister?

2. What are some of the likely blessings that would come from being a bivocational minister?

3. When you think about the cross and the future of your ministry, what is your initial response?

4. What is one personal application of the gospel that you will put into practice this week? How?

5. How many bivocational ministers have you known? Do you think bivocational ministry has been increasing, decreasing, or staying about the same in your lifetime?

6. Do you think that the churches you have been a part of have been mostly growing, decreasing, or staying about the same in attendance in your lifetime?

7. Look at the annual church budget from your church or a church you are familiar with. What is the amount of the total expenses budgeted for the year? What are the three biggest expenses on the budget? What is the annual amount budgeted for each of those expenses?

8. Besides bivocational ministry, what are some other ways a struggling church might cut back on expenses without compromising New Testament standards or ministry effectiveness?

9. According to 1 Corinthians 15, what is the message of the gospel and why does Paul describe it as a message of "first importance"?

10. What does it look like for Christians today to "stand" in the gospel and "hold fast" to it? Give an example.

11. How is the gospel a message of good news for both the local church and the local community?

12. How can the message of the gospel help us when we are facing difficult decisions in life?

# CHAPTER 3

REVIEWING VOCATION

"It was for this He called you through
our gospel, that you may gain the glory
of our Lord Jesus Christ."
—2 Thessalonians 2:14

If the Lord makes you a plumber, be a plumber for the Lord.
If the Lord makes you a drummer, be a drummer for the Lord.
If the Lord has need of plumbers, He has need of drummers too.
Yes, everyone created has a special job to do.
—author unknown

I remember singing this song in Sunday school and then asking my mother, "Did the Lord make daddy a janitor or a preacher?" My mother wisely responded, "Both!"

Some people when they hear the word "bivocational" they have no idea what it means. When I told one of my coworkers that I was doing research on bivocational ministry he responded by asking, "Oh really? What other languages do you speak?" Most people, however, understand that bivocational has something to do with having two jobs. When people find out that I am both a preacher and a school bus driver, they usually know what I mean when I say that I am a bivocational minister. They understand that I have two occupations. However, they rarely conclude that I have two callings.

Did the Lord call me to be both a preacher and a bus driver? How I answer that question will have a major impact on my effectiveness and fulfillment in ministry. Bivocational ministers need to see both their ministry and their work outside the church as part of their calling. However, terms like job, career, vocation, calling, and ministry are often used with some underlying assumptions that we need to reconsider or at least clarify. In this chapter, we will examine the current understanding of the term "vocation." We will consider the original meaning of the term as well as the biblical concepts of vocation and calling. We will look for connections between the calling we receive through the gospel and what we commonly think of as our vocation. Finally, we will challenge the tendency many people have of dividing work into the categories of "secular" and "sacred."

## THE COMMON UNDERSTANDING OF VOCATION

According to the *Merriam-Webster Dictionary*, the definition of "vocation" is,

1a: a summons or strong inclination to a particular state or course of action; *especially*: a divine call to the religious life

b: an entry into the priesthood or a religious order

2a: the work in which a person is employed: occupation

b: the persons engaged in a particular occupation

3: the special function of an individual or group[21]

While the first definition points to the original meaning of the term, the most common usage of this word today is found in the second definition referring to a person's job or career without any reference to a divine call or a ministry in the church. The *Oxford Dictionary* takes God completely out of the picture in its definition:

1 A strong feeling of suitability for a particular career or occupation. "Not all of us have a vocation to be nurses or doctors."

1.1 A person's employment or main occupation, especially regarded as worthy and requiring dedication. "Her vocation as a poet…"

---

21. "Definition of Vocation," *Webster English Dictionary*, accessed March 4, 2018, https://www.merriam-webster.com/dictionary/vocation.

1.2 A trade or profession. "GNVQs in Leisure and Tourism will be the introduction to a wide span of vocations."[22]

In contrast, the etymology of the word shows us that it originally referred to a divine calling. It comes from the Latin word *vocatio* from which we also get the English cognates "voice" and "vocal."[23] These definitions help us to see how the meaning of vocation has gone through a radical shift from one extreme to the other. The original Latin word had virtually nothing to do with the work a person did outside of a religious context. However, the more modern *Oxford* definition focuses only on the work a person does outside of a religious context. The *Oxford* definition has replaced the idea of a divine calling with a "strong feeling."

In his book *The Call*, Os Guinness observes how this shift in our understanding of vocation was partly due to the secularization that took place in the modern world following the Reformation. He explains,

> Slowly such words as work, trade, employment, and occupation came to be used interchangeably with calling and vocation. As this happened, the guidelines for calling shifted; instead of being directed by the commands of God, they were seen as directed by duties and roles in society. Eventually, the day came when faith and calling were separated completely.[24]

Your vocation will not be a truly fulfilling experience unless it is seen as a calling from God and answered in response to the gospel. However, many bivocational ministers do not see their work outside the church as a calling from God. In fact, most practicing Christians view the work of pastors as "more important than their own career or vocation."[25]

The second survey I conducted for this project revealed a strong connection between a minister's view of calling and his sense of effectiveness in ministry.[26]

---

22. "Vocation - Definition," *Oxford English Dictionary*, accessed March 4, 2018, https://en.oxforddictionaries.com/definition/vocation

23. Richard A. Muller, *Dictionary of Latin and Greek Theological Terms: Drawn Principally from Protestant Scholastic Theology* (Grand Rapids, MI: Baker Book House, 2006), 329.

24. Os Guinness, *The Call: Finding and Fulfilling the Central Purpose of Your Life* (Nashville, TN: Thomas Nelson, 2003), 39.

25. David Kinnaman, *The State of Pastors: How Today's Faith Leaders Are Navigating Life and Leadership in an Age of Complexity* (Ventura, CA: Barna Group, 2017), 130.

26. Kennedy, 235-36.

Questions 6-9 of the survey were specifically about their calling and effectiveness in ministry.

### QUESTION #6:

**Do you believe God has called you to the church where you currently serve?**

Out of the 194 bivocational ministers who took the survey, 162 answered, "yes" to this question, 9 said, "no," and 23 left it blank or indicated that they were, "not sure."

### QUESTION #7:

**Do you believe God has called you to the work you do outside the church?**

In reply to this question, 108 said, "yes," 40 said, "no," and 46 either left it blank or indicated that they were, "not sure." While 84% of bivocational ministers believe that they have been called to their current ministry, only 56% believe that they have been called to the work they do outside of their church ministry. Bivocational ministers tend to be confident about their calling to ministry and if they have doubts concerning their calling it is more likely to be in the area of the work they do outside the church.

**HOW BIVOCATIONAL MINISTERS VIEW THEIR CALLING**

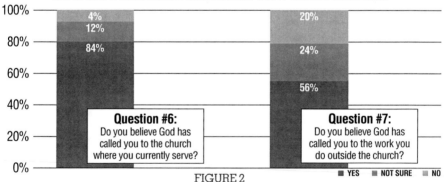

FIGURE 2

### QUESTION #8:

**How effective do you believe your ministry has been?**

In response to this question, 2 said, "not very effective," 34 said, "somewhat effective," 85 said, "more effective than not," 72 said, "very effective," and 1 left this question blank. The 72 ministers who answered, "very effective" to this question also answered "yes" to the previous questions about their calling. Most of the ministers who said they were not very effective or only somewhat effective were also ministers who said that they were not called to the work they are doing outside the church.

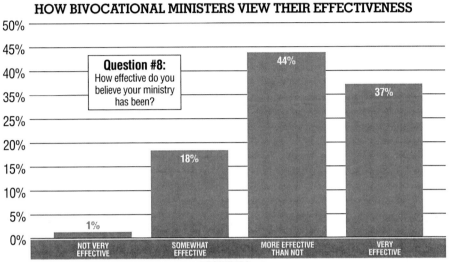

HOW BIVOCATIONAL MINISTERS VIEW THEIR EFFECTIVENESS

**Question #8:**
How effective do you believe your ministry has been?

FIGURE 3

## QUESTION #9:

**As a bivocational minister, how often do you have a sense of fulfillment and satisfaction?**

In response to this question, 2 ministers said, "almost never," 23 said, "sometimes," 93 said, "often," 75 said, "almost always," and 1 left this question blank. A comparison of the results from this question and questions 6 and 7 shows another correlation between our view of calling and our sense of fulfillment in ministry. Almost all of the ministers who answered "yes" to question 6 also said that they often or almost always have a sense of fulfillment and satisfaction as a bivocational minister. Furthermore, all the ministers who said that they almost always have a sense of fulfillment and satisfaction in ministry also answered "yes" to question 7. This survey does not indicate whether our view of calling is the cause or the result of our sense of fulfillment in ministry, but it does indicate that there is a correlation.

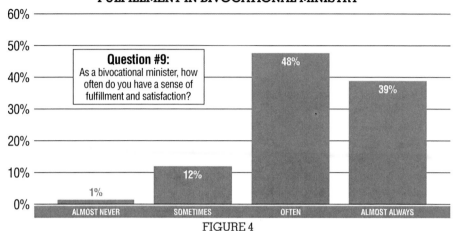

FIGURE 4

# A BIBLICAL VIEW OF CALLING

Most of us have heard sermons on our calling in Christ. A common outline that I have seen and even used myself is that we are called to salvation, sanctification, and service. While that is a fair summary of our divine calling with solid biblical support, we quickly realize that the idea of calling gets much more complicated when we try to be more specific about what kind of service God is calling us to do and where He is calling us to do it. Does God always call individuals to specific ministries in specific places? What if I don't feel called to any ministry? Does that mean that God wants me to just sit on a pew until I do feel called before I start serving in a specific ministry?

The "call to ministry" is a difficult discussion because people have various ideas of what that means. For some people, it is a subjective inward feeling that God is leading them into ministry. For others, it is a mystical or even miraculous experience that in some way convinces them that God is calling them to ministry. Certainly, God can call individuals in many ways. God called Moses from a burning bush (Ex. 3:2). God called Samuel with an audible voice in the temple (1 Sam. 3:10). Saul of Tarsus was called to be an Apostle when the resurrected Christ blinded him with a bright light (Acts 9:3-8). However, the Bible presents these as unique events and not the typical way that God leads people into opportunities to serve. Gary Johnson brings up an interesting question as he considers some of the miraculous callings in the Bible.

It is interesting to note unique aspects of God's leadership calls to Moses, Paul, and Samuel. For example, when God called each of these men to lead, He said their names twice (Ex 3:4, "Moses, Moses"; 1 Sam 3:10, "Samuel, Samuel"; Acts 9:4, "Saul, Saul"). Is there something in us men that we do not hear very well?[27]

Perhaps God called their names twice because He was calling them to do something they didn't want to do. On the other hand, perhaps God called their names twice because their calling would be an important part of their unique identity. As we will see later, before we can understand what God is calling us to do, we must first understand who God is calling us to be. Concerning Moses, Samuel, and Paul, these were unique events. These people were resistant to accept the job God was calling them to do. And the miraculous nature was probably because God was calling these men to a prophetic role where they would be speaking and writing the authoritative word of God. We don't need a miraculous event or a subjective mystical experience to have confidence that God is calling us to do something. And we certainly shouldn't wait around doing nothing until we experience a subjective inward feeling.

God called Paul to preach the gospel in Macedonia by giving him a vision in the night (Acts 16:9-10). However, from the context of the passage, we see that Paul was not sitting on his hands waiting for an inward feeling or a miraculous experience when he received the call to go to Macedonia. He had tried to preach in Asia, but he was forbidden by the Holy Spirit (Acts 16:6). He also tried to go into Bithynia, but the Spirit of Jesus stopped him (Acts 16:7). He was proactive in his search for opportunities to preach the gospel, even when he didn't know specifically where God wanted him to go.

While it is possible for God to call people to ministry in several different ways, we need to focus our understanding of calling on an objective evaluation of things like our gifts, abilities, experiences, passions, qualifications, and current opportunities. This seems to be the focus in the New Testament when it gives us instructions about appointing leaders in the church (1 Tim. 3:1-13; Titus 1:5-9). In his book *Decision Making and the Will of God*, Garry Friesen laments the fact that many evangelicals make a subjective experience an essential sign of a person's call to ministry. He writes,

---

27. Jim Estep, David Roadcup, and Gary Johnson, *Answer His Call* (Joplin, MO: College Press, 2009), 20.

31

The traditional view of guidance so permeates evangelical thinking that the validity of a vocational call is not only assumed for all believers, it is actually required for "full-time ministers." When a candidate is examined for ordination into the gospel ministry, the council usually questions him with respect to three key areas: (1) his experience of conversion; (2) his call to ministry; and (3) his doctrinal positions.[28]

Later, in the same chapter, Friesen recounts the awkward examination he went through before his ordination. Since his decision to go into the ministry was not based on an "inward feeling" or a "mystical calling," some of the leaders examining him were suspicious and reluctant to sign off on his ordination.[29]

So how is our calling to a ministry in the church or to a career in the world related to the general calling we receive through the gospel? Gordon Smith provides an outline of divine calling that gives us a little more clarity on how individuals are called in specific areas of life. He breaks it down this way:

### CALLED OF GOD: THE THREE EXPRESSIONS OF VOCATION

- The general call—the invitation to follow Jesus, to be Christian
- The specific call—a vocation that is unique to a person; that individual's mission in the world
- The immediate responsibilities—those tasks or duties God calls us to today[30]

The general call or invitation to follow Jesus and be Christian is a calling we receive through the gospel (2 Thess. 2:14). This is not just a call to be saved; it is also a call to sanctification and service as well. Through the gospel, God is calling all people to be saved (1 Tim. 2:4; 2 Peter 3:9). He is calling all people to be sanctified (1 Thess. 4:7). And He is calling all people to serve (Mark 10:45; Eph. 2:10; 4:11-12).

The specific call is God's call for each individual. This is the overall purpose or mission that God has for specific individuals. Since every person has a unique combination of abilities, experiences, physical traits, personality traits, passions, convictions, resources, and opportunities, God is going to use everyone in different

---

28. Garry Friesen, *Decision Making & the Will of God* (Portland, OR: Multnomah, 1982), 314-15.
29. Friesen, 319.
30. Gordon T. Smith, *Courage and Calling: Embracing Your God-Given Potential*, Revised and Expanded edition. (Downers Grove, Ill: IVP Books, 2011), 10.

ways. However, before people can understand their specific call and purpose, they must first answer the general call of the gospel. After they become Christians they are encouraged to discover and evaluate their spiritual gifts and serve in ways that are consistent with the gifts and opportunities that God gives them (Romans 12:6-8). In his comments on this passage, Jack Cottrell notes that there are several sample lists in the New Testament of the various gifts that God gives to Christians as He calls them to unselfish service. Cottrell writes,

> In Rom 12 Paul calls them gifts of grace rather than gifts of the Spirit, but the point is the same. Other listings of such gifts are found in 1 Cor 12:8-10, 28-30; Eph 4:11; and 1 Pet 4:10-11. Some gifts appear in more than one list; others appear in only one. No list is exhaustive in itself, and probably all taken together are not exhaustive.[31]

We should also note that these passages about spiritual gifts are only focusing on one aspect of our identity. When we are trying to determine our specific calling including where and who we should serve, we also need to take into consideration our personality, experiences, resources, passions, and relationships.

While this specific call is based on the unique identity of an individual and looks for the overall purpose God has for that person, it is not so rigid that it cannot change or be adjusted as the person goes through different stages of life. In the first survey I conducted, 47 ministers said that they were called into ministry after they had retired from a "secular" career. Technically, they are not "bivocational" ministers because they currently only have one vocation. These pastors are often called "second-career" ministers. A recent report put out by the Barna Group notes this growing trend:

> More specific to church ministry, the percentage of "second-career clergy" has been increasing over the past two decades, particularly in non-mainline churches and historically black congregations; more pastors are coming to ministry later in life, having first pursued a non-ministry career.[32]

---

31. Jack Cottrell, *The College Press NIV Commentary Romans Vol 2: Chapters 9-16* (Joplin, MO: College Press, 1996), 318.
32. Kinnaman, Brown, and Brown, *The State of Pastors*, 14-15.

I don't like the implications of the phrase, "non-ministry" career. Many of these workers had fulfilling careers outside the church where they were using their God-given gifts to be a blessing to their community. They answered God's call to serve Him in the community even though their jobs were not in a church. God is now calling them and using them as pastors in churches that may not be able to pay a full-time wage with benefits. Smith notes that we need to evaluate our specific calling as we approach transitional periods of life.

> It has been commonly assumed that vocational counseling was provided in high schools for those seeking to choose a career. But in a true understanding of vocation, we discover that vocational questions follow us throughout the course of our lives—and that perhaps vocational counsel needs to be present at each transition. The questions remain the same: Who am I, and who has God called me to be?[33]

Our general calling to follow Jesus and be a Christian is clearly defined in the New Testament. That calling is the firm foundation that never changes and as such we must always anchor our specific calling to that general calling. Our specific calling may change as our gifts, abilities, and opportunities change, but if we are making those adjustments in response to the gospel, then we are answering God's call. When we base our specific calling on an "inward feeling" or a mystical experience our anchor may be slipping away from the foundation. R. Paul Stevens observes,

> There is no need to be 'called' through an existential experience to an occupation in society. God gives motivation and gift. God guides. Work, family, civil vocation and neighboring are encompassed in our total response to God's saving and transforming call in Jesus.[34]

The third category in Smith's outline of divine calling is "the immediate responsibilities." These are the things God calls us to do in the specific situations

---

33. Smith, *Courage and Calling*, 78.
34. R. Paul Stevens, *The Other Six Days: Vocation, Work, and Ministry in Biblical Perspective* (Grand Rapids, MI: Eerdmans, 2000), 82.

we face each day. The daily decisions we make as we live our lives must be based on the general calling we have received through the gospel. In Ephesians 4:1, Paul says, "I urge you to live a life worthy of the calling you have received." In chapter 5 he tells his readers to, "find out what pleases the Lord" (Eph. 5:10, NIV). A few verses later, he says,

> Be very careful, then, how you live—not as unwise but as wise, making the most of every opportunity, because the days are evil. Therefore do not be foolish, but understand what the Lord's will is. Do not get drunk on wine, which leads to debauchery. Instead, be filled with the Spirit. —Ephesians 5:15-18 (NIV)

Understanding our calling in life includes the process of evaluating our daily decisions and finding out what pleases the Lord. This process must be in cooperation with the Holy Spirit as He is at work producing the fruit of the Spirit in our lives. This requires wisdom and an understanding of the overall purpose God has for us. It also requires us to evaluate the time and the opportunities God has given us. The book of Esther is a good example of this principle. Esther saw no bright light or burning bush. She heard no audible voice from God calling her to be the Queen of Persia who would save God's people from genocide. In fact, the name of God does not even appear in the book. And yet the prophetic voice of Mordecai encourages Esther to assume that a providential plan may be calling her to action. When Mordecai asked Esther to tell the king about Haman's evil plan to kill all the Jews he concluded with this observation, "And who knows but that you have come to royal position for such a time as this?" (Esther 4:14, NIV). Timothy Keller shows how this is a statement of God's providence and grace bringing Esther to an opportunity to understand God's will and respond. Keller writes,

> The Hebrew word translated as "come" is a passive verb. It would be better translated: "Who knows but that you were not *brought* to your royal position because of this?" He is reminding Esther that she did not get to the palace except by grace. She did not develop or earn her beauty, nor did she produce this opportunity; they were given to her.[35]

---

35. Timothy Keller, *Every Good Endeavor: Connecting Your Work to God's Work* (New York, NY: Penguin Books, 2014), 120.

This is also true for us. Whether we are fully funded ministers, bivocational ministers, or volunteer ministers, by grace God has called each of us to serve in His kingdom. The positions of influence that we achieve both in the community and in the church are by God's grace and we should respond as "good stewards of the manifold grace of God" (1 Peter 4:10).

## A BIBLICAL VIEW OF WORK

An understanding of our specific calling and our immediate responsibilities must be firmly based on the general calling we have received through the gospel. This is true whether we are talking about understanding God's will for our ministries in the church or our job opportunities outside the church. The labels "secular" and "sacred" make it easier for us to divide our activities and responsibilities into separate categories. Sometimes we need to distinguish between the jobs we are doing for the church and the jobs we are doing for some other organization. However, the Bible clearly teaches us that, as Christians, all our work needs to be seen as sacred. "For we are His workmanship, created in Christ Jesus for good works, which God prepared beforehand so that we would walk in them" (Eph. 2:10). Whether we are getting paid for our work or not, God has created all of us to work. Whether we are working at a ministry in a church or at a job in the community, God calls all of us into a partnership with Him where He works through our work to accomplish His will.

Many people think that work was a part of the curse that came upon mankind because of the first sin. However, the Genesis account shows us that work is a wonderful and sacred gift from God. While work is discussed in Genesis 3 when God describes the consequences of sin, that is not the first time we read about work in the Bible. We are introduced to work when we are introduced to God in Genesis 1:1. Keller observes, "The Bible begins talking about work as soon as it begins talking about anything—that is how important and basic it is."[36] Genesis 1 begins with a description of God working, creating the heavens and the earth and caring for all that He created. Our God is a working God, and He delights in His work. The last verse in Genesis 1 describes God examining all His work and calling it "very good" (Gen. 1:31). Our God is also a relational God. The work we see the Father planning

---

36. Keller, *Every Good Endeavor*, 19.

and performing in Genesis is in partnership with the Word and the Spirit. God said, "Let Us make man in Our image, according to Our likeness; and let them rule over the fish of the sea and over the birds of the sky and over the cattle and over all the earth, and over every creeping thing that creeps on the earth" (Gen. 1:26). The work of God is an avenue for Him to demonstrate and share His relational nature with us.

From the very beginning, God created us to join with Him in doing His work. Part of the delight God has in His work comes from His love and care for His creation. However, as a relational being, God also delights in His work by working in partnership with us. He enjoys working both for us and with us. Gene Edward Veith notes that "human work is an imitation of God's work, a participation in God's creation and His creativity. Ruling, subduing, multiplying, causing plants to grow, making things—these are what God does, and yet God gives them as tasks to human beings."[37]

Work was not assigned to us as a punishment for Adam's sin. Work was given to us as a good gift to bring us dignity, purpose, and fulfillment in life. Work is a part of the sacred image of God that makes us who we are. Only when we have a biblical view of work can we reflect the image of God and experience the partnership of work that God wants to share with us. The work of "ruling over" creation was designed to be a partnership of management where God works through us to care for and cultivate the physical world. "Then the LORD God took the man and put him into the garden of Eden to cultivate it and keep it" (Gen. 2:15). Notice that this work assignment of cultivating and keeping took place before the fall in chapter 3. All the work God gives us to do is sacred because He is working with us and through us to continue to care for and cultivate His creation.

The Garden of Eden was perfect in the sense that there was nothing wrong with it and it was the ideal environment for Adam and Eve. However, God intentionally created the Garden of Eden to be incomplete. He created the garden with the potential for cultivation, growth, and creative new ideas. The work God entrusted to Adam began with the creative task of naming all the animals (Gen. 2:19). The commands in Genesis 1:28 to "multiply," "fill the earth," "subdue it," and "rule," are sometimes called the "cultural mandate." God was not just telling mankind to increase in number. He was entrusting us with the opportunity to create good cultures and societies and cultivate them to make them even better. In the

---

37. Gene Edward Veith Jr, *God at Work: Your Christian Vocation in All of Life* (Wheaton, IL: Crossway, 2011), 62.

book *Culture Making: Recovering our Creative Calling*, Andy Crouch notes how all our work as Christians should be a partnership with God to create and cultivate culture. He writes,

> I wonder what we Christians are known for in the world outside our churches. Are we known as critics, consumers, copiers, condemners, of culture? I'm afraid so. Why aren't we known as cultivators—people who tend and nourish what is best in human culture, who do the hard work and painstaking work to preserve the best of what people before us have done? Why aren't we known as creators—people who dare to think and do something that has never been thought or done before, something that makes the world more welcoming and thrilling and beautiful?[38]

Another reason all our work must be seen as sacred is because of the two greatest commandments. When Jesus was asked about the greatest commandment He said, "'Love the Lord your God with all your heart and with all your soul and with all your mind.' This is the first and greatest commandment. And the second is like it: 'Love your neighbor as yourself'" (Matt. 22:37-39, NIV). He also said, "All the Law and the Prophets hang on these two commandments" (Matt. 22:40, NIV). That means that all the commands and principles about work in the Bible depend on and exemplify loving God and loving others. When I drive a school bus full of rebellious and ungrateful middle school students, it is an opportunity for me to allow God to work through my work to show those students love.

Psalm 145:15-16 says, "The eyes of all look to You, And You give them their food in due time. You open Your hand And satisfy the desire of every living thing." Keller notes, "So how does God 'feed every living thing' (Psalm 145:16) today? Isn't it through the farmer, the baker, the retailer, the website programmer, the truck driver, and all who contribute to bring us food?"[39] Even in the most mundane occupations, we have opportunities to display the image of God by loving people in the same way that God loves us.

All our work is sacred because we were created in the image of God, entrusted to care for and cultivate His creation, and commanded to love God and love our

---

38. Andy Crouch, *Culture Making: Recovering Our Creative Calling* (Downers Grove, Ill.: IVP Books, 2013), 97-98.
39. Keller, *Every Good Endeavor*, 60.

neighbor through our good works. However, as Christians, all the work we do must also be seen as sacred because of the work Christ has accomplished for us. Jack Cottrell writes,

> But there is another aspect of the God-dimension of work. Through it, we honor God not only as our Creator but also as our Redeemer. The Christian's job or occupation is one of the ways in which he fulfills his *main* calling, which is to bring glory and honor to the one who has saved us from sin. Sometimes we think of our work in terms of vocation, a word which literally means "calling." As Christians, we actually have *two* vocations or callings.[40]

Our main calling is the general calling we have received through the gospel. Our secondary calling may be a career in the world, a ministry in the church, or some combination of the two, but whatever it is, it must be based on our main calling. Before we can truly understand what God wants us to do, we must understand who God wants us to be in Christ.

We have seen in this chapter that the way we view our vocation will have a major impact on our sense of fulfillment and our effectiveness in ministry. When we have a biblical view of calling, we can find out what pleases the Lord and make wise decisions about our ministries and occupations that are based on the objective realities of who we are called to be in Christ. When we have a biblical view of work, we are able to experience joy and fulfillment in our work as we reflect the image of God. This involves working together with God to create and cultivate culture, and loving all people through our work both in the church and in the world.

---

40. Jack Cottrell, *Tough Questions Biblical Answers/Part 1* (Joplin, MO: College Press, 1985), 61.

## DISCUSSION QUESTIONS

1. What do you typically think of when you hear the word "vocation"?

2. Do you think that it is important for Christians to see their occupations as a calling from God? Why or why not?

3. Do you believe God has called you to the church where you currently serve? Why or why not?

4. Do you believe God has called you to the work you do outside the church? Why or why not?

5. How could a bivocational minister's calling for his job outside the church be a benefit to his ministry within the church?

6. Have you ever been certain that God was calling you to do something specific that is not specifically stated in the Bible? If you have, what helped you come to that conclusion? If you haven't, what would it take for you to come to that conclusion?

7. Why is it unwise for people to base their callings primarily on their feelings?

8. What are some of the objective things we need to evaluate in order to better understand our calling?

9. Why should people answer the general call in their lives before they answer the specific call in their lives?

10. How is the message of the gospel not only a call to salvation and sanctification, but also a call to service? (Support your answer with Scripture.)

11. How can the gospel help us to see the blessings God has given to us in our work?

12. What can you do to remember and maintain a biblical perspective of work?

# CHAPTER 4

"for our gospel did not come to you in word only,
but also in power and in the Holy Spirit and with
full conviction; just as you know what kind of men
we proved to be among you for your sake."
—1 Thessalonians 1:5

His dying crimson, like a robe,
Spreads o'er his body on the tree;
Then I am dead to all the globe,
And all the globe is dead to me.
—Isaac Watts

I began this book with a story about a mission trip that prompted me to ask myself, "What does it mean to be a minister of the gospel?" That is a difficult question to answer in a specific way because, as we saw in the previous chapter, *every* Christian is called through the gospel to serve in various ways. The Greek verb "to serve" (*diakoneo*) is the same word translated "to minister." Therefore, in a general sense, all Christians are called to be ministers of the gospel. However, what that gospel ministry is going to look like for a specific person at a specific stage in life is going to vary depending on that person's specific calling. Paul said that he was made a minister of the gospel "according to the gift of God's grace" (Eph. 3:7).

Undoubtedly, Paul's specific ministry was unique to him in many ways.

In the previous chapter, we also established that every Christian's specific calling, regardless of whether it is a ministry in the church or a career in the community, must be based on his or her general calling through the gospel. In this chapter, we will consider five principles that will keep our ministries centered on the gospel. These are principles that all Christians should recognize and apply to their lives as ministers of the gospel.

## GOSPEL PERCEPTION

First, we must look at all of life from the perspective of the cross. We must have a gospel perception. There is no such thing as a view from nowhere. Everyone views the world through the lenses of their experiences in life including things like the jobs they have had, their accomplishments and failures, the relationships they have had, the books they have read, the movies they have watched, and all the different classes they have taken. But we must allow the gospel to transform the way we see the world. We must intentionally and consistently put on the gospel glasses and look at everything in the light of the gospel.

Many preachers have used the phrase "gospel glasses" as a sermon illustration. However, it first caught my attention when I was taking a class on "Christ-Centered Preaching."[41] The professor used this word picture to show how we could read virtually any text of Scripture and discover how the text points us to Christ and God's overall redemptive plan.

This word picture of the gospel glasses applies not only to how we view Scripture but also to the way we view everything in life, including our ministries and careers. Every struggle I face as a bus driver, the elementary students using profanity, the middle school students fighting, the traffic jams and mechanical problems, the drama in the breakroom, the disagreements in the office, as well as my own failures and weaknesses, are all reminders that I live in a messed-up world. But God has a plan of redemption and restoration for this messed up world. My work as a bus driver is not the redeeming work of the gospel, and neither is my work as a preacher. However, the gospel glasses help me to remember that God is working through both of my jobs to communicate and illustrate the redemptive

---

41. Bryan Chapel taught the course PTS 730 "Christ-Centered Preaching" June 20-23, 2016 at Western Seminary in Portland, OR.

love of God. Amy Sherman underscores this important principle when she writes, "To steward their vocations well, Christians need to have a big conception of God's redemptive work."[42]

In his book *Shaped by the Gospel*, Timothy Keller makes the point that while the gospel is not everything, it still affects everything. He applies this principle to specific jobs and ministries when he writes,

> People naturally want to go deeper into various topics and ministry disciplines. But this tendency can cause us to lose sight of the whole. Though we may have an area or a ministry that we tend to focus on, the gospel is what brings unity to all that we do. Every form of ministry is empowered by the gospel, based on the gospel, and is a result of the gospel.[43]

This does not mean that we should never specialize in a certain field of work or ministry. It does not mean that we should never focus our attention on the details of those things that are not specifically proclaiming the gospel. But it does mean that we need to intentionally and consistently step back and look at the big picture of the gospel and consider how the details of our lives fit into the big picture. From my own experience as well as from the surveys I have conducted I get the impression that most Christian ministers firmly believe in the gospel and see it as a matter of "first importance" just as Paul describes it in 1 Corinthians 15:3. However, I'm afraid that many ministers see the gospel as such a huge overarching principle that they rarely bring it into the smaller details of life and really think about how it applies to specific situations in ministry.

In the second survey I conducted I asked the following questions about the gospel and ministry:

17. How (if at all) did the gospel influence your decision to be bivocational?

18. How (if at all) does the gospel help you as a bivocational minister?

19. How (if at all) has your bivocational ministry provided opportunities for you to proclaim the gospel?

---

42. Amy L. Sherman, Steven Garber, and Reggie McNeal, *Kingdom Calling: Vocational Stewardship for the Common Good* (Downers Grove, IL: IVP Books, 2011), 235.

43. Timothy Keller, Michael Horton, and Dane Calvin Ortlund, *Shaped by the Gospel: Doing Balanced, Gospel-Centered Ministry in Your City* (Grand Rapids, MI: Zondervan, 2016), 43.

20. How (if at all) has your bivocational ministry provided opportunities for you to demonstrate or live out the gospel?[44]

I did not give them any boxes to check or suggested answers to consider. I intentionally left these questions open because I wanted to get a sense of how natural it was for them to think of specific aspects of their jobs and ministries from a gospel perspective. I'm sure many of the participants were in a hurry and didn't have time to give specific answers. Many of them spoke of the gospel in very general terms without giving specific examples. However, some ministers spoke with passion about the role the gospel has played in their lives and ministries. They did not see these questions as a waste of their time; they were eager to share details. These ministers gave specific testimonies about the how the gospel influenced their decisions in ministry and empowered them in difficult times. It was obvious that they were in the habit of looking at life through the gospel glasses. That gospel perspective created a gospel motivation within them that was evident in their responses. In chapter 8, I will share some of those testimonies of how the gospel is being applied to bivocational ministry.

## GOSPEL MOTIVATION

The WHY of our ministry is our motivation. And our WHY must be clearly understood and communicated. In his 2009 "TED Talk," Simon Sinek explained the relationship between the WHAT, the HOW, and the WHY with a diagram he calls "The Golden Circle" (figure 5).[45] The diagram shows three concentric circles. The largest outer circle is the WHAT. It is the largest circle because most people and organizations know what they do. The middle circle is the HOW. It is the medium size circle because some people and organizations know how they do what they do. The smallest inner circle is the WHY. It is the smallest because fewer people and organizations know why they do what they do. Sinek observes,

> When most organizations or people think, act or communicate they do so from the outside in, from WHAT to WHY... But not the inspired companies. Not the inspired leaders. Every single one

---

44. Kennedy, 245-49.
45. Simon Sinek, *How Great Leaders Inspire Action*, 2009, accessed June 14, 2018, https://www.ted.com/talks/simon_sinek_how_great_leaders_inspire_action.

of them, regardless of their size or their industry, thinks, acts and communicates from the inside out.[46]

**"THE GOLDEN CIRCLE" by Simon Sinek**

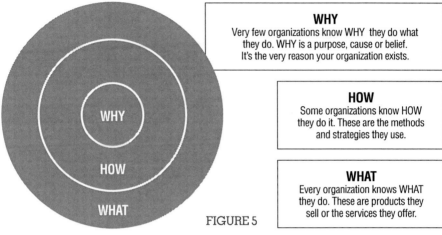

**WHY**
Very few organizations know WHY they do what they do. WHY is a purpose, cause or belief. It's the very reason your organization exists.

**HOW**
Some organizations know HOW they do it. These are the methods and strategies they use.

**WHAT**
Every organization knows WHAT they do. These are products they sell or the services they offer.

FIGURE 5

When Sinek talks about the WHY of what we do he is not referring to the natural results or the effects of our work. The WHY in Sinek's model is a powerful belief and a firm conviction that inspires and motivates people to get onboard and support whatever it is that we do. As a school bus driver, I transport students to get them from their homes to their school and back home safely. That's the result of what I do, but it's not a powerful belief or a firm conviction that motivates what I do. I am a school bus driver because I firmly believe that children are the most precious cargo anywhere in the world. I am convinced that the children in school today are the future leaders of our communities tomorrow. And I am persuaded that these precious children need a safe and encouraging environment on their way to school and back home every day. Jesus said, "See that you do not despise one of these little ones, for I say to you that their angels in heaven continually see the face of My Father who is in heaven" (Matt. 18:10). When it comes to my divine calling as a school bus driver, that is my WHY.

As ministers of the gospel, we must have a powerful belief that motivates all that we do. Our WHY must be firmly grounded in the gospel. What we do and how

46. Simon Sinek, *Start with Why: How Great Leaders Inspire Everyone to Take Action* (New York, NY: Portfolio, 2011), 39.

we do it is certainly important. However, the WHAT and the HOW of ministry will never inspire us, motivate us, and drive us forward in those difficult times when we feel like giving up. We need a powerful WHY. There is no WHY more powerful than the gospel. The gospel is "the power of God for salvation" (Rom. 1:16). Looking at our ministries with a gospel perception creates within our hearts a dynamic and relentless gospel motivation for everything we do. When we, like Isaac Watts, "survey the wondrous cross" and allow the sacrificial love of God to penetrate our hearts, we will be overwhelmed with a sense of humble gratitude and divine purpose.

When Paul was in his first Roman imprisonment, contemplating his future and whether he was going to live or die, he encouraged the Christians at Philippi to "let your manner of life be worthy of the gospel of Christ, so that whether I come and see you or am absent, I may hear of you that you are standing firm in one spirit, with one mind striving side by side for the faith of the gospel," (Phil. 1:27, ESV). "Your manner of life" is the WHAT and the HOW of your Christian life but what makes it "worthy" is the WHY or the motivation for "your manner of life." The WHY that makes your manner of life "worthy" is "the gospel of Christ."

We see the what, the how, and the why even more clearly in the second half of the verse. The WHAT is "standing firm in the spirit." Paul is hoping and praying for the result of his exhortations to the Philippians to be their spiritual growth and stability. That is the product, or the goal Paul wants the Philippians to have. The HOW is "with one mind striving side by side." If these Christians are going to remain faithful and grow spiritually in Paul's absence this is how they are going to do it. As a church, they will need to have unity as they work together toward their goal. Both the WHAT and the HOW are important. However, even more important than the WHAT and the HOW is the WHY. The WHY is "for the faith of the gospel." The gospel must be our driving motivation for what we do and how we do it. And what greater motivation could we have?

I began this chapter with an obscure verse from the hymn, "When I Survey the Wondrous Cross" by Isaac Watts.

> His dying crimson, like a robe,
> Spreads o'er his body on the tree;
> Then I am dead to all the globe,
> And all the globe is dead to me.

46

I say this is an obscure verse because most people in the last two centuries have never heard it. The hymn originally had five stanzas and this verse was the fourth. However, George Whitefield did not like this verse because he thought it was too graphic and gory. Unfortunately, as a result of Whitefield's influence, most hymnals have eliminated this verse.[47] It is unfortunate because this is the focal point of the hymn that emphasizes the gospel motivation which comes from having a gospel perception. The word "then" here in verse 4, refers back to the first word of the first verse "when." "WHEN I survey the wondrous cross…THEN I am dead to all the globe."

The WHY of the gospel is the sacrificial love of God. Jesus said that the divine motivation for His gospel mission was because "God so loved the world" (John 3:16). Later, John would write, "We love, because He first loved us" (1 John 4:19). Are you allowing the powerful love of God demonstrated in the gospel to be the driving motivation in your life?

## GOSPEL PROCLAMATION

When we have a gospel perception that creates within us a gospel motivation, that naturally generates enthusiasm in us about this good news so much so that we want to share it with others. As ministers of the gospel, all Christians must proclaim the good news. The gospel is a message and as such it must be proclaimed. The gospel means "good news" but even the best news is useless unless it is reported. The gospel is the good news that Jesus died for our sins, was buried, and then three days later, raised from the dead (1 Cor. 15:1-4). Certainly, the main reason Jesus came to earth as a man was to *do* the work of the gospel for our salvation. However, it was also His purpose and His pleasure to *proclaim* this good news.

Shortly after He was baptized, Jesus began preaching the gospel. "Now after John had been taken into custody, Jesus came into Galilee, preaching the gospel of God, and saying, 'The time is fulfilled, and the kingdom of God is at hand; repent and believe in the gospel'" (Mark 1:14-15). When Jesus came to the synagogue in His hometown of Nazareth, they handed Him the scroll of Isaiah and He read this passage:

---

47. Jerry Rushford, "The Wondrous Cross of Christ," *Heartlands Church*, last modified 2011, accessed June 14, 2018, http://www.heartlandschurch.org/sermons/2011/9/11/the-wondrous-cross-of-christ.

> The Spirit of the Lord is on me, because he has anointed me to preach good news to the poor. He has sent me to proclaim freedom for the prisoners and recovery of sight for the blind, to release the oppressed, to proclaim the year of the Lord's favor (Luke 4:18-19, NIV).

Jesus kept on preaching the good news in towns throughout Galilee and Judea. He even told His disciples that His purpose was to preach the good news. "But he said, 'I must preach the good news of the kingdom of God to the other towns also, because that is why I was sent.' And he kept on preaching in the synagogues of Judea" (Luke 4:43-44, NIV). And at the end of His ministry on earth, Jesus gave us the great commission, commanding us to "Go into all the world and preach the gospel to all creation" (Mark 16:15).

The gospel is good news. However, the scope and purpose of this good news are much larger than most of us realize. The gospel is a good news message of forgiveness and salvation for the lost (Rom. 1:16). The gospel is also a good news message of redemption and restoration for the entire creation that has been cursed by sin (Rom. 8:20-21). The gospel is also a good news message of ongoing transformation and meaningful purpose for the saved (1 Peter 2:9). This passage in First Peter emphasizes our new purpose and our new identity as "a chosen race, a royal priesthood, a holy nation, a people for his own possession, that you may proclaim the excellencies of him who called you out of darkness into his marvelous light" (1 Peter 2:9, ESV). All Christians, as ministers of the gospel, are royal priests called to speak up and tell people the good news. Our ministry as priests requires us to interact with people outside the church. Cottrell notes that a greater appreciation of the gospel will help with that ministry. He writes,

> We must realize that priesthood is what we do OUTSIDE the church building when we are mixing with the world of unbelievers. To be able to offer the sacrifice of praise in such situations, we must concentrate upon overcoming our fear of talking about our faith and developing more gratitude for our salvation.[48]

---

48. Jack Cottrell, *Studies in First Peter: 35 Lessons for Personal or Group Study* (Mason, OH: Christian Restoration Association, 2017), 155.

All Christians, as ministers of the gospel, must look for opportunities in every area of life to proclaim the good news. As we preach the gospel to ourselves and meditate on how good the good news is, we will develop a greater appreciation for the gospel and a greater boldness to share it with others.

## GOSPEL DEMONSTRATION

Having a gospel perspective produces within us a gospel motivation. That, in turn, leads us to proclaim the gospel to others. And gospel proclamation leads us to gospel demonstration. Being ministers of the gospel means that we live out the gospel so that people don't just hear it in our words, but they also see it in the way we live. Many of the situations we face in life are opportunities to communicate the message of the gospel not just in our words but also in our actions and attitudes of love and sacrifice. This principle was made especially clear to me in a course I took called "A Jesus-Shaped Life."[49] In that class, Paul Miller shared an illustration of the gospel he calls the "J-curve"®[50] (see fig. 6). It is a directional pattern for us to follow based on the life, death, and resurrection of Jesus. While the gospel certainly is the power of God for salvation, it is also a pattern for life that God wants to use in us to illustrate the gospel.

Most people live for themselves trying to achieve success as the world defines it. They are climbing up the I-chart (see fig. 6). At the top of the I-chart, you have honor, success, and boasting. At the bottom of the I-chart, you have failure, shame, and humility, things we want to avoid at any cost. Many people are willing to step on others in order to get to the top of the I-chart. This is the wisdom of the world. But Jesus, in His paradoxical teaching, turns the wisdom of the world upside down. In the wisdom of the gospel, we see that the way up is down because it is based on sacrificial love.

---

49. Paul Miller taught the course PTS 750 "A Jesus-Shaped Life" November 9-12, 2015 at Western Seminary in Portland, OR. In class, Paul Miller called the first chart, "the Failure/Boasting Chart." I changed the name to "the I-Chart" to emphasize the fact that people living by the first chart are focused more on themselves than on Jesus.
50. J-Curve is a registered trademark of seeJesus.net, Inc. Used with permission.

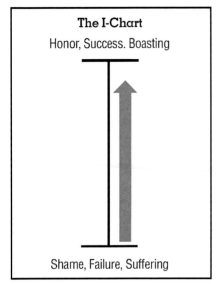 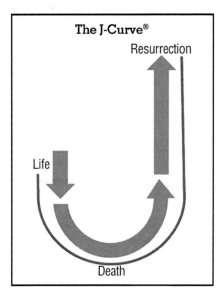

FIGURE 6

The principle of the J-curve® is seen on virtually every page of the Bible. In the book, *A Loving Life*, Paul Miller illustrates how this principle can be seen in the life of Ruth.[51] When Naomi had given up all hope, God worked through Ruth to demonstrate the sacrificial love of the gospel. God wants to do the same thing through us. Miller explains,

> Within seconds of Naomi's charge that "the hand of the Lord has gone out against me," Ruth's hands are clinging to Naomi in a fierce grip of love. Ruth is the face of God to Naomi. Our faces— how we reflect Christ in our gentleness, boldness, and love—are God's best picture of himself on earth. Ruth embodies the gospel. All acts of love done in faith are small pictures of the gospel. Our dying love replicates the dying love of Jesus.[52]

Jesus demonstrated this dying love when He went to the cross. He went down the curve sacrificing His honor, glory, and life for us. He willingly took the shame and punishment for our sins and hit the bottom of the curve when He cried out, "My

51. Paul E. Miller, *A Loving Life: In a World of Broken Relationships* (Wheaton, IL: Crossway, 2014), 68.
52. Miller, 41.

God, My God, why have You forsaken Me." Then God brought Him up the other side of the curve when He raised Him from the dead and gave Him life, power, and honor. However, even before He went to the cross, Jesus commanded us to follow His example of sacrificial love. Jesus said, "If anyone wishes to come after Me, he must deny himself, and take up his cross and follow Me. For whoever wishes to save his life will lose it, but whoever loses his life for My sake and the gospel's will save it" (Mark 8:34-35).

Everyone who wants to follow Jesus must give up their own self-promotion and live for the sake of Jesus and the gospel. When we stop trying to promote ourselves and just love people the way Jesus loved us, we are giving up our lives for Jesus and sometimes it feels like dying. However, this is how we experience true joy and fulfillment in life. And this is how God demonstrates the power of the gospel in our lives. The Apostle Paul said, "I have been crucified with Christ; and it is no longer I who live, but Christ lives in me; and the life which I now live in the flesh I live by faith in the Son of God, who loved me and gave Himself up for me" (Galatians 2:20). Peter taught the same principle when he wrote, "For you have been called for this purpose, since Christ also suffered for you, leaving you an example for you to follow in His steps," (1 Peter 2:21).

Later in First Peter, he tells us that we need to have a perspective of suffering that sees it as normal and even as an opportunity to participate with Christ in His sufferings.

> Beloved, do not be surprised at the fiery ordeal among you, which comes upon you for your testing, as though some strange thing were happening to you; but to the degree that you share the sufferings of Christ, keep on rejoicing, so that also at the revelation of His glory you may rejoice with exultation. —1 Peter 4:12-13

When we look at our times of suffering as sharing in the sufferings of Christ, we experience a union with Christ that helps us to grow spiritually and become more like Christ. This enables us to rejoice throughout the whole process, even when we are at the bottom of the curve. We also need to remember that the curve up into resurrection is not always a removal of the suffering. Many times, the suffering is chronic and never seems to go away in this life (2 Cor. 12:8-9). The life-changing experience in the J-Curve® of suffering is the work of the same Spirit that raised Christ from the dead. And the primary work of the Spirit in our lives is the development of Christ-like character (Gal. 5:22-23).

By God's grace, I learned this lesson in a very practical way as a bivocational minister. About seven years ago the church youth group attendance was going down and kids were getting discouraged. I started praying for the youth group because most of the teens were graduating and going off to college and we only had five preteens in the congregation to take their place. Just a couple weeks after I started praying, my middle school bus route was altered. I was given two bus stops in the same neighborhood as our church, one right in front of the church building. I really didn't think much of it because public school employees are not allowed to share their faith on the job and most teenagers pay little or no attention to the bus driver anyway. That bus route had several students who were especially challenging and consistently disrespectful. I decided that no matter what, I would greet every student with a smile and an encouraging word. Most of the students would completely ignore me and walk right past me as if I was just a piece of equipment on the school bus. But I figured that even if I was only able to encourage one student, at least I know God has worked through me to make a positive difference in that one student's day.

The Sunday after I got those new bus stops, a girl from my middle school route was babysitting her younger siblings. Her parents told her to take them to church, probably to get the kids out of the house for couple hours. Kassie was one of those more challenging students on the bus. When I saw her walk through the front door of the church I said, "Hi Kassie." She looked surprised and asked, "How do you know my name?" I said, "Kassie, I'm your bus driver." At that, she was even more surprised and said, "Mr. Mike, what are you doing here?" I told her that I was one of the preachers. The next day on the bus, Kassie started telling all her friends that the bus driver was her pastor. The next Wednesday evening at youth group, Kassie showed up with half a dozen of her friends from the neighborhood. Over the next few weeks, the youth group grew to about 25 teens.

Greeting students with a smile and an encouraging word may not seem like a big sacrifice when we think of what Christ has done for us, but that's the point. Following the pattern of the gospel is not meant to draw attention to us. It is meant to point people to Jesus. It is by God's grace that He uses our sincere sacrifices— regardless of how big or small they are—to demonstrate His love and the message of the gospel.

## GOSPEL TRANSFORMATION

The gospel is an unending source of divine power for meaningful transformation. As we maintain a gospel perception and continue to develop a gospel motivation, gospel proclamation and gospel demonstration start to become more natural to us. In this process there is an ongoing gospel transformation taking place within us. As ministers of the gospel, we need to trust in the power of God to help us live a Jesus-shaped life. The gospel not only provides us with the Jesus-shaped *pattern* for how to live a fulfilling life, but it also provides the divine *power* we need to live that life.

In their book on *The Meaning of Marriage*, Kathy and Timothy Keller show us how the gospel provides both the *pattern* and the *power* for a healthy and fulfilling marriage. They write, "So, what do you need to make marriage work? You need to know the secret, the gospel, and how it gives you both the power and pattern for your marriage."[53] This same gospel principle is true concerning *every* area of life including our careers and our ministries. When we completely trust both the pattern and the power of the gospel, then we will, by God's grace, experience fulfilling and effective ministries.

The gospel is the power of God as Paul boldly declares, "For I am not ashamed of the gospel, for it is the power of God for salvation to everyone who believes, to the Jew first and also to the Greek" (Rom. 1:16). In First Corinthians, he writes, "For the word of the cross is foolishness to those who are perishing, but to us who are being saved it is the power of God" (1 Cor. 1:18). The salvation we experience through the power of the gospel is not just the forgiveness of sins. In his book, *Set Free: What the Bible Says About Grace*, Jack Cottrell describes how the gospel is the power of a double cure to heal the double trouble caused by our sin. He writes,

> Long ago I noticed a phrase in the first verse of the hymn, "Rock of Ages," that has shaped my thinking considerably. The hymn calls upon the blood of Christ to "be of sin the double cure," thereby saving us from sin's guilt and sin's power. (Another version says the double cure is being saved from God's wrath and being made pure, which is a different way of saying the same

---

53. Timothy Keller and Kathy Keller, *The Meaning of Marriage: Facing the Complexities of Commitment with the Wisdom of God* (New York, NY: Penguin Books, 2013), 43-44.

thing.) The words of the hymn are simply telling us that God's grace as the content of salvation contains two main components.[54]

Cottrell is referring to the blessings of justification and sanctification, blessings that we can only enjoy because of the power of the gospel. Our sin makes us legally guilty before God and deserving of death (Rom. 6:23). At the cross, Jesus paid the just wages for our sin by providing a way for us to be justified or declared, "not guilty." However, our sin also causes a problem in our hearts. Our sin makes our hearts spiritually sick with sinfulness. The more we sin the more we develop a greater tendency to sin. So even if all our sins are forgiven, we are still spiritually sick and enslaved to our sinfulness. Unless we renew our minds and allow the Holy Spirit to transform our hearts, we will continue to be slaves to the power of sin (Rom. 12:2). This second part of the double cure is the ongoing work of sanctification that takes place by the power of the Holy Spirit.

Cottrell notes the significance of the form of the verbs in Romans 12:2.[55] The commands "do not be conformed" and "be transformed," are both passive in voice indicating that we are not the ones doing the actions of the verbs but rather we are the ones receiving the action of the verbs. However, these verbs are in the imperative mood indicating that they are commands to us that we, in some way, have a responsibility to obey. We must allow the Holy Spirit to transform us. These verbs are also in the present tense, emphasizing ongoing action. These are commands that we must continue to obey throughout our lives. But how do we allow the Holy Spirit to continue to transform us? Paul says, "by the renewing of your mind." We must continue to preach the gospel to ourselves every day. This is how we continue to renew our minds and reinforce our trust in the power of God.

For those of us who are often overwhelmed with the demanding schedule of a bivocational ministry, this principle is crucial. In bivocational ministry, we are at a greater risk of feeling isolated and without the spiritual support and shepherding that Christians need. In the book, *Dangerous Calling*, Paul David Trip warns us, busy pastors, to take the time to renew our minds by preaching the gospel to ourselves. He writes,

> Because there will be many times when no one knows what you are
> thinking and therefore cannot interrupt your private conversation,

---

54. Jack Cottrell, *Set Free! What the Bible Says About Grace* (Joplin, MO: College Press, 2009), 67-68.
55. Cottrell, *The College Press NIV Commentary Romans Vol 2: Chapters 9-16,* 314.

you need to be committed to preaching the gospel to yourself. You need to preach a gospel that finds its hope not in your understanding and ability but in a God who is grand and glorious in every way and who has invaded your life and ministry by his grace. You need to preach a gospel to yourself that does not find its rest in you getting it right but in the righteousness of Jesus Christ. You need to preach a gospel to yourself that does not get its motivation from human success, respect, and acclaim but from plenteous grace, which you could never have earned. You need to tell yourself again and again that there is no pit of life or ministry so deep that Jesus isn't deeper. You need to call yourself to rest and faith when no one else knows that private sermon is needed.[56]

Tripp is not suggesting that we use the gospel like a doormat of cheap grace on which we casually wipe off our sins. The gospel underscores both the holy justice of God and the loving mercy of God. Tripp is showing us how preaching the gospel to ourselves is the way we renew our minds and allow the Holy Spirit to transform our hearts (Rom. 12:2). Meditating on the kindness of God at the cross, leads us to sincere and humble repentance (Rom. 2:4). Remembering the amazing grace of God displayed in the gospel, teaches us to deny ungodliness and worldly desires (Titus 2:11). The gospel is a powerful, life-transforming message.

All Christians are called to be ministers of the gospel in a general sense because we are all called through the gospel (2 Thess. 2:14) to live for the sake of the gospel (Mark 8:35) and preach the gospel to all creation (Mark 16:16).

In this chapter, we have explored what it means to be a minister of the gospel in a general sense. As ministers of the gospel, we must put on the "gospel glasses" and view all of life from the perspective of the cross. This gospel perception will develop within us a gospel motivation to share this good news with others. We must proclaim the gospel message to all creation, including ourselves, our brothers and sisters in the church, and especially to those outside the church. We must also follow the gospel pattern in the way that we live and demonstrate the sacrificial love of God in our actions and attitudes. We must also trust in the power of the gospel, by renewing our minds with the message of the gospel and allowing the

---

56. Paul David Tripp, *Dangerous Calling: Confronting the Unique Challenges of Pastoral Ministry* (Wheaton, IL: Crossway, 2015), 136.

Holy Spirit to transform our hearts. We can focus on and experience growth in any one of these gospel principles. They do not always develop in a certain order. However, when we look at all five gospel principles together, we see how they feed into and enhance each of the other principles. Figure 7 illustrates the cycle of a gospel-centered ministry.

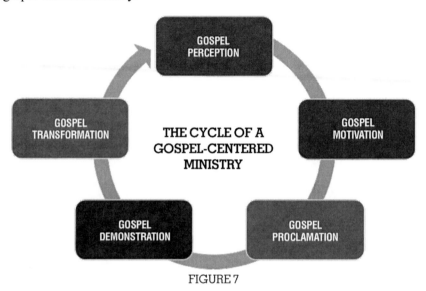

FIGURE 7

These are foundational principles for every ministry. These principles must be established before we move on to talk about the more specific aspects of bivocational ministry. Later in chapter 8, we will look at some specific applications of the gospel to bivocational ministry. However, before we get into the practical applications of the gospel to bivocational ministry, we need to consider the biblical foundations for bivocational ministry.

# DISCUSSION QUESTIONS

1. What does it mean to have a "gospel perception" in every area of life?

2. What can Christians do to develop and maintain a gospel perception of their work?

3. What is the connection between a gospel perception and a gospel motivation?

4. In his diagram, "the Golden Circle," Simon Sinek says that most organizations work from the outside in, emphasizing the WHAT and the How more than the WHY. He also contends that those organizations that are more inspiring and effective, operate from the inside out, emphasizing the WHY more than the WHAT or the HOW. Do you agree with his analysis? Why, or why not?

5. If Sinek's observations are generally true, what would be some important implications for church leaders to consider?

6. The author maintains that "the gospel must be our driving motivation for what we do and how we do it." Do you agree? Why or why not?

7. If someone asked you how the gospel is good news to you personally, what would you say?

8. What does the author mean when he talks about gospel demonstration?

9. What would be an example of gospel demonstration in your work or ministry?

10. What does the author mean when he talks about gospel transformation?

11. If spiritual transformation is the work of the Holy Spirit, what is our part in the process of "being transformed by the renewing of our mind"? How does the gospel help us in that process?

# CHAPTER 5

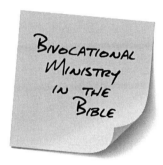

"So he was reasoning in the synagogue with the Jews and the God-fearing Gentiles, and in the market place every day with those who happened to be present."
—Acts 17:17

It was an exciting time for Peter, Andrew, James, and John. They had left the fishing business of their families and boldly accepted the invitation of Jesus to follow Him and be "fishers of men." But what did that mean? Peter didn't know what he was getting himself into. All he knew was that Jesus was the Christ, the Son of the living God. And even in those times when he didn't understand what Jesus was saying (which was often) he still knew that no one but Jesus had the words of eternal life.

On the day when Jesus preached the "Sermon on the Mount," the crowd was hanging on every word that Jesus spoke. But there was still something nagging Peter in his heart. He knew Jesus was the Messiah. No one could do the amazing miracles that Peter saw with his own two eyes. But Peter still wondered if Jesus made the right choice in calling a sinful fisherman to be His disciple. Peter's mind began to wander as he wondered, "Am I really cut out to be the disciple of any Rabbi, let alone the Messiah? And where is all this going anyway? I have a family to provide for and my mother-in-law is constantly struggling with health problems."

Jesus was seated just down the hill from Peter. As Peter watched Jesus preaching to the people, some movement caught his eye off in the distance where the bottom of the hill met the seashore. Some fishermen were cleaning their nets and getting their boats ready for the evening shift. "What am I doing?" Peter thought to himself. "Did I really think this through, or am I just being impulsive? I can't feed my family this way." Just then, the words of Jesus caught his attention and brought his heart back to the most important thing.

> "Do not worry then, saying, 'What will we eat?' or 'What will we drink?' or 'What will we wear for clothing?' For the Gentiles eagerly seek all these things; for your heavenly Father knows that you need all these things. But seek first His kingdom and His righteousness, and all these things will be added to you."
> —Matthew 6:31-33

I don't know if Peter was struggling with the worries Jesus mentioned that day. But at times, Peter seemed to be concerned about the financial security of his future (Matt. 19:27). And many preachers today wrestle with similar concerns. Certainly, Jesus wants us to make the Kingdom of God our priority. However, as we will see in this chapter, Jesus was not telling us that bivocational ministry is forbidden or a sign of weak faith.

Bivocational ministry is nothing new; in fact, it is a biblical idea. We see several examples of what we might call "bivocational ministers" throughout the Bible. In this chapter, we will examine the ministries of several people in the Bible who also had other occupations. Some of these people had clearly defined responsibilities both as ministers in God's kingdom and as workers in non-religious occupations. Some of these people took on these different roles at different times in their lives. And others were used by God to minister in special ways for brief periods of time while they were still working their regular jobs. This chapter will explore biblical principles that apply to bivocational ministry and show how God often calls people to bivocational ministry.

## WORK AND MINISTRY IN BIBLE TIMES

Before we look at the examples of bivocational ministers in the Bible we need to consider how the culture was different in ancient times. Both work and ministry are very different in our 21ˢᵗ century, first-world culture than they were in Bible times. We must also remember that the Bible covers four thousand years of human history and multiple cultures on three different continents. All that to say, we must be careful not to force our 21ˢᵗ century thinking into the text.

By our standards, the cultures we read about in the Bible would be similar to a third-world impoverished nation today. One of the most common and acceptable forms of work in the first century was slavery. We must also remember that slavery in the Bible was very different from the slavery in early American history. Slaves in the Roman Empire could own property, including their own slaves. With their master's permission, they could also work another job and save up money to purchase their own freedom. Some people would sell themselves into slavery to pay off debts and enjoy a higher standard of living than they had as a free person. Andrew Lincoln notes that slaves were in engaged in a wide variety of occupations. He writes,

> One-third of the population of Greece and Italy was enslaved. The work of these slaves covered the whole range of activities in the ancient world—from privileged positions in the household of the emperor to working in the mines. In between came such work as the civil service, medical care, teaching, accountancy, business, domestic work, and agricultural employment.[57]

For most people in the ancient world, work was a matter of survival rather than personal fulfillment. While there were many different occupations mentioned in the Bible, the people of ancient Israel did not have the career choices we have today. Ralph Gower makes the following observations about craftsmen in the early history of Israel. He writes, "After individuals developed skills, the skills were transmitted to their own families and groups until it became customary for groups of craftsmen to be found together."[58] Most boys grew up learning the same trade as their father and grandfather without any thought of choosing a career outside the family.

The most common jobs in ancient Israel centered around livestock and agriculture. John Beck notes that "Growing food was a necessity for most people living in Bible times. Virtually everyone was intimately connected with the family

---

57. Dr. Andrew T. Lincoln, *Word Biblical Commentary: Ephesians* (Grand Rapids, MI: Zondervan, 2014), 417-18.
58. Ralph Gower, *The New Manners & Customs of Bible Times* (Chicago, IL: Moody Publishers, 2005), 135.

grain and fruit production that provided ancient households with their food."[59] As we will see, many people were multi-vocational by necessity. While a person would be known by his primary trade of being a carpenter, a fisherman, a tanner, etc., he would also have other agricultural responsibilities to engage in or manage which would be an additional way to provide for his family. The same would also be true of those who were known by their religious roles such as prophets and priests.

## THE OLD TESTAMENT

In the patriarchal age of the Old Testament, the spiritual leaders were the fathers. The author of Hebrews reminds us that God "spoke long ago to the fathers in the prophets in many portions and in many ways," (Heb. 1:1). While God undoubtedly took care of these faithful fathers, we can also see that they were hard workers who provided for their families by working in common occupations of their time and culture. Noah was a farmer with a vineyard (Gen. 9:20). Abraham, Isaac, and Jacob all raised livestock for a living. While these fathers were working in these common occupations, God called them to special roles in His redemptive plan. They were all ministers of the gospel while they were faithfully working in their regular jobs.

Joseph is a good example of a man who had several different jobs, though not by his choice. He went from being a slave to being a prisoner and from being a prisoner to being the second in command of all Egypt. Regardless of the situations he faced in life and the roles that were given to him, he remained faithful to God. By his faith and God's grace, he prospered in each of those positions. Even though Joseph did not understand what God was doing until the end, God was still working in each of those roles to carry out His redemptive plan for His people. In each of his jobs, Joseph was also a minister of the gospel. Joseph's colorful career path provides a practical lesson for us. Many times, we won't be able to see the redemptive plan that God has for our work, but we still need to trust Him and remain faithful with the responsibilities He has given us.

During the time of Abraham, there was a bivocational minister who served as a picture of Jesus in Hebrews 7:1. Melchizedek was the king of Salem and a priest of God Most High (Gen. 14:18). This is another example of a cultural difference

---

59. John A. Beck, *The Baker Illustrated Guide to Everyday Life in Bible Times* (Grand Rapids, MI: Baker Books, 2013), 141.

foreign to our way of thinking, especially in America. It was common in ancient cultures for kings to be entrusted with the responsibilities of spiritual leadership as well as civil leadership.[60] Later, when God gave instructions for leadership in the nation of Israel, He did set up a separation of powers but even then, the separation was not purely between civil leadership and spiritual leadership. Many of the priests and prophets were called to be civil leaders and many of the kings were called to be spiritual leaders. For us today, we need to remember that God can still use civil leaders as spiritual leaders.

Melchizedek is the only biblical example from this period of someone receiving financial compensation as a minister of God. Abraham gave him a tenth of all the spoils from the war with the kings. The offering Melchizedek received as a priest was just supplemental to his main source of income as a king. It wasn't until the Mosaic age when God organized the Levitical priesthood that we see financial compensation prescribed for God's ministers. The tribe of Levi did not receive a portion of the Promised Land in the same way that the other tribes had. God told them that He was their inheritance and as such, they would be provided for by the tithes and offerings of the nation (Num. 18:20-21 and Deut. 18:1-8). However, God did not forbid the Levites from owning land, farming, or raising livestock to supplement their income. In fact, the Levites were given cities with pasture lands to work (Num. 35:2-3).

Like Joseph, Moses had several occupations over the course of his life, all of which God used to accomplish His redemptive plan for His people. As the first leader of God's people, Moses wore many occupational hats. He was a religious leader, a civil leader, and a military leader. He served as a lawgiver, a judge, and a prophet. Like many bivocational ministers today, Moses took on more than he could handle until his father-in-law talked some sense into him and told him how to delegate (Ex. 18:17-26). Delegation is the most important principle from the life of Moses for bivocational ministers to learn and put into practice. Jethro warned Moses that if he didn't learn how to delegate some of his responsibilities to others, both he and the congregation would suffer. Jethro said, "You will surely wear out, both yourself and these people who are with you, for the task is too heavy for you; you cannot do it alone" (Ex. 18:18).

During the time of the Judges, Israel had no king and no central government

---

60. John H. Walton, ed., *Zondervan Illustrated Bible Backgrounds Commentary Vol 1: Genesis, Exodus, Leviticus, Numbers, Deuteronomy* (Grand Rapids, MI: Zondervan, 2009), 82.

to maintain the stability and structure of the nation. The summary statement of the period was "In those days there was no king in Israel; everyone did what was right in his own eyes" (Judges 17:6 and 21:25). Throughout the book of Judges, we see God raising up people from various stations in life and using them, for a period, to deliver Israel from an oppressor. Gideon was a farmer threshing out his wheat when the Lord called him. After he defeated the Midianites, he turned down the opportunity to rule over Israel and "went and lived in his own house" (Judges 8:29). Each of the judges responded to God's call out of faith rather than a need for financial compensation. They did not see their calling as a career change. However, answering God's call, in faith, did change their identity as Fleenor notes concerning Gideon.

> To conclude the story of Gideon, the narrator switches to calling him Jerub-baal. The unexpected name change is the author's way of mocking Baal a final time. At the beginning of life as a judge, Gideon is renamed by his Baal-worshiping father Joash in a way that reflects a contest between Gideon and Baal. Gideon's new name challenges Baal to a confrontation. In 8:29, "Let Baal Strive" goes home in peace after having torn down Baal's altar and defeated Canaanite armies.[61]

This same principle is true for Christians today. The gospel calls us to a new identity in Christ. That new identity doesn't mean that we must change our career. It may be that God wants us to live out our new identity and be ministers of the gospel without changing our careers.

When we come to the period of kings and prophets, we see God expanding the list of roles and vocations that He calls people to fulfill. Again, these vocations are examples of God's grace working in the lives of people to help them fulfill their calling for the glory of God and God's overall redemptive plan. These were servants of God responding to God's calling out of faith and obedience regardless of any financial compensation. The first three kings of Israel were bivocational in the sense that they were all called to be kings of Israel, but they also served in a prophetic role. Saul's role as a prophet was temporary and mainly seen as a sign showing that God had chosen him to be the king. However, David and Solomon were both used by God to write Scripture. When we evaluate our gifts and ministry options and

---

61. Rob Fleenor and Mark S. Ziese, *The College Press NIV Commentary: Judges & Ruth* (College Press, 2008), 140.

we understand what God is calling us to do, we need to respond in faith and do it regardless of any financial compensation.

In the ancient near east, prophets often served as advisors employed by the crown. This was probably the case in 1 Kings 18:19 where it describes the 400 prophets of Baal and the 450 prophets of Asherah as those who "eat at Jezebel's table."[62] The true prophets of Yahweh accepted their calling regardless of any compensation. However, some of them were probably supported by the crown. In 2 Chronicles 22, when Jehoshaphat forms an alliance with Ahab, Jehoshaphat wants Ahab to inquire a word from Yahweh concerning their plans to join forces. Ahab brings in 400 prophets who all agree that the battle plans are a great idea but none of the prophets are prophets of Yahweh and Jehoshaphat knows it. When Jehoshaphat asks Ahab why he doesn't have any prophets of Yahweh in his court, Ahab basically says, "I have this one guy, Micaiah, but I hate him because he never tells me what I want to hear." Perhaps Ahab had Micaiah on a retainer for the sake of those 7,000 Israelites who had not bowed the knee to Baal. However, I'm sure Micaiah would have given Ahab the same message even if he wasn't paid to say it.

Another interesting bivocational minister from that same time was an official in the household of King Ahab by the name of Obadiah (not to be confused with the minor prophet). 1 Kings 18:3-4 says, "Ahab called Obadiah who was over the household. (Now Obadiah feared the LORD greatly; for when Jezebel destroyed the prophets of the LORD, Obadiah took a hundred prophets and hid them by fifties in a cave, and provided them with bread and water)" (1 Kings 18:3-4). Here is a man who "fears the LORD greatly" and even puts his life on the line to rescue and care for God's prophets and yet he is working for the most corrupt king in the history of Israel. Jesse Long notes the implied comparison between Elijah and Obadiah when he writes,

> Obadiah sustained (kûl; cf. 17:4,9) the prophets of Yahweh with bread and water. The reader hears the allusion to Yahweh's provisions for Elijah, with the theme of eating and drinking (17:1-16). Has Yahweh commanded Obadiah to provide for the prophets as he commanded the ravens and the widow of Zarephath to provide for Elijah?[63]

62. John H. Walton, ed., *Zondervan Illustrated Bible Backgrounds Commentary Vol 3: 1 & 2 Kings, 1 & 2 Chronicles, Ezra, Nehemiah, Esther* (Grand Rapids, MI: Zondervan, 2009), 76.

63. Jesse C. Long, *The College Press NIV Commentary: 1 & 2 Kings* (Joplin, MO: College Press, 2002), 211.

Many times, Christians complain about how ungodly the people are at their place of work and how corrupt their supervisors are. However, it may be that God wants to use us in those dark places like He used Obadiah in the palace of the wicked king Ahab. God is working through Christians in those unpleasant work environments to rescue and care for people in those dark corners of our world.

Isaiah may have been bivocational. The comments made about the writings of Isaiah in 2 Chronicles 26:22 and 32:32 indicate that Isaiah had an official position not just as a prophet but also as the palace historian. Jeremiah may have also had an official position in the palace. Jeremiah had a major role in the funeral of King Josiah (2 Chron. 35:25). The evil kings after Josiah refused to follow the word of the Lord that Jeremiah brought to them. However, King Zedekiah made sure that Jeremiah did not starve to death during the Babylonian siege (Jer. 37:21).

While some of the Old Testament prophets may have been on the king's payroll most of the prophets were probably more like Amos. Amos was a farmer and a shepherd in Judah, but God called him to go up to Bethel in Israel and prophesy against the house of Jeroboam (Amos 7:12-15). Amaziah, the priest at Bethel told Amos to go back to Judah "and there eat bread and there do your prophesying!" Amos responded by saying, "I am not a prophet, nor am I the son of a prophet; for I am a herdsman and a grower of sycamore figs." Amaziah was accusing Amos of trying to get a job in Israel as a prophet. But Amos told him that his call to preach was not a call to make a career change. The way he earned his bread was still through his work on the farm. However, his ministry as a prophet of the LORD was no less important simply because it was not his career.

Ezra is a good example of a bivocational minister in an Old Testament context. He was a priest and a scribe when he was commissioned by the government to be a civil leader. After the Babylonian exile, Jews in the Persian empire were concerned about the welfare of their brethren in Palestine. Harrison writes, "in 458 B.C. Artaxerxes I, who was sympathetic to their requests, appointed Ezra, a member of a Jewish priestly family, to go to Jerusalem as a royal commissioner to establish Jewish law there."[64] Ezra did not abandon his priestly duties when he accepted this position of civil authority. He saw it as an opportunity to partner with God in the redemptive plan God had for His people. He continued to serve both as a religious leader and as a civil leader.

---

64. R. K. Harrison, *Old Testament Times: A Social, Political, and Cultural Context* (Grand Rapids, MI: Baker Books, 2005), 286.

## THE NEW TESTAMENT

The New Testament identifies several church leaders who were employed in vocations outside of the church. In fact, that was the normal pattern for church leadership in the New Testament. The qualifications for overseers and deacons listed in 1 Timothy 3 include being a "husband of one wife," managing "his children and household well," and having a "good reputation with outsiders" (1 Timothy 3:1-12). These are all indications that the leaders of the early church were productive members of society, proving for their families, and living out a good work ethic in the community before they were appointed to leadership in the church. While these spiritual leaders often received monetary compensation for their ministries in the church, there is no indication from Scripture that they had to give up all other sources of income. Terry Dorsett urges Christians today to change their thinking about church leadership and recognize that bivocational ministry is the New Testament pattern. He writes,

> The New Testament reflects bivocational ministry as normative for the church. Modern church attendees have come to expect pastors to devote all of their time to the ministry of the church. As a result, many modern church attendees do not understand that New Testament churches were often led by bivocational pastors. This misunderstanding has created unrealistic expectations for bivocational pastors because of their additional employment outside the church. If bivocational pastors are going to lead their churches effectively, they will first have to educate their congregation in how New Testament churches were led.[65]

Before we look at the examples of bivocational ministry in the New Testament church, let's consider the testimony of the four gospels. The preaching and teaching ministry of Jesus only lasted about three years. But before He was known as the teacher, Jesus was known as the carpenter. When Jesus preached in the synagogue at Nazareth, the people from his hometown could not believe what they were seeing. The said, "Is not this the carpenter, the son of Mary, and brother of James and Joses and Judas and Simon? Are not His sisters here with us?" (Mark 6:3). While Jesus

---

65. Terry W. Dorsett, *Developing Leadership Teams in the Bivocational Church* (Bloomington, IN: Crossbooks, 2010), 7.

probably gave up His carpentry work to focus those last three years on preaching the gospel and training His disciples, it is interesting that He spent so many years of His life on earth as a carpenter. Joseph, the earthly stepfather of Jesus taught Jesus the family trade. The last time we hear about Joseph is when Jesus was twelve (Luke 2:48). We don't know what happened to Joseph during those 18 years before Jesus began His ministry. We don't know when Joseph died, but we can safely assume that for many of those years Jesus ran the carpentry business and worked as the breadwinner for the family. Tom Nelson notes that this situation does not reflect our typical view of manual labor when he asks,

> How did Jesus' brilliance fit in with a carpentry career? At first glance, this doesn't seem to be a very strategic use of the Son of God's extraordinary gifts or his important messianic mission. Why was it the Father's will for Jesus to spend so much time in the carpentry shop instead of gracing the Palestinian countryside, proclaiming the gospel and healing the multitudes?[66]

Perhaps Jesus spent all that time doing hard manual labor because He loved His family and He wanted to take care of them. Perhaps He spent all that time in the carpentry shop because He understood the value of making things that were useful and He enjoyed creating things that would benefit the community and the culture. And perhaps He wanted to fully experience humanity so that we would know that He understands all the struggles we go through in this life.

The author of Hebrews wrote, "For we do not have a high priest who cannot sympathize with our weaknesses, but One who has been tempted in all things as we are, yet without sin" (Heb. 4:15). And Paul said, "although He existed in the form of God, did not regard equality with God a thing to be grasped, but emptied Himself, taking the form of a bond-servant, and being made in the likeness of men" (Phil. 2:6-7). The Greek word here for bond-servant is *doulos* or slave. Our Lord and Master became a slave for us. This principle of incarnation is important for all ministers of the gospel to remember and practice. When we, as ministers, are willing to do hard work in the world with the people we are reaching out to, we are demonstrating the gospel. When the people in the pews listening to us on Sunday see us working beside them Monday through Friday, they know that we understand

---

66. Tom Nelson, *Work Matters: Connecting Sunday Worship to Monday Work* (Wheaton, IL: Crossway, 2011), 88.

what they are going through every day. And they will be far more likely to believe what we preach when they see it demonstrated in their world.

We now turn our attention to the twelve Apostles. Did Jesus call them to permanently leave their occupations for the sake of their new ministries? Was Jesus asking them to put their occupations on hold temporarily while they train for their new ministries? Or was Jesus just giving them a general principle about priorities rather than a command to permanently leave their occupations? And what are the practical implications for ministers of the gospel today?

The gospels mention the fact that at least four of the Apostles (Peter, Andrew, James, and John) were fishermen and one was a tax collector (Matthew, AKA Levi). The first time the fishermen expressed an interest in following Jesus is recorded in John 1:35-42. This event preceded their calling recorded in the synoptic gospels (Matt. 4:18-22; Mark 1:16-20; and Luke 5:1-11). The calling of the tax collector is recorded in Matthew 9:9-12; Mark 2:13-17; and Luke 5:27-32. One might assume that since Luke's account says, "they left everything" (Luke 5:11 and 5:28) a call to ministry is a call to "full-time" ministry. While Jesus certainly teaches us to make God's kingdom our priority (Matt. 6:33), He is by no means prohibiting bivocational ministry.

Concerning the fishermen, there are several things we need to remember about the context of their calling. First, Jesus was in the process of selecting twelve men to train for three years to be the Apostles of the New Testament church. While there are some principles about calling that we can learn from this and apply to our ministries today, we must recognize that their calling was unique. None of us are being called to live with Jesus for three years and learn how to be one of the twelve Apostles in the New Testament church.

Second, these men understood this calling in the Jewish context of the rabbi-disciple relationship. In that culture, Jewish boys (and men) who wanted further training after they completed their education in the school at the local synagogue would seek out a rabbi who would agree to train them. The rabbis of that time almost always had supplemental employment as Edersheim points out when he writes,

> Still, the great Hillel was a wood-cutter, his rival Shammai a carpenter, and among the celebrated Rabbis of after times we find shoemakers, tailors, carpenters, sandalmakers, smiths, potters,

builders, etc.—in short, every variety of trade. Nor were they ashamed of their manual labour.[67]

However, Jesus was not a typical rabbi as Chouinard explains,

Unlike typical rabbinic practice, Jesus takes the initiative to select his own followers by confronting them with an unconditional demand to join him in ministry. It is clear, in Matthew's story, that discipleship, in the sense of accompanying Jesus, arose primarily through his authoritative call (cf. 8:19-22; 9:9).[68]

Jesus was the Messiah selecting specific men to be the leaders of His new kingdom. He was calling these men to be much more than just disciples of a typical Jewish rabbi.

A third point to consider is that there are no commands anywhere in Scripture prohibiting ministers from having employment outside the church. Even in the case with the Apostles, we have strong evidence that these fishermen did not permanently leave their former occupations. In John 21:1-14, all four fishermen plus three other disciples are back out on the Sea of Galilee fishing. And in Matthew 17:24-27, Jesus commands Peter to go fishing for supplemental income in order to pay the temple tax.

All three points mentioned above also apply to Matthew's calling. Some people may object to the idea of Matthew ever going back to earning money as a tax collector on the grounds that it was an occupation of greed and dishonesty. However, when the tax collectors sincerely asked John the Baptist what they needed to do in order to "bear fruits in keeping with repentance," he did not tell them to leave their sinful occupations and find some honest work to do. He simply said, "Collect no more than what you have been ordered to" (Luke 3:13). On the other hand, Mark Moore takes the position that Matthew could not have gone back to collecting taxes because of the competitive nature of the business. Comparing the different occupations of the disciples, Moore writes,

We have seen four fishermen leave their private business in the hands of their father. However, they always have the option

---

67. Alfred Edersheim, *Sketches of Jewish Social Life: Updated Edition* (Peabody, MA: Hendrickson Publishers, 1994), 174.
68. Larry Chouinard, *The College Press NIV Commentary: Matthew* (Joplin, MO: College Press, 1997), 86.

to return. In fact, after the resurrection, the Apostles return to Galilee and spend their time fishing as they wait for Jesus. Levi is different—he has no other options. When he steps out of that tax collector's booth, it is for the last time. He is a small member of a large corporate structure. There are eager young publicans itching to sit in his lucrative seat. When he leaves, he leaves for good.[69]

While that may be the case, the Bible doesn't tell us about the employment options Matthew may have considered after that point. However, the Bible does tell us that the relationships Matthew had with his former business associates was good and he maintained those connections for the sake of the gospel. All three accounts of Matthew's calling place a strong emphasis on how Jesus and Matthew worked together and used Matthew's work connections for the sake of the gospel. In the book *Eats with Sinners*, Arron Chambers describes how this passage applies to us when he writes,

> Levi and his tax-collector friends were definitely "people of the soil," but Jesus didn't care. He accepted Levi, and Levi in turn accepted Jesus and threw a banquet in his honor, which made the legalists mad. "Why do you eat and drink with tax collectors and 'sinners'?" they asked (Luke 5:30).
> Good Question.
> Jesus ate with tax collectors and sinners because, unlike the Pharisees, teachers of the law, and some Christians, he wanted to have an intimate relationship with all sinners—including us.[70]

The principle for us today is that instead of cutting ourselves off from the connections we have with people through work, we need to allow Jesus to work through us and those connections for the sake of the gospel.

Now let's consider some of the bivocational ministers in the early church. Acts 18:1-3 indicates that Paul, Priscilla, and Aquila were professional tentmakers in addition to their ministry roles in the early church. Some people object to the notion of comparing Paul and his co-workers to modern bivocational ministers. In a response

69. Mark Moore, *The Chronological Life of Christ* (Joplin, MO: College Press, 2007), 138.
70. Arron Chambers, *Eats with Sinners: Reaching Hungry People Like Jesus Did* (Cincinnati, OH: Standard Publishing, 2009), 85-86.

to an article by Thom Rainer, Christopher wrote, "Using Paul as an example of a bi-vo pastor is just not accurate. Paul may have worked from time to time, but he was not a full time tent-maker with a church on the side."[71] It is true that Paul, Priscilla, and Aquila were missionaries and not pastors working in one congregation for a long period of time. However, I have yet to find a New Testament example of a fully funded pastor. The New Testament gives no instructions prohibiting ministers or pastors from working outside the church, so we must look at the examples we do have and go from there.

The Greek word for tentmaker is *skenopios* and it only occurs this one time in the New Testament. Because of the limited times it occurs outside the Bible, there is some dispute concerning its meaning. Bruce believes that "This trade was closely connected with the principal product of Paul's native province, a cloth of goats' hair called *cilicium*, used for cloaks, curtains, and other fabrics designed to give protection against wet."[72] However, other scholars give convincing evidence that the term was more general referring primarily to leather work. Michaelis states that "It is more probable that Paul and Aquila were 'leather-workers' or 'saddlers' and that as such they manufactured tents, for which there was considerable use in antiquity."[73]

This leatherworking trade would require a few small tools that could easily be packed up and carried to new locations. Leather tents and awnings would be needed by all the different merchants in the marketplaces of every city Paul went to. Gloer describes how Paul and his tent-making co-workers probably used their trade as an opportunity for a marketplace ministry for the sake of the gospel. He writes,

> If Acts 18:2 represents a typical pattern, it is possible that Paul, upon arriving at a new city, sought out a fellow artisan with whom he might practice his trade. Such association might have provided Paul with his first contacts in a new city. Furthermore, Paul's workshop may have been the locus of much of his missionary preaching and teaching (17:17). Certainly the nature of his trade would have allowed him to engage in conversation, lecturing, and teaching while working.[74]

---

71  Rainer, "Eight Characteristics of the New Bivocational Pastor."
72  F. F. Bruce, *The Book of the Acts* (Grand Rapids, MI: Eerdmans, 1988), 346.
73  Gerhard Kittel and Gerhard Friedrich, eds., *Theological Dictionary of the New Testament: Vol. VII* (Grand Rapids, MI: Eerdmans Pub Co, 1979), 394.
74  Geoffrey W. Bromiley, *The International Standard Bible Encyclopedia Vol. Four: Q-Z* (Grand Rapids, MI: Eerdmans Pub Co, 1995), 792.

A practical principle for us is that if we are going to be bivocational we should look for a job that helps us to make connections with people and gives us opportunities to proclaim and demonstrate the gospel.

Paul also used his vocation outside the church to serve as an example for Christians to follow. In 2 Thessalonians, he specifically states that one of the reasons he chose to keep his tent-making job while in ministry was to be a model for other Christians to follow.

> For you yourselves know how you ought to follow our example, because we did not act in an undisciplined manner among you, nor did we eat anyone's bread without paying for it, but with labor and hardship we *kept* working night and day so that we would not be a burden to any of you; not because we do not have the right *to this,* but in order to offer ourselves as a model for you, so that you would follow our example (2 Thess. 3:7-9).

In Acts 20, Paul meets with the elders from Ephesus and he reminds them of his work ethic. In this passage, Paul points out that we have an obligation to use our vocation for the common good of "helping the weak."

> "I have coveted no one's silver or gold or clothes. You yourselves know that these hands ministered to my *own* needs and to the men who were with me. In everything I showed you that by working hard in this manner you must help the weak and remember the words of the Lord Jesus, that He Himself said, 'It is more blessed to give than to receive'" (Acts 20:33-35).

The principle for bivocational ministers today is that our jobs outside the church give us an opportunity to be a blessing to the community and provide an example of vocational stewardship that the Christians in our congregations can follow.

In 1 Corinthians 9:6, Paul identifies Barnabas as a church leader who earned his living from another vocation. The name Barnabas means "son of encouragement." We learn in Acts 4:36-37 that his real name was Joseph. He was a Levite from Cyprus. The Apostles in Jerusalem probably gave him the nickname Mr. Encouragement because of his generosity. Anthony Thiselton suggests that Barnabas and Paul may have established a "pay your own way" policy when they were called to go on their first mission together. Thiselton writes,

> The allusion to Barnabas is not arbitrary. Barnabas disposed of his own source of business income to support the church (Acts 4:36-37), and his introduction of Paul to the missionary staff of the churches (Acts 11:22-26) may have implied that they shared the policy of trying to "pay their way" as part of their joint missionary strategy, whether or not other co-workers did the same.[75]

As bivocational ministers, we can learn from the example of Barnabas to use what might seem to be an unfavorable situation to be an encouragement to the church. Our positive attitude about our work and our generosity with our time and money will be contagious.

Undoubtedly, the way we work and do ministry has changed dramatically since Bible times. However, in this chapter, we have seen from both the Old Testament and the New Testament that God is fully capable of using people to carry out His will in many kinds of ministries and occupations. We have seen that it is often the case that God calls people to be ministers of the gospel in bivocational ways. We have also seen several biblical principles that are helpful and practical for bivocational ministers today. In the next chapter, we will consider how God has used bivocational ministry in the last two thousand years.

---

75. Anthony C. Thiselton, *The New International Greek Testament Commentary: The First Epistle to the Corinthians* (Grand Rapids, MI: Eerdmans, 2013), 679.

# DISCUSSION QUESTIONS

1. How is work in our culture today different from what it was in Bible times?

2. How did God use Joseph's work as a slave, a prisoner, and an administrator to advance His redemptive plan?

3. Many ministers today are busy trying to do too many things at once. What should busy ministers learn from the advice Jethro gave to Moses?

4. Read 1 Kings 18:3-4. How can Obadiah be an encouragement for Christians who feel like they are trapped working in a spiritually dark place for an ungodly employer?

5. Why do you think Jesus spent so much time as a carpenter and only three years proclaiming the gospel and healing the multitudes?

6. How can bivocational ministry provide us with an opportunity to demonstrate the incarnation of Jesus?

7. What principle was Jesus teaching the apostles when He called them to leave their current occupations to follow Him? How (if at all) does this principle apply to Christians today?

8. What evidence do we have to suggest that the Apostles did not permanently leave their occupations when they decided to follow Jesus?

9. How did Jesus use Matthew's connections with other tax collectors as an opportunity for ministry?

10. How did Paul's job as a tentmaker give him opportunities for evangelism?

11. How did Paul use his tentmaking job as an opportunity for discipleship?

# CHAPTER 6

BIVOCATIONAL MINISTRY IN CHURCH HISTORY

"Remember the days of old, Consider the years of all generations. Ask your father, and he will inform you, Your elders, and they will tell you."
—Deuteronomy 32:7

And since we cannot deceive the whole human race all the time, it is most important thus to cut every generation off from all others; for where learning makes a free commerce between the ages there is always the danger that the characteristic errors of one may be corrected by the characteristic truths of another. But thanks be to our Father and the Historical Point of View, great scholars are now as little nourished by the past as the most ignorant mechanic who holds that "history is bunk."

Your affectionate uncle,
SCREWTAPE[76]

C. S. Lewis wrote the first edition of *The Screwtape Letters* back in the 1940s. Some people might say that his writings are dated and no longer relevant for Christians today, thus, making his critique of the Historical Point of View another victim of the Historical Point of View. The idea of senior demons explaining

---

76. C.S. Lewis, *The Screwtape Letters* (New York, NY: HarperOne, 2015), 151.

philosophical strategies to junior demons may be speculative, but the point Lewis makes about learning from previous generations is both biblical and relevant for Christians in every century.

This chapter is a brief overview of church history looking at examples of bivocational ministry as well as the beliefs and practices that have shaped our current view of the ministry of the gospel. In the previous chapter, we saw that the Bible contains many examples of what we could call bivocational ministry. We saw that bivocational ministry was probably the most common way of doing ministry in the New Testament church. In this chapter, we will see that bivocational ministry was also quite common throughout church history. But when and why did fully funded ministers become the norm for local churches? Under what circumstances were the different ministries in church history fully funded, bivocational, or volunteer based? Were the examples of bivocational ministry in church history simply due to the economic constraints of the time? How did bivocational ministers in church history leverage their occupations in the community for the sake of the gospel?

Some people in the Restoration Movement see studies in church history as a waste of time. Ironically, that sentiment is largely due to our history. The Restoration Movement was born out of a frustration that several ministers were experiencing in the early 1800s. They were frustrated with the sectarian attitudes and the divisiveness seen in the different denomination. They were also frustrated because so many of those divisions were based on unbiblical theology. They thought that Christian unity and doctrinal purity could be accomplished by simply inviting all churches to abandon their denominational creeds and traditions and just go back to New Testament Christianity. That conviction soon developed into a tendency to be suspicious of anything that happened in church history As C. Leonard Allen writes,

> This sense of historylessness works in powerful and subtle ways. In the process it creates exhilarating (and damaging) illusions. Among Churches of Christ it often has meant that we simply discounted eighteen centuries of Christianity as, at worst, a diseased tumor or, at best, an instructive failure.[77]

However, I am convinced that a better understanding of church history is both

---

77. C. Leonard Allen, *The Cruciform Church: Becoming a Cross Shaped People in a Secular World* (Abilene, TX: Abilene Christian University Press, 1990), 5.

practical and beneficial for our ministries today and in the future. This study of church history is essential to our discussion about bivocational ministry and the ministry of the gospel for three reasons.

First, when we are not aware of church history, we tend to think that the way we do ministry is the only way it has ever been done. One of the goals of this chapter is to show that bivocational ministry was the norm up until the twentieth century. Our purpose here is not to use history to define bivocational ministry but to note the changes in ministry over the years. Just as ministry and work changed throughout Bible times, they have gone through radical transformations in church history as well. Understanding the transitions of the past will help us to navigate the inevitable transitions we will face in the future.

Second, a study of church history gives us an opportunity to learn from the mistakes and the successes of the past. As we examine both good and bad examples from church history, we will note lessons that may help us to be more effective as ministers of the gospel.

Third, in order to understand who we are and where we are going, we must know something about where we have been and how the changes in culture over the years have shaped us. The Bible says that the men of Issachar "had understanding of the times, to know what Israel ought to do," (1 Chron. 12:32, ESV). The same is true for our understanding of the ministry of the gospel and bivocational ministry. In America today, 64% of the Churches of Christ and Christian churches have a fully funded minister.[78] Whenever I share that statistic with Christian leaders, they usually ask the same question, "Why are so few of our preachers fully funded?" But no one ever asks, "Why are so many of our preachers fully funded?" How did fully funded ministry get to be the norm? Why do ministry students come out of Bible college thinking that if they don't get a full-time ministry position then God must not be calling them to ministry?

## THE EARLY CHURCH

We already saw how bivocational ministry was the norm in the New Testament. Granted, the option of fully funded ministry was simply not available for most congregations for financial reasons. And the situation did not change during the first three centuries of the early church. McCarty writes, "Before Constantine

---

78. Kennedy, 228.

legalized Christianity in the fourth century, there were few 'paid' clergy."[79] Luther Dorr states that "The testimony of research is almost universal that bivocationalism was the normal practice in the early church."[80] And James Lowery writing about bivocational ministry says, "It is a historic form of ministry and was the norm in the first three or four centuries of church history."[81]

Bivocational ministry was the norm in the early church for more than just financial reasons. The certain aspects of both the Jewish and Greek cultures during that time reinforced the practice of bivocational ministry. Bruce believes that Paul was influenced early in life by the rabbinic values of that period. He writes,

> Paul had been brought up to believe that the teaching of the Torah should not be made a means of livelihood or personal aggrandizement. "He who makes a worldly use of the crown of the Torah will waste away," said Hillel; and so Paul, whether he was a Hillelite or not, was by manual occupation a tent-maker.[82]

This Jewish work ethic continued to be taught by the rabbis in the second century. The *Tosefta* exhorts, "Whoever does not teach his son a craft teaches him to be a robber."[83] And the *Mishna* proclaims, "Excellent is the study of the Torah together with worldly occupation."[84]

The Greek work ethic (or lack thereof) influenced bivocational ministry in the early church from the opposite direction. The Greeks despised manual labor. They saw it as the demeaning activity of slaves and those simple-minded people who could not contribute meaningful ideas to their philosophy-centered culture. As Keller notes,

> The ancient Greeks, who also thought that the gods made human beings for work, saw this as no blessing. Work was demeaning… In fact, Aristotle said that unemployment—by which he meant the ability to live without having to work—was a primary qualification for a genuinely worthwhile life.[85]

---

79   McCarty, *Meeting the Challenge of Bivocational Ministry,* 26.
80   Luther M. Dorr, *The Bivocational Pastor* (Nashville, TN: B&H Publishing Group, 1988), 22.
81   James L. Lowery, *Case Histories of Tentmakers* (Wilton, CT: Morehouse-Barlow Co., Inc., 1976), v.
82   F.F. Bruce, *Paul: Apostle of the Heart Set Free* (Grand Rapids, MI: Eerdmans, 1994), 107-108.
83   Herbert Danby, *Tractate Sanhedrin, Mishnah and Tosefta: The Judicial Procedure of the Jews* (Forgotten Books, 2008), Qidd. 1-11-73.
84   Danby, Abot 2:2-74.
85   Keller, *Every Good Endeavor,* 32-33.

We know that Paul's decision to be bivocational was not just because of his financial needs. On more than one occasion Paul used his manual labor to teach and demonstrate a biblical work ethic to Christians who were being influenced by the Greek culture to avoid manual labor (Acts 20:33-35; 1 Thess. 2:9; and 2 Thess. 3:6-12). The practice and teaching of the early church fathers are consistent with the work ethic taught and exemplified by Paul. The *Didache* (AD 80-140) records this instruction concerning the hospitality given to a prophet: "If a prophet desires to abide with you, and if he is a tradesman, let him work and eat. However, if he has no trade, according to your understanding see to it that as a Christian, he will not live with you idle."[86] Here we see that it was not unusual for traveling preachers to also have a trade and if they didn't they were still expected to do some kind of work for their room and board. In fact, the Christian host was instructed to hold these prophets accountable in this area.

The church was born in a Jewish culture with a biblical work ethic. As the early church continued to become more and more Gentile it held on to that biblical work ethic even when it was in opposition to the dominant Greek culture. It did so through bivocational ministers who taught and demonstrated a good work ethic. For those early church leaders, that work ethic was empowered and motivated by the message of the gospel. There is a practical application here for bivocational ministers today. Many of us older preachers grew up with a work ethic like that of the Jewish culture in Paul's day. However, "the times they are a changing." We are now finding ourselves in a culture that places extremely low expectations on youth and young adults. In their book, *Do Hard Things*, Alex and Brett Harris write about how our society has lowered the bar so much for teenagers and young adults that we have a generation of unmotivated low achievers with little or no work ethic. They share their research about this trend when they write,

> In 2005, *Time* magazine ran a story on "kidults," a new breed of
> adolescents in their mid- to late twenties and beyond who offer
> convincing evidence that the modern concept of adolescence is
> not a biological stage, but a cultural mind-set. It doesn't stop when
> you graduate from high school, or when you turn twenty-one.

---

86    David W. Bercot, ed., *A Dictionary of Early Christian Beliefs: A Reference Guide to More Than 700 Topics Discussed by the Early Church Fathers* (Peabody, MA: Hendrickson Pub, 1998), 229.

"Everybody knows a few of them," the article pronounced. "Full-grown men and women who still live with their parents, who dress and talk and party as they did in their teens, hopping from job to job and date to date, having fun but seemingly going nowhere."

Kidults generally have neither clear direction nor a sense of urgency. "Legally, they're adults, but they're on the threshold, the doorway to adulthood, and they're not going through it," says Terri Apter, a psychologist at the University of Cambridge. In other words, they're standing on the end of the diving board, but they won't jump in.[87]

What a great opportunity we have as bivocational ministers in a culture that desperately needs to see a gospel empowered Christian work ethic not just preached but exemplified in real life. We need to show and tell the current generation how the gospel gives us purpose and fulfillment in our work. When we talk about our work, is our conversation filled with complaints and negative remarks or do we inspire and motivate people to see work as a gift from God that helps us to reflect His image? If you are a bivocational youth leader, are you using your testimony and example of work to help young people see that manual labor is not a curse but a blessing from God? If you are a bivocational minister with children, are you looking for creative and positive ways to include your children in your work and ministry?

## THE MIDDLE AGES

After the rise of Constantine and the legalization of Christianity, the roles of ministry in the church began to go through radical changes. Most of the Christian leaders in the west had already abandoned the New Testament model of local autonomy with a plurality of elders leading each congregation. The western church developed a pyramid model of organization with a fully funded bishop exercising authority over multiple congregations in his region. When the Roman Empire began to support the church, these roles of church leadership became even more lucrative positions of power and influence.

---

87. Alex Harris and Brett Harris, *Do Hard Things: A Teenage Rebellion Against Low Expectations* (Colorado Springs, CO: Multnomah, 2008), 50-51.

However, things were different in the east, particularly in Persia. Soon after Rome legalized Christianity, Persia took a hardline stance against Christianity. Christy Wilson describes the struggles of the Christian ministers in Persia and how many of them were bivocational.

> Under the persecution of Christians by Zoroastrians in Persia between A.D. 339 and 448, hundreds of thousands were martyred. Many were also exiled. These, like those in the early church, went everywhere preaching the gospel. Most of them were lay people who had to work for their living. Supporting themselves by the labor of their own hands or filling appointments as secretaries, physicians, or stewards in the households of the nobles and princes of those lands to which they went, they were one and all missionaries of the cross.[88]

While there were undoubtedly some Christian leaders during this period (especially in the western church) who were greedy for wealth and power, we do find some examples of bishops and priests who were bivocational. Dorr identifies several Christian leaders during the dark ages who also worked outside the church. He writes,

> Chrysostom (ca. 347-407) mentioned some rural clergymen as yoking the oxen and driving the plow. Spyridon, a bishop of Cyprus, was also a shepherd. Zeno, whose church in Gaza was quite large, was a linen weaver. One named Dionysius was a presbyter/silversmith. Basil reported that his priests were working and earning their bread.[89]

One of the issues discussed at the Council of Chalcedon (AD 451) was concerning the kind of employment bishops, priests, and deacons could have outside the church. Among new regulations the council came up with "listed professions and activities forbidden to clerics such as money-lending, holding public office, or administering property."[90] The implication is that clerics were permitted to keep

---

88. McCarty, *Meeting the Challenge of Bivocational Ministry,* 58.
89. Dorr, *The Bivocational Pastor,* 22.
90. Everett Ferguson, ed., *Encyclopedia of Early Christianity, Second Edition* (New York, NY: Routledge, 1990), 266.

other occupations not forbidden by the new rule. Later, as the church continued to gain more political power, church leaders were entrusted with more responsibilities of civil leadership as Lowery observes:

> In the medieval western church where church and state were effectively one, many priests in effect earned their living as government officials, (canon) lawyers, and (because they could read and write), clerical workers (hence the title <u>clerk</u> or cleric in Old English. Thus many early tentmakers were government bureaucrats.[91]

The examples we have considered so far in the medieval period do not seem to be based on the gospel. In many cases, these bivocational ministries seem to be motivated by greed and a lust for power. As a result, this often led to an abuse of power and further corruption of the church.

However, there is another example of bivocational ministry from this period that we need to consider. Monasticism was born out of a sincere desire to live out the gospel and the words of Jesus when He said, "If anyone wishes to come after Me, he must deny himself, and take up his cross daily and follow Me" (Luke 9:23). At first, the monastic movement consisted of individual hermits living out in the desert, trying to deny themselves any of the pleasures of life. They were trying to recapture the devotion and sincerity displayed in the lives of Christian martyrs back when Christians were being persecuted by the Roman government. However, they were unorganized individuals who had not considered the redemptive and productive purposes God has for Christians in this world. Eventually, Christian leaders like Pachomius, Basil, and Benedict saw the passion of this movement and organized it into productive ways to be a blessing to both the church and the culture. Shelley writes,

> A former soldier named Pachomius instituted the first Christian monastery. Instead of permitting the monks to live singly or in groups of hermits, each a law to himself, Pachomius established a regulated common life, in which the monks ate, labored, and worshiped. His plan called for fixed hours, manual work, dress in uniform garb, and strict discipline.[92]

91. James Lowery, *Bi-Vocationals: Men And Women Who Enrich the Human Ecology And the World Surrounding* (West Conshohocken, PA: Infinity Publishing, 2006), 2.
92. Bruce Shelley, *Church History in Plain Language: Fourth Edition* (Nashville, TN: Thomas Nelson, 2012), 128.

In AD 358, Basil, the Bishop of Caesarea established a monastery in Pontus. He wrote up a Rule that would forever change monasticism in the east. James North describes the goals of Basil:

> He wanted to transform the institution from a life of bizarre competition in outlandish asceticism to a devotion to the common life of the monastery. Basil designed his Rule to do four things. (1) Suppress the anchorites, bringing them into monasteries. (2) Remove the monasteries from the deserts to the cities. (3) Restrict the austerities and the self-inflicted suffering.... (4) Encourage learning. By these measures, Basil directed much of the energy of monasticism into more productive channels.[93]

In AD 529, Benedict of Nursia established a monastery in Monte Casino. The Rule he established became the foundation for monasticism in the west. Williston Walker writes,

> To Benedict's thinking, worship was undoubtedly the prime duty of a monk. Its daily common observance at least four hours, divided into seven periods. Almost as much emphasis was laid on work. "Idleness is the enemy of the soul." Hence Benedict prescribed manual labor in the fields and reading.[94]

In addition to their religious duties, these monasteries required monks to do manual labor that would help support the monastery and be a blessing to the outside community. While the monastic life was separate from the world, in many ways, the monks were still serving their communities and proclaiming the gospel. James Goehring notes, "They were instrumental in the spread of Christianity, particularly in the countryside."[95] Justo Gonzalez describes how the bivocational work of these monks was used by God to cultivate and bless most of Europe. He writes,

> Eventually, monasteries also had a profound economic impact,

---

93. James B. North, *A History of the Church from Pentecost to Present* (Joplin, MO: College Press Publishing Company, Inc., 1991), 116-17.
94. Williston Walker, *A History of the Christian Church* (New York, NY: Simon Schuster Trade, 1970), 127.
95. Ferguson, *Encyclopedia of Early Christianity, Second Edition,* 774.

for many were established on marginal lands that were brought into productivity by the labor of the monks. Thus, countless acres were added to the agricultural land of Europe. Furthermore, in a society where the wealthy considered manual labor demeaning, the monasteries showed that the highest intellectual and spiritual achievements could be coupled with hard physical labor.[96]

Of course, the monks were not perfect. Many times, monasteries became wealthy from the donations of others. With their growing wealth and influence came the temptation to abuse their power. Shelley states that "The history of the Middle Ages shows constant efforts toward their reform and the foundation of new houses designed to eliminate the corruption of the older ones."[97] An important principle for us to remember is that we need to constantly check our motives for pursuing and accepting positions of leadership. As we noted in chapter four, we must constantly preach the gospel to ourselves. Only when our jobs and ministries are grounded in the gospel will we be able to effectively guard against the temptations to pursue wealth and power.

## THE REFORMATION

There are several examples of bivocational ministry from the period of the Reformation. Many of these were due to the economic struggles of the various groups that came out of the Reformation as John Elliott notes,

> The Reformation excluded many preachers and church leaders from the blessing of the church. The new churches were led by clergy outside of apostolic succession. Once again the Dual Role minister emerged out of necessity to survive, because the new congregations did not have the resources to support full-time clergy, and some of the groups were "underground."[98]

However, the greatest shift in how Christians view work and ministry took place during the reformation. One of the major themes of the Reformation was "the

---

96. Justo L. Gonzalez, *The Story of Christianity, Volume 1: The Early Church to the Dawn of the Reformation* (San Francisco, CA: Harper & Row, 1984), 241.
97. Shelley, *Church History in Plain Language*, 132.
98. Elliott, *Our Pastor Has an Outside Job*, 18.

priesthood of all believers." The Roman Catholic church had exalted the clergy to a superior spiritual status over and above anyone who was not ordained. The work of clergy was seen as spiritual and eternal, but the work of all other Christians was worldly and temporal. Martin Luther railed against this false teaching in his address *To the Christian Nobility of the German Nation.* He wrote,

> It is pure invention that pope, bishop, priests, and monks are called the spiritual estate while princes, lords, artisans, and farmers are called the temporal estate. This is indeed a piece of deceit and hypocrisy. Yet no one need be intimidated by it, and for this reason: all Christians are truly of the spiritual estate, and there is no difference among them except that of office. Paul says in I Corinthians 12 that we are all one body, yet every member has its own work by which it serves the others. This is because we all have one baptism, one gospel, one faith, and are all Christians alike; for baptism, gospel, and faith alone make us spiritual and a Christian people.[99]

Notice that Luther tied the value of all Christians along with the value of their work to three things: one baptism, one gospel, and one faith. In his mind, the message that unifies all Christians and gives our work value is the message of the gospel. Luther went on to show how God uses the work of all Christians including that of tailors, cobblers, stonemasons, carpenters, cooks, innkeepers, farmers and all the craftsmen to accomplish His will and advance His Kingdom.

Despite Luther's teaching on the subject, most of the denominations that came out of the Reformation continued to hold on to a distinction of importance between the clergy and the laity. Of course, the New Testament gives clear instructions about the organization and qualifications of local church leadership (Acts 20:28; 1 Tim. 3:1-13; Titus 1:5-9; and 1 Peter 5:1-4). And the New Testament commands Christians to follow, respect, and financially support these spiritual leaders (1 Cor. 9:1-18; Gal. 6:6; 1 Thess. 5:12-13; 1 Tim. 5:1-18; and Heb. 13:17). Clearly, there is a distinction in the New Testament given to those who have been appointed (set apart) as leaders in the local church. They have a heavier weight of responsibility on their shoulders for which God is holding them accountable (Heb. 13:17 and James 3:1).

---

99. Martin Luther, *Three Treatises* (Philadelphia, PA: Fortress Press, 1990), 12.

Protestant denominations have struggled to communicate the distinct authority in the roles of church leadership without giving everyone else the impression that other roles and occupations are not as important or spiritual. This is still a common perception that people have today. Researchers at the Barna Group state that,

> according to most U.S. adults—especially (and paradoxically) practicing Christians—pastors' work is more important than their own career or vocation.... three-quarters of practicing Christians say a pastor's vocation is more important than their own (51% much more, 22% a little more).[100]

Perhaps the question on their survey set people up to think about this issue from an unbiblical perspective. It is in our nature to compare ourselves to others, sometimes, to boost our self-worth, and at other times to punish ourselves or engage in false humility. Paul said that this practice of comparing ourselves to others is not wise (2 Cor. 10:12).

In the context of bivocational ministry, this perception gives people the impression that the work a bivocational minister does for the church is important but the work he does outside the church is at best a financial necessity and at worst a waste of his time. There have been times when people have tried to encourage me by saying things like, "Mike, I hope God works things out, so you can get off that school bus and start using that time for work in God's Kingdom." I understand what they are trying to say. And frankly, sometimes I feel the same way. But we don't have to tear down the work Christians are doing in the community in order to build up the work pastors are doing in the church.

## THE RESTORATION MOVEMENT

Many of the early leaders of the Restoration Movement were opposed to positions of paid ministry in the local church. They were reacting to the abuses of the paid clergy they saw in the denominations they came out of. Early in his ministry, Alexander Campbell wrote: "The Third Epistle of Peter, to the Preachers and Rulers of Congregations." It was a satirical piece meant to rebuke the greed and abuse of the paid clergy. The last section was specifically about the monetary wages of ministry.

---

100. Kinnaman, *The State of Pastors*, 130.

"IN all your gettings" get money! Now, therefore, when you go forth on your ministerial journey, go where there are silver and gold, and where each man will pay according to his measure. For verily I say you must get your reward.

Go you not forth as those that have been sent, "without two coats, without gold or silver, or brass in their purses; without scrip for their journey, or shoes, or staves;" but go you forth in the good things of this world.

And when you shall hear of a church that is vacant and has no one to preach therein, then be that a call to you, and be you mindful of the call, and take you charge of the flock thereof and of the fleece thereof, even of the golden fleece.

And when you shall have fleeced your flock, and shall know of another call, and if the flock be greater, or rather if the fleece be greater, then greater be also to you the call. Then shall you leave your old flock, and of the new flock shall you take the charge.

Those who have "freely received" let them "freely give," and let not men have your words "without money nor without price," but bargain you for hundreds and bargain for thousands, even for thousands of silver and gold shall you bargain.

And over and above the price for which you have sold your service, take you also gifts, and be you mindful to refuse none, saying, "Lo! I have enough!" but receive gifts from them that go in chariots, and from them that feed flocks, and from them that earn their morsel by the sweat of their brow.

Yea, take you gifts of all, and take them in gold and in silver, and in bread; in wine and in oil; in raiment and in fine linen.

And the more that the people give you the more will they honor you; for they shall believe that "in giving to you they are giving to the Lord;" for behold their sight shall be taken from them, and they shall be blind as bats, and "shall know not what they do."

And you shall wax richer and richer, and grow greater and greater, and you shall be lifted up in your own sight, and exalted in the eyes of the multitude; and lucre shall be no longer filthy in your sight. And verily you have your reward.

In doing these things you shall never fail. And may abundance of gold and silver and bank notes, and corn, and wool, and flax, and spirits and wine, and land be multiplied to you, both now and hereafter. Amen.[101]

Other leaders in the early years of the Restoration Movement were not as outspoken against paid clergy as Alexander Campbell was, however, none of the other leaders were as influential as Campbell. In the early years of the movement, the local congregations were led only by the elders of the church and when, in the 1850s, some churches started paying one man to be the full-time pastor it was viewed by many people as an unscriptural innovation. [102]

Our views and practices concerning paid ministry have changed over the years, and they can and will continue to change in the future. In some circles of the movement, it seems like the pendulum has swung the other way and the idea of bivocational ministry is looked upon as if we are not fully committed to the Lord's work. However, the movement has great potential to be blessed by the developing trend of bivocational ministry if local churches and church leaders are willing to prepare for it.

In the past, the Restoration Movement placed a strong emphasis on a leadership structure in the local church consisting of a plurality of elders who are active in the ministries of leading and teaching the congregation. Such a structure is especially important when a congregation has a bivocational minister because the elders are helping to share the load of ministry. Churches in the Restoration Movement should already have this structure and this value for the New Testament model of church leadership. Christian leaders in other traditions have noted the importance of this biblical strategy in the context of bivocational ministry. Dorsett writes,

The New Testament demonstrates a shared pastoral leadership model as normative for the church. In modern times, many North American Protestant churches have become accustomed to a single-pastor model of church leadership.... The solo pastor, or

---

101. Alexander Campbell, *Christian Baptist* (Joplin, MO: College Press Pub Co, 1983), 219.
102. James B. North, *Union in Truth: An Interpretive History of the Restoration Movement*, (Cincinnati, OH: Standard Publishing, 1994), 168.

the senior pastor in a large church, is often expected to do almost all of the preaching and pastoral care.

When the bulk of the preaching and pastoral care is centered on one person, it creates the impression that the person has more authority than the New Testament grants. Once the congregation perceives that the pastor has all the authority, it follows that the pastor also bears all the responsibility for everything done.[103]

The Bible does not say that preachers must be bivocational. However, churches in the Restoration Movement should recognize the biblical model of local church leadership where a plurality of pastors are all equipping the members for works of service (Eph. 4:11-13). Our perception of bivocational ministry should take into consideration the potential it has to encourage the biblical model of church leadership.

A more important issue in the Restoration Movement that affects our perception of work and ministry is the message of the gospel. We need to adjust our view of bivocational ministry not just in the light of the New Testament pattern for church leadership but also in the light of the gospel. As we will see in the next two chapters bivocational ministry provides us with a unique opportunity to both proclaim and demonstrate the message of the gospel in powerful ways. But is gospel proclamation and demonstration a core value of the Restoration Movement today?

An important book for all preachers to read is *The Core Gospel* by Bill Love. While he is approaching this topic from the perspective of the Acapella Churches of Christ, the research he has conducted includes an examination of the preaching of Restoration leaders in the early years of the movement, a heritage that also belongs to the Christian Churches and instrumental Churches of Christ. In this study, Love reports the percentage of sermons in each generation of the Restoration Movement that specifically and intentionally proclaim the message of the gospel. After analyzing the first three generations of the movement he writes,

> In this third generation we see further decline in the percentages of sermons with references to the core gospel. The rate of mention declined from 56 in the first generation to 46 in the second to 26 in the third. Even that low figure does not truly indicate the poverty

---

103. Dorsett, *Developing Leadership Teams in the Bivocational Church*, 10.

of their preaching regarding the cross. One notices a continuing lack of references to the metaphors of the atonement. Only three times was there any reference to the story line of Jesus' life leading to the cross. There was no mention of the Suffering Servant and a single reference to the scandal of the cross.[104]

Love also examines the preaching that took place in the fourth generation of the movement and reports that the percentages continued to drop. Some may look at the conclusions Love has made about preaching in the Restoration Movement with shock and disbelief. Is it really possible that only 26% of the sermons in the third generation of the movement made references to the gospel? And how is it even possible to know that statistic? Obviously, Bill Love did not sit down and read every sermon ever preached in the Restoration Movement. It is outside the scope of this book to give a detailed critique or defense of Bill Love's research. However, he gives a thorough explanation of his assumptions and the methodology of his research.[105] It was not his goal to be judgmental but rather to warn preachers about the trends of past generations and encourage them to be more focused on the gospel.

As preachers in the Restoration Movement, we need to restore our passion for proclaiming the message of the cross not only from our pulpits but also in the way we live our lives. C. Leonard Allen agrees when he writes,

> The most pressing question facing the Churches of Christ today is the question, can we recover the "word of the cross" in its biblical fullness? No other question even comes close to this one…. "the word of the cross" has been significantly displaced in the history of Churches of Christ. Throughout four generations since Stone and Campbell we have tended to push the cross into the background and thus to proclaim an anemic and distorted gospel.[106]

Never has there been a time in our history when the proclamation and demonstration

---

104 Bill R. Love, *The Core Gospel* (Abilene, TX: ACU Press, 1992), 207.
105 Love, 315. For each generation, Love chose five well-known preachers in the Restoration Movement who also had published sermons. He did not "cherry-pick" certain sermons to support his thesis. He read and evaluated all the published sermons of each of those five preachers from each of the first four generations of the Restoration Movement. His research is unbiased and peer reviewed.
106 Allen, *The Cruciform Church*, 113.

of the gospel have been so crucial. As the culture around us continues to become more and more post-Christian, it becomes more and more in need of the gospel.

We have seen from this brief overview of church history that our roles in bivocational ministry can be leveraged for the sake of the gospel. As church membership in America continues to decline, the necessity for bivocational ministry will continue to increase. However, we have also seen in this chapter that we can learn some important lessons from history that will help us to face the challenges of the future with confidence. Bivocational ministry does not have to be an option to consider only as a financial necessity. In the next chapter, we will explore in greater detail the potential bivocational ministry has to proclaim and demonstrate the message of the gospel.

# DISCUSSION QUESTIONS

1. What value do you see in the study of church history?

2. Why were there relatively few fully funded ministers during the first three centuries of church history?

3. In ancient times, how was the Greek philosophy of work different from the Jewish philosophy of work?

4. How did the *Didache* (AD 80-140) encourage traveling preachers or prophets to be bivocational?

5. How can bivocational ministers use their employment to teach and encourage a good work ethic in our culture?

6. At various times in church history, volunteer or bivocational ministry was necessary because of persecution and financial hardships. Yet, the church was growing in those difficult times. What principles from those examples can we apply to the trials we face in ministry today?

7. How was monasticism a blessing to both the church and the community?

8. What caused some monasteries to fall into the temptation of abusing their power?

9. Why were many of the church leaders during the Reformation volunteer or bivocational ministers?

10. What do you think determines how "spiritual" our work is to God?

11. Bill Love and C. Leonard Allen believe that important gospel themes have declined in the sermons of the Restoration Movement. Do you think that there needs to be a stronger emphasis on the gospel in the churches you are familiar with? Why or why not?

# CHAPTER 7

"I do all things for the sake of the gospel,
so that I may become a fellow partaker of it."
—1 Corinthians 9:23

The scriptures are pretty clear about who the heroes
were and are. They are those who have sacrificed
for the Gospel, who have stood faithful in view of
physical death, and who have given up everything
for their love of the king and his kingdom.[107]

Chapters 3-7 of this book are focused on exploring the biblical and historical foundations for bivocational ministry and the ministry of the gospel. So far, we have examined the biblical ideas of vocation and calling. We have considered what it means for every Christian to be a minister of the gospel. We have looked at several examples of bivocational ministry in the Bible. And we have heard the testimony of bivocational ministry from church history. However, we still need to explore the biblical connections between bivocational ministry and the gospel. How can the gospel help us to make decisions about our vocational ministries? Does the Bible make any connection between the gospel and bivocational ministry? In this

---

107. Hugh Halter, *Bivo: A Modern-Day Guide for Bi-Vocational Saints* (Littleton, CO: Missio Publishing, 2013), 130.

chapter, we will be taking a closer look at the ministry of Paul and how the gospel helped him to make decisions about his ministry to the church as well as his work in the world.

The title of this book is *Bivocational Ministry for the Sake of the Gospel*. By that, I am not suggesting that ministry must be bivocational or else it is not really "for the sake of the gospel." Rather, if a Christian is considering bivocational ministry, he or she must make that decision for the sake of the gospel. If we are truly "ministers of the gospel" then every ministry decision we face should be run through the filter of the gospel. As "ministers of the gospel" we should decide to pursue a fully funded ministry, a bivocational ministry, or a volunteer ministry not for the sake of financial needs or career goals, but primarily for the sake of the gospel.

## THE GOSPEL CONNECTION

Recently I was slapped in the face with a biblical truth that I should have seen years ago. I had been struggling to find fulfillment and effectiveness in a bivocational ministry for several years without seeing any connection between bivocational ministry and the gospel. I discovered, quite by accident, that there is a significant connection between bivocational ministry and the gospel.

I had been taking classes at Western Seminary, a school that prides itself on being "gospel-centered." Indeed, every class I took seemed to drill into us the importance of making every ministry a "gospel-centered" ministry. One of the classes I took was on "Preaching the Gospel from the Old Testament."[108] I was already aware of the centrality of the gospel in all of Scripture, but I was amazed by the different ways the gospel could be seen in virtually every chapter of the Bible. I was also impressed by how often the gospel was mentioned in the Bible. The Greek word for gospel is *euangelion*, and it literally means "good news."[109] This Greek word is used 75 times in the New Testament. The verb form *euangelizo* (preach the good news) is used 61 times. And the New Testament uses the noun, *euangelistes* (one who proclaims the good news) 3 times.

The whole Bible is a book of good news from God that we should be excited

---

108. Ray Ortlund Jr. taught the course PTS 732P "Preaching the Gospel from the Old Testament" April 21-24, 2014 at Western Seminary in Portland, OR.
109. Walter Bauer and F. Wilbur Gingrich, *A Greek-English Lexicon of the New Testament and Other Early Christian Literature*, ed. William F. Arndt and Frederick W. Danker, 2nd edition. (Chicago, IL: The University Of Chicago Press, 1979), 317.

to share. This inspired me to go through my Bible and underline in red the word "gospel" wherever it appeared and put a little red cross in the top corner of the page. I realize that there are many other words and phrases that proclaim the message of the gospel without using the Greek word *euangelion*. However, the word "gospel" has become so common in our Christian vocabulary that there have been times when I have read a passage and completely missed the fact that it mentioned the gospel. So, I wanted the word "gospel" to jump off the page and grab my attention whenever it was in the text! I wanted an alarm to go off in my head reminding me to slow down and think about why and how the author or speaker was using the word "gospel."

After I filled my Bible with little red crosses, I became curious about which chapters in the Bible contained the most references to the gospel. I was expecting one of the chapters in the book of Romans to be the winner. However, much to my surprise, I discovered that 1 Corinthians 9 uses the word "gospel" more than any other chapter in the Bible. 1 Corinthians 9 is where Paul defends his freedom to either refuse or accept payment for preaching the gospel. In this chapter, Paul uses the word "gospel" nine times. It seemed like the Holy Spirit was shouting, "YOUR MINISTRY MUST ALWAYS BE FOR THE SAKE OF THE GOSPEL!" Granted, the purpose of this text is not to teach us about bivocational ministry. Paul was explaining his strategy for why he usually refused payment for his ministry because some of his critics were using that as an accusation against him. However, the overall principle is that all ministry decisions must be firmly grounded in the gospel.

## PAUL'S GOSPEL STRATEGY FOR MINISTRY

The culminating verse of 1 Corinthians 9 says, "I do all things for the sake of the gospel, so that I may become a fellow partaker of it" (1 Cor. 9:23). Paul made strategic decisions about when he would spend time working as a tentmaker, when he would focus on preaching and teaching, when he would accept money for his ministry, and when he would refuse money that was offered to him. Some people might read verse 18 and just assume that Paul never accepted financial support for preaching the gospel. However, Paul did not have a blanket policy of never accepting money for ministry (2 Cor. 11:7-9). Steve Nerger points out that Paul was flexible enough to use three different strategies for ministry depending on which one would work best at the time. Nerger writes,

You see, Paul worked, he received, and he also ministered for free. What a blessed combination. Today, we make a trichotomy of pastors: fully-funded = pastor; partially-funded = bivocational pastor; no funding = lay minister or pastor. This is understandable for conversing and writing; however, we find it interesting that the apostle Paul was just interested in doing whatever it took to plant churches and disciple people—and he was in all three![110]

Paul thought about the people and the cultures he was reaching out to, he carefully considered his ministry plans, and he examined his options through the lens of the gospel. While standing firm on the unchanging message of the gospel, Paul was flexible with his methods of ministry and adjusted his strategies based on what would be most effective in the culture of the people he was reaching out to (1 Cor. 9:19-23). Do we choose our ministry strategies and methods based on how well they help us to effectively proclaim and demonstrate the gospel?

While the word "gospel" occurs nine times in this chapter, it is interesting to note that those occurrences take place in only five verses. Those five verses contain important gospel principles that helped to shape Paul's gospel strategy for his ministry. These are important gospel principles that can help bivocational ministers today. I call these "Gospel Ministry Principles" or GMPs for short. 1 Corinthians 9 does not contain all the Gospel Ministry Principles in the Bible, but the ones we will look at in this passage are absolutely essential regardless of whether your ministry is full-time, bivocational, or voluntary.

### GMP 1: We Must Cause No Hindrance to the Gospel.

In verses 1-11, Paul established the fact that as the Apostle who planted the church in Corinth, he had the right to expect payment from the Corinthians for his work in ministry. However, in verse 12 he says that he relinquished that right in order to "cause no hindrance to the gospel of Christ." The Greek word for "hindrance" (*enkopto*) carries a vivid word picture. The *New International Dictionary of New Testament Theology* says this word "originally meant to knock in or cut into. The meaning 'hinder' arose out of its military use. During a retreat, the road might be cut

---

110. Steve Nerger, *Bivocational Church Planters*, (Alpharetta, GA: North American Mission Board of the Southern Baptist Convention, 2007), 22.

into (i.e. broken up), in order to delay the pursuing enemy."[111]

Anthony Thiselton notes how this word picture may be connected to the gospel prophecy in Isaiah 40:3-4 when he writes,

> The metaphor is drawn from a military context of blocking enemy advance. Yet for Paul there may be a resonance with disrupting the level pathway for the messengers of good news in Isa 40:3-4 ("prepare the way of the Lord…make uneven ground level"), which suggests avoiding **any** (*tina*) **cut** (*cutting into* or *cutting up*) which roughens the path for **the gospel of Christ**.[112]

Many people today see the work a bivocational minister does outside the church as a hindrance to the gospel. But that's not how Paul saw it. Paul saw his tent-making job not as a hindrance but as a means to advance the gospel. He was moving the gospel into enemy territory without giving the enemy any tools to break up his path or impede his progress.

As a minister of the gospel Paul often had difficult decisions to make about things like when he would accept financial support, and when he would work as a tentmaker. Mark Moore believes that Paul had three financial rules that he always followed when making these decisions:

> (1) He never took money from a church he was planting. He boasted about this to the Thessalonians (1 Thess 2:9-10), the Corinthians (1 Cor 9:15-19; 2 Cor 11:7-13), and the Ephesians (Acts 20:35). (2) He was not opposed to "tent-making," but always preached full-time when he had the resources. A Christian worker is certainly worthy of wages (1 Cor 9:14; Gal 6:6; 1 Tim 5:17). (3) He expected the churches he planted to participate in funding other church plants (Rom 15:27; Phil 4:10-19).[113]

However, Paul did not have a "one size fits all" financial policy for all the churches he worked with and every situation he faced. Contrary to the first rule on Moore's list, Paul accepted financial support from the very first convert in Philippi when she was still dripping wet from her baptism (Acts 16:15). Concerning the

---

111. Verlyn Verbrugge, ed., *New International Dictionary of New Testament Theology: Abridged Edition.* (Grand Rapids, MI: Zondervan, 2003), 160.

112. Anthony C. Thiselton, *The First Epistle to the Corinthians* (Grand Rapids, MI: Eerdmans, 2013), 691.

113. Mark Moore, *The College Press NIV Commentary: Acts* (Joplin, MO: College Press, 2011), 314.

second rule, Paul *was* a tentmaker, but we don't know if he "always" put away his tent-making tools when he had other resources. I'm sure that if we ever get the opportunity to talk to Paul about his "full-time" status, he will tell us that he was always a full-time preacher of the gospel regardless of whether he was preaching while making tents in the marketplace or while he was addressing the Jews in the synagogue (Acts 17:17).

Paul's primary concern was the gospel. The principle of not causing a hindrance to the gospel was a solid conviction that Paul would never compromise. This was a principle that would require a careful evaluation of each situation. In the case of his ministry at Corinth, Paul knew that accepting money from them for his ministry would be a hindrance to the gospel. This was probably because of the patron/client mentality which we will discuss in more detail when we get to the fifth principle. In order to avoid being a hindrance to the gospel Paul chose to work as a tentmaker in Corinth (Acts 18:1-4) until Silas and Timothy arrived from Macedonia with financial support, probably from the Christians in Philippi (Acts 18:5; 2 Cor. 11:8-9; Phil. 4:16). After that Paul may have quit his tent-making job for a year and a half and devoted his time in Corinth to preaching and teaching the word of God (Acts 18:11). However, the text does not specifically say that Paul was not doing *any* work as a tentmaker during this time.

The principle for us is that we need to discover and use the ministry strategy that will best help us to remove any hindrance to the gospel. Instead of having a set of rigid rules for our ministry strategy, we need to be flexible for the sake of the gospel. We need to be willing to make sacrifices and work hard in order to make a clear way for the gospel to come into the lives of the people in our community. Many times, Paul worked hard "night and day" in order to make a clear path for the gospel (1 Thess. 2:9).

**GMP 2: We Must Value People More Than our Rights.**
This is the overall principle of chapters 8-10. In chapter 9, Paul was using his decision to preach the gospel without accepting wages for his ministry as an example of this principle. 1 Corinthians 9:14 says, "So also the Lord directed those who proclaim the gospel to get their living from the gospel." This verse seems to say that Jesus commanded preachers to earn their living by preaching the gospel. However, in this context, Paul was explaining why he gave up his right to accept

wages for preaching the gospel (1 Cor. 9:18). If this was a command given to all preachers to earn their living from the gospel, then Paul was not just giving up his rights, he was refusing to obey the Lord's command. Obviously, Paul would never do that. However, New Testament scholars have noted that the Greek word translated as "directed" in verse 14 can refer to how something is organized rather than a command that must be obeyed.[114]

An examination of what Jesus commanded sheds even more light on Paul's strategy for ministry. Paul was most likely referring to the instructions Jesus gave His disciples when He would send them out on short-term preaching tours (Matt. 10:5-15; Mark 6:7-13; Luke 9:1-6; and 10:1-12). We should remember that this was before the beginning of the New Testament church. Jesus was not sending preachers out into long-term pastoral ministries where they would be hired by congregations. Jesus was sending His disciples on short-term mission trips into towns and villages that had not yet heard the gospel. Paul took a general principle from that context—namely, preachers should be paid for preaching the gospel— and applied it to Christian ministry. However, that does not mean that Jesus was forbidding bivocational or volunteer ministry in the church.

A closer look at the short-term mission trips recorded in Gospels indicates that Jesus was more concerned about the relationships His disciples were forming with others than about finances. He was teaching His disciples to trust God to take care of them as they seek first His kingdom and His righteousness. Jesus told His disciples that "the worker is worthy of his support" (Matt. 10:10). He also told them not to take money with them (Matt. 10:9; Mark 6:8; Luke 9:3; Luke 10:4). This instruction was not given as a command for the disciples to demand wages for their preaching, nor was it a command for the disciples to abstain from all other work except preaching. In fact, Jesus entrusted His disciples with a bivocational ministry consisting of both preaching the gospel and healing the sick. "Departing, they began going throughout the villages, preaching the gospel and healing everywhere" (Luke 9:6). Their living expenses were being paid by the people in the communities they were serving. "Whatever city you enter and they receive you, eat what is set before you; and heal those in it who are sick, and say to them, 'The kingdom of God has come near to you'" (Luke 10:8-9).

Jesus commanded His disciples to find the "worthy" people (Matt. 10:11) or

---

114. David E. Garland, *Baker Exegetical Commentary on the New Testament: 1 Corinthians* (Grand Rapids, MI: Baker Academic, 2003), 415.

the "man of peace" (Luke 10:6) whenever they came to a new city. These were the hospitable people in the community who would accept the message of the gospel and invite the disciples to stay. Jesus said, "Stay in that house, eating and drinking what they give you; for the laborer is worthy of his wages. Do not keep moving from house to house" (Luke 10:7). Notice that Jesus did not tell His disciples to request or demand a minimum wage. He did not tell them to move around from one house to another until they find the one that pays the best wage. It wasn't about the money; it was about the people. Jesus was telling His disciples to develop relationships with the hospitable people in the community trusting that God would work through those people to take care of their needs.

The Bible clearly states that those who are taught the gospel must offer hospitality or some kind of payment to their teacher (Gal. 6:6). In 1 Corinthians 9, Paul presents the principle of remuneration as a right that the preacher of the gospel can either accept or decline. The principle for us is that we should value the people we serve even more than our right to receive financial support. We should choose ministry strategies that help us to cultivate good relationships with people in the church and in the community. Sometimes inviting people (both in the church and in the community) to partner with us through their financial support improves our relationships with them and opens a door for the gospel. However, when a preacher is more concerned about getting what he deserves than he is about serving people, he is not demonstrating the attitude of Christ or the message of the gospel (Phil. 2:5-8).

### GMP 3: We Must Preach the Gospel.

We also see Paul's gospel perspective in verse 16 when he writes, "For if I preach the gospel, I have nothing to boast of, for I am under compulsion; for woe is me if I do not preach the gospel." In Paul's mind, the urgency of the gospel message demanded that his ministry of preaching the gospel also be urgent. Whether or not God still wanted him to continue to preach the gospel was never determined by his financial support. Richard Oster points this out when he writes,

> He states explicitly that preaching the gospel is not grounds of his boasting. The reason that preaching is disqualified as a reason to boast is because he must preach out of necessity. Paul's reasoning says that there is nothing virtuous in performing the ministry

received from God because that was what he was commanded to do. Moreover, Paul is so convinced about the divine mandate that lies behind his apostolic preaching that he pronounces a woe upon himself (οὐαὶ γάρ μοί ἐστιν, *ouai gar moi estin*) if he were to fail to follow God's commandment in this matter.[115]

Paul placed his ministry of preaching the gospel at the top of his "to do" list every day. Earlier in this letter, Paul said, "For Christ did not send me to baptize, but to preach the gospel, not in cleverness of speech, so that the cross of Christ would not be made void" (1 Cor. 1:17). Just a few verses later, Paul said, "but we preach Christ crucified, to Jews a stumbling block and to Gentiles foolishness, but to those who are the called, both Jews and Greeks, Christ the power of God and the wisdom of God" (1 Cor. 1:23-24). In the next chapter he claimed, "For I determined to know nothing among you except Jesus Christ, and Him crucified" (1 Cor. 2:2).

The passion Paul had for preaching the gospel was partly due to the unique calling he received. Perhaps Paul saw his calling to preach the gospel as part of his conversion. As Carson notes, "Paul cannot abandon his preaching without abandoning his salvation; to him, the two are of a piece. Thus Paul never volunteered. He was simply captured by Christ for salvation and apostolic ministry in one blinding act of self-disclosure by the glorified Christ."[116]

God did not remove Paul's free will choice to either accept or reject the gift of salvation. But Paul knew that rejecting God's commission to preach the gospel would also be a rejection of his own salvation. None of us can claim to have the same specific apostolic calling that Paul had on his life. However, the great commission to "preach the gospel" is given to all Christians (Mark 16:16). The exhortation Paul gave Timothy to "preach the word, in season and out of season" (2 Tim. 4:2) is applicable to all ministers of the gospel regardless of whether we are fully funded, bivocational, or volunteers.

Some people have used this principle to argue against bivocational ministry. They claim that ministers with a second job are not "fully devoted" to preaching the gospel "full-time." In the first survey I conducted, a fully funded minister in a large church shared this response:

---

115. Richard E. Oster, *1 Corinthians* (Joplin, MO: College Press, 1995), 217.
116. D. A. Carson, *The Cross and Christian Ministry: Leadership Lessons from 1 Corinthians* (Grand Rapids, MI: Baker Books, 2004), 128.

My opinion is that it is not possible to do well in ministry today while doing another job. I cannot imagine it being done well. The pastors in [name of city] who do so, all serve churches that are not growing. It requires that the pastor focus internally only and eats up the time that would be spent focusing outward. I grieve whenever I hear someone trying to do this... I followed a man in [name of state] who did this and he took the church from 170 down to 25 when he left because he was divided. I took over and took the church as my sole focus and we grew to 500.[117]

While in some cases that may be true, I have found that with most bivocational preachers it is just the opposite. Several bivocational ministers I know have encouraged and equipped church members to be more involved in ministry making the congregation more effective both in its ministry to members and in its witness in the community. Like Paul, most bivocational ministers are willing to make hard financial sacrifices and put in extra hours to make sure that a struggling church will have a qualified leader preaching and teaching the gospel even if that church cannot afford a "full-time" preacher. This principle is not a principle about "full-time" versus "part-time." This principle is about the commitment to preach the gospel regardless of whether we get paid for it.

Consider your calling. Have you been called to preach the gospel? You may not be called to "full-time" ministry. You may not be called to bivocational ministry. However, all of us have been called to proclaim the gospel to someone in some way (Mark 16:16). All of us have been called to demonstrate the gospel and live for the sake of the gospel (Mark 8:34-35). That is the general calling given to all Christians. We saw back in chapter 3 that our specific calling must be grounded in the general calling. We would never tell God that we can't obey His calling to follow Jesus unless we get paid for it. Why would we ever tell God that we can't obey our calling to preach the gospel unless we get paid a "full-time" wage?

Bivocational minister and author, Dennis Bickers tells the story of a time he was shopping in a Christian bookstore. He writes,

Another customer was asking an employee of the store if he had talked to any churches since his recent graduation from seminary. I

---

117. Kennedy, 104.

will never forget his answer: "All the churches that have contacted me have been small churches out in the country. I am not going to waste my time on such churches. I would rather work here." Such an attitude has no place in the heart of a pastor.[118]

Actually, I would say that this store employee made the right decision concerning his career choice. The preacher who lacks the conviction to preach the gospel regardless of the wage he earns or the size of the church he serves is not ready for leadership in the Lord's church.

**GMP 4: We Must Demonstrate the Gospel in our Ministries.**

While verse 16 shows us the urgency of the gospel in Paul's ministry decisions, verse 18 displays the glorious grace of the gospel from Paul's perspective of his ministry. Paul writes, "What then is my reward? That, when I preach the gospel, I may offer the gospel without charge, so as not to make full use of my right in the gospel." Paul saw God's amazing grace at multiple levels in his ministry of preaching the gospel. First, the message he preached was a message of God's grace. Second, the privilege to preach the gospel was an amazing honor that he didn't deserve. And third, the decision to preach the gospel free of charge underscored the nature of grace. Leon Morris makes an important observation about Paul's gospel perspective when he states that,

> He did not see this simply as good strategy. He has already said that it is his boast (v. 15), something he delights in. Now he says it is his reward: his pay is to serve without pay! Preaching without pay is his privilege. The gospel gave him rights, but he chose not to use them.[119]

Undoubtedly Paul was using his ministry decision to forego his rights as an example of a Christian principle he wanted his readers to follow in other areas of life. Both chapters 8 and 10 deal with the Corinthians' right to eat meat from the pagan temples and the principle of Christian love that gives up that right for the sake of the weaker brother. Bruce Winter makes the following observation about Paul's

---

118. Dennis W. Bickers, *The Tentmaking Pastor: The Joy of Bivocational Ministry* (Grand Rapids, MI: Baker Books, 2000), 18-19.
119. Leon L. Morris, *1 Corinthians* (Downers Grove, Ill: IVP Academic, 2008), 136.

gospel perspective on this issue:

> In contrast to the 'confident' Christians Paul explains that he
> chooses not to exercise certain rights he has (9:4-6) and that he
> is keen to make his gospel without charge, so as not to use to the
> full his right (εξουσια) in the gospel (9:18). There were some
> Christians who decided that they would exercise a particular right
> that they possessed to eat in the idol temple.[120]

Paul made it a point to live out the message of the gospel and even point out the pictures of the gospel that God was painting in his life. Likewise, we should make ministry decisions that help us to both preach and demonstrate the grace of God.

This is another example of the J-curve® we discussed in chapter 4. When out of love, we sacrifice our rights, when we suffer and die for the sake of others, we are giving people a picture of what Christ did for us and we are helping people to see practical examples of what it means to take up our cross daily and follow Jesus. Bivocational ministers have a unique opportunity to demonstrate the gospel at multiple levels. When people see us making sacrifices in ministry like Paul talks about in 1 Corinthians 9 it assures them of our love for them. And when they see us making sacrifices in the workplace it gives them a model of the gospel that is much easier for them to relate to and follow.

In the second survey, I asked bivocational ministers, "How (if at all) has your bivocational ministry provided opportunities for you to demonstrate or live out the gospel?" Here are some of their responses:

> A minister in Ohio said, "I think it is encouraging for people from
> our church to see me living out my faith in the public square. They
> see me as a player and a coach. It's not that they hear me telling
> THEM to live out their faith in everyday life — they can see me
> do it, too!"

> Donnie Collings, a minister in Kentucky, said, "I live out the gospel
> in a bivocational sense because the people I work with have seen
> me 'not as a minister' and 'as a minister.' They can see that I'm

---

120. Bruce W. Winter, *After Paul Left Corinth: The Influence of Secular Ethics and Social Change* (Grand Rapids, MI: Wm. B. Eerdmans Publishing Co., 2001), 280.

essentially the same...many have concluded that Christians aren't a lot of the things that the media portrays them to be."

Fred Nelson, a minister in North Carolina, said, "Working diligently among lazy people has really demonstrated a stark difference, especially when others realize that I am a Christian and that my diligence is accompanied with a measure of joy and (most of the time) a lack of complaining."

Jeff Blaine, a minister in Missouri, said, "I find that as I see routine life experiences in my other roles, I get to use them as a great illustrative quality to convey the love of Jesus in every day practical ways. Each time I work in those roles, it allows the fruit of the Spirit to be seen in my life as a means to work with integrity, encourage, be kind, and love others in the uniqueness of their moment."[121]

Demonstrating the gospel is never easy, even for Christian leaders. David Fisher describes how this calling is often more demanding and difficult for those who are in ministry when he writes,

Pastoral ministry, whether in the first century or the twenty-first, requires those of us who have been captured by Christ to lead God's people by climbing up on the altar as a way of life. It is the call given to all God's people but uniquely experienced by Christian leaders, especially pastors. Our master also calls us to carry his cross (Luke 9:23). By the use of this double sacrificial metaphor Paul indicates that our pastoral ministry, like his, is uniquely sacrificial and therefore painful.[122]

While the demonstration of the gospel in our work and ministry is often painful, it is always worth it. As the J-Curve® diagram illustrates (see fig. 6), going down into suffering and sacrifice leads to the death of ourselves. However, by God's grace, He brings us up into resurrection power, abundant life, and joy as we see a

---

121. Kennedy, 107.
122. David C. Fisher, *21st Century Pastor* (Grand Rapids, MI: Zondervan, 1996), 103-104.

transformation taking place in our own lives as well as in the lives of the people we are leading.

## GMP 5: We Must Know the Culture and How to Adjust for the Sake of the Gospel.

Paul was a student of culture and he always adjusted his ministry strategy to fit the culture. When we compare the sermon, he preached to the Jews in the synagogue (Acts 13:16-41) to the sermon he preached to the Greek philosophers in Athens (Acts 17:22-31), we see two very different strategies with the same gospel message. Paul did this not only with the way he preached but also with the way he did ministry.

> To the Jews I became as a Jew, in order to win Jews. To those under the law I became as one under the law (though not being myself under the law) that I might win those under the law. To those outside the law I became as one outside the law (not being outside the law of God but under the law of Christ) that I might win those outside the law. To the weak I became weak, that I might win the weak. I have become all things to all people, that by all means I might save some. I do it all for the sake of the gospel, that I may share with them in its blessings. —1 Corinthians 9:20-23

Paul's analysis of the culture helped him to decide when to earn his money as a tentmaker and when to accept monetary support for his ministry. Paul took into consideration how deeply the people had bought into the patron-client mentality of the Greco-Roman culture. In a patron-client relationship, the patron was a wealthy sponsor of the client. The client could be an artist, a philosopher, a teacher, or someone in virtually any lower-class vocation. In return for the patron's financial support, the client was expected to always speak favorably of the patron and pay back the patron's support in whatever way the patron saw fit.

Paul accepted financial support from the church at Philippi on multiple occasions (Phil. 4:14-16). Lydia, Paul's first convert at Philippi, was a wealthy businesswoman who insisted on showing hospitality to the missionaries and taking them into her home (Acts 16:15). Paul saw from her maturity and the culture at Philippi that receiving financial support from them would not in any way hinder their understanding of the gospel. However, things were different at Corinth. Ben Witherington notes that,

> In a society where, by and large, it was patrons and not banks that loaned money, and where there was no adequate government social safety-net, patronage and clientage were necessary for the survival of many of those of lower social status. So in Corinth Paul was diligent in avoiding "gifts" and patronage since they always came with strings attached. Because of the party spirit of the Corinthians, if Paul had accepted patronage there, he would have only exacerbated a spirit of rivalry. Patronage was not simply a matter of economic or social power and control. It was a matter of honor and shame, and even of spiritual or religious control. Paul had to tiptoe carefully through the minefields of this social network to make sure the gospel was not seen as a commodity to be bought, and its apostle was not seen as a gun for hire.[123]

Many of the Corinthians were so entrenched in the patron-client mentality that they were offended when Paul refused to accept payment for his ministry there. They thought that if a speaker or a teacher is not being paid for his services, he must not be very good. Paul's critics claimed that he couldn't possibly be an authentic apostle if he was conducting his ministry for free. The attitudes fostered by the patron-client mentality were in direct opposition to the gospel of grace. We see Paul addressing these anti-gospel attitudes in 2 Corinthians 11:7-9.

> Or did I commit a sin in humbling myself so that you might be exalted, because I preached God's gospel to you free of charge? I robbed other churches by accepting support from them in order to serve you. And when I was with you and was in need, I did not burden anyone, for the brothers who came from Macedonia supplied my need. So I refrained and will refrain from burdening you in any way.—2 Corinthians 11:7-9

We see from this text that Paul did not have an across-the-board policy of never

---

123. Ben Witherington III, *A Week in the Life of Corinth*, First edition. (Downers Grove, IL: IVP Academic, 2012), 39-40.

accepting wages for his preaching ministry. He admits here that he refused financial support from the Corinthians while accepting it from the Macedonians. This was not duplicity or favoritism on Paul's part. This was based on a strategic analysis of the culture and an evaluation of what would work best for the sake of the gospel. Witherington explains Paul's analysis of the Corinthian culture when he writes,

> Paul would not take certain kinds of support from the Corinthians because of the elitists, benefactor attitudes and obligations that would come with such support. Such attitudes kept the Corinthians from seeing the gospel of grace and Paul as their patron or benefactor. They were tied too much into the conventional system of reciprocity to understand Paul's approach.[124]

The practical application for us is that we need to understand the culture and adjust our ministry strategies for the sake of the gospel. This is a crucial principle that we desperately need to put into practice if we want to effectively proclaim and demonstrate the gospel to the current generation. Jesus rebuked the religious leaders in Jerusalem for being able to predict the weather but not being able to understand the signs of the times (Matt. 16:3). The Bible commends the sons of Issachar because they were "men who understood the times, with knowledge of what Israel should do" (1 Chron. 12:32). It is important for us to understand the communities we are reaching out to and how the culture is changing. We need to study the trends in our society and be flexible enough in our methods to adjust our ministry strategies while holding firm to the consistent truth of God's word.

The Barna Group has identified 9 cultural trends that pastors need to understand (see Table 3).[125] If we are going to effectively reach out to our communities with the gospel, we must be familiar with how our communities are changing. Several of these trends indicate that bivocational ministry is more relevant than ever. In chapter nine, we will explore some of these trends and the potential opportunities they are presenting for gospel-centered bivocational ministry.

In this chapter, we have seen that the decisions Paul made about his work and ministry were not just a matter of exercising good strategies. Paul evaluated his ministry methods and options in the light of the gospel. He removed anything that

---

124. Ben Witherington, *Conflict and Community in Corinth: A Socio-Rhetorical Commentary on 1 and 2 Corinthians* (Grand Rapids, MI: Carlisle: Eerdmans, 1995), 448.
125. Kinnaman, *The State of Pastors*, 154.

| 9 CURRENT TRENDS PASTORS NEED TO UNDERSTAND | |
|---|---|
| 1. Demographic | Not only are Millennials the largest adult generation in terms of sheer numbers, they are also the most ethnically, culturally and spiritually diverse (unlike many of our churches). |
| 2. Social | Young people are generally going through the shaping experiences of adulthood at later ages than did previous generations—yet most of our churches are designed with families in mind. |
| 3. Economic | The economic pressures on middle-class and working families are being passed on to local churches, and the financial and ministry implications are immense. |
| 4. Vocational | The landscape of work is shifting toward a gig-oriented, multi-careering, freelance terrain, and there is profound need for a robust theology of vocational discipleship. |
| 5. Institutional | People get the information they want, when they want, for the price they want to pay. "Disintermediated institutions"—including churches—are no longer the sole mediators of knowledge, and pastors no longer the chief authority. |
| 6. Legal | Particularly when it comes to holding historically orthodox beliefs about human sexuality, Christian institutions are at increasing risks of running afoul of the law. |
| 7. Digital | The "screen age" requires adaptive approaches to community and discipleship. "Digital Babylon" is an always-on, hyperlinked, immersive culture where Christians must learn to live and thrive as exiles. |
| 8. Moral | Society's moral center is shifting away from external sources of authority (the Bible, Christian tradition) to the self: You look inside yourself to find what's best for you. |
| 9. Spiritual | "Nones" or the religiously unaffiliated, are the fastest growing religious group in the nation. Nominal, cultural Christianity is no longer the "default position" of Americans—and this reality is challenging the Church to reevaluate faith formation. |

TABLE 3

might be a hindrance to the gospel even if that required hard work and sacrifice. He valued the relationships he was building with people more than his right to earn money for preaching. He also studied the cultural trends of the people he was reaching out to and adjusted his ministry strategies for the sake of the gospel. He had a gospel perspective of his vocations both as an Apostle and as a tentmaker. That perspective gave him joy and fulfillment as the gospel continued to be proclaimed and demonstrated in every area of his life.

# DISCUSSION QUESTIONS

1. How has the gospel recently helped you to make decisions in work or ministry?

2. Mike Kennedy identifies 1 Corinthians 9:23 as the "culminating verse" of the chapter. Do you agree? Why, or why not?

3. What is the first GMP (gospel ministry principle) from 1 Corinthians 9? Give an example of how this principle might be seen in a ministry today.

4. Why did Paul refuse to accept money from the Corinthian church while accepting money from the Macedonian churches (2 Cor. 11:7-9)?

5. What is the second GMP from 1 Corinthians 9? Give an example of how this principle might be seen in a ministry today.

6. Do you think that 1 Corinthians 9:14 is a command for preachers to only earn their living by preaching the gospel? Why or why not?

7. What is the third GMP of 1 Corinthians 9? Give an example of how this principle might be seen in a ministry today.

8. What would you say to someone who claims that bivocational ministers are not "fully devoted" to their ministry?

9. What is the fourth GMP of 1 Corinthians 9? Give an example of how this principle might be seen in a ministry today.

10. How can giving up our right to receive a full-time wage in ministry serve as an example for other Christians to follow in other areas of life?

11. What is the fifth GMP of 1 Corinthians 9? Give an example of how this principle might be seen in a ministry today.

# CHAPTER 8

"Only conduct yourselves in a manner worthy
of the gospel of Christ, so that whether I come
and see you or remain absent, I will hear of you
that you are standing firm in one spirit, with one
mind striving together for the faith of the gospel."
—1 Philippians 1:27

Near the cross! O Lamb of God,
Bring its scenes before me;
Help me walk from day to day,
With its shadows o'er me.
—Fanny Crosby

Although she was physically blind, Fanny Crosby could see that the gospel had practical applications for the decisions she made from day to day. This chapter is a transition from the theological foundations of gospel-centered bivocational ministry to the practical application of doing bivocational ministry for the sake of the gospel. While we will occasionally refer back to the biblical foundations we established in chapters 2-7, in chapters 8-13 we turn our attention to the more current and practical questions concerning bivocational ministry for the sake of the gospel. In this chapter, we will consider some of the ways bivocational ministers can be specifically and intentionally gospel centered.

At the end of chapter 4, I introduced a diagram illustrating the progress of a cycle in a gospel-centered ministry. As ministers of the gospel, we need to be intentional and specific in our application of the gospel to life and ministry. There are five different ways we can focus on the gospel in our ministry. Each of these applications of the gospel can take place independently from the others and they don't always take place in a certain order, but when we see them as stages of gospel application, they naturally prepare us and move us into a cycle of becoming more and more gospel-centered in our ministries.

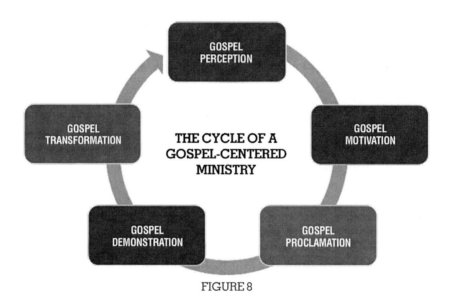

FIGURE 8

## GOSPEL PERCEPTION

Gospel perception is looking at all of life through the lens of the gospel. This principle is especially important when we are making decisions about our calling in life. The decisions about being fully funded, bivocational, or volunteer ministers do not always feel like options from which we can choose. Many times, the situations we face don't give us the luxury of having all those options available to us. However, when we do have a choice, we must look at those options through the lens of the gospel. We need to evaluate the culture in which we live, we need to carefully consider the perceptions of the church we are serving and the community we are reaching out to, and we need to make our ministry decisions for the sake of the gospel (Mark 8:35 and 1 Cor. 9:23).

As I mentioned in chapter 4, I conducted a survey of bivocational ministers in which I asked the following questions about the gospel and ministry:

17. How (if at all) did the gospel influence your decision to be bivocational?

18. How (if at all) does the gospel help you as a bivocational minister?

19. How (if at all) has your bivocational ministry provided opportunities for you to proclaim the gospel?

20. How (if at all) has your bivocational ministry provided opportunities for you to demonstrate or live out the gospel?[126]

These four questions are based on four of the five principles in the cycle of a gospel-centered ministry. These principles are gospel motivation, gospel transformation, gospel proclamation, and gospel demonstration.

I'm sure all the ministers that responded to the survey believe in the gospel and are committed to preaching and living out the message of the gospel. However, many of the responses I got were very general, lacking any specific examples or details. These responses illustrate a common tendency we have when it comes to applying the gospel to our ministries. Our gospel perception gets blurred unless we focus on specific applications of the gospel to the specific situations we face in ministry. We often see the gospel as this great overarching plan of redemption that generally applies to all aspects of our ministry, but in our generalization of the gospel, we fail to intentionally apply it to specific areas of ministry in specific ways. One minister replied to question 18 with the following comment, "It is hard to specify since the gospel is my ministry."[127] Another bivocational minister responded by saying, "I won't go into how the gospel is a help to all of us. I have no answer that is specific to being bivocational."[128] And one minister answered all four questions (17-20) by saying, "I have not regarded this (bivocational ministry) as a 'gospel' thing other

---

126. Kennedy, 245-49.
127. Kennedy, 115.
128. Kennedy, 115.

than the fact it was a medium often used by the Apostle Paul and others in the New Testament."[129]

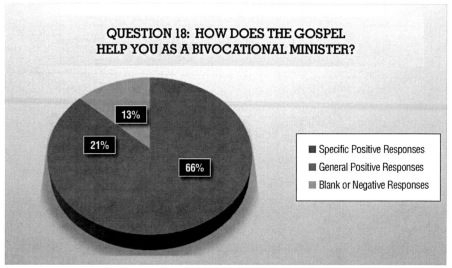

QUESTION 18: HOW DOES THE GOSPEL
HELP YOU AS A BIVOCATIONAL MINISTER?

- Specific Positive Responses
- General Positive Responses
- Blank or Negative Responses

13%
21%
66%

FIGURE 9

The majority (66%) of those who responded to question 18 gave specific positive comments about how the gospel was helping them as bivocational ministers. 21% responded with general yet positive comments about how the gospel helps them. For example, several ministers answered question 18 with comments like "in many ways," or "a lot." 13% of the participants left question 18 blank or responded with a negative comment like "not sure," "not much," or "not at all" (figure 6). Those ministers who gave specific positive responses to question 18 also believe that their ministries are "very effective" or "more effective than not" (figure 3). These ministers also said that they "often" or "almost always" have a sense of fulfillment and satisfaction in their ministries (figure 4). These survey results suggest that ministers who often consider the specific ways that the gospel helps them and are willing and eager to talk about it are also enjoying effective and fulfilling ministries. This observation indicates that there is a connection between being intentionally and specifically gospel-centered in ministry and experiencing effectiveness and fulfillment in ministry.

---

129. Kennedy, 116.

The following four principles will help us to be gospel-centered in specific and intentional ways. These gospel-based ministry principles are good for any time and any culture. For each of these principles, I will also include some of the more specific responses I received to questions 17-20 of the second survey. The testimonies and ministry examples given in this chapter illustrate some of the specific ways bivocational ministers are applying those principles in their unique situations.

## GOSPEL MOTIVATION

Why we do what we do makes all the difference in the world. There are several powerful motivations given in the Bible as good reasons to obey God. We are motivated to obey God by the fear of punishment (John 5:15) and the hope of rewards (Matt. 6:4). However, God wants us to grow spiritually and develop more mature motivations. He wants us to obey Him primarily because we love Him (John 14:15). And when we develop that kind of love-based motivation, our obedience to God becomes more natural and fulfilling. The same is true concerning our motivations for what we do in ministry. There are several valid reasons why a minister may choose to be bivocational. However, as ministers of the gospel, we need to make ministry decisions for the sake of the gospel. That doesn't mean that we can't have other motivations that influence our decisions. But we need to evaluate our motives and be willing to adjust them or change them so that the gospel is the primary empowering motivation for why we do what we do.

What does it mean to have the gospel as our primary empowering motivation for our ministries? It means two things. First, it means that we are motivated by our love for God because of all that He has done for us through the gospel. "We love because He first loved us" (1 John 4:19). Gospel motivation means that we are empowered in our ministries with an overwhelming sense of gratitude and love for God. It means that we renew our minds every day by considering the specific and undeserved blessings we have received through the gospel and the love Jesus demonstrated for us on the cross. Look at the way Paul expressed this gospel motivation for his ministry in 1 Timothy 1:12-17.

I thank Christ Jesus our Lord, who has strengthened me, because He considered me faithful, putting me into service, even though

> I was formerly a blasphemer and a persecutor and a violent aggressor. Yet I was shown mercy because I acted ignorantly in unbelief; and the grace of our Lord was more than abundant, with the faith and love which are found in Christ Jesus. It is a trustworthy statement, deserving full acceptance, that Christ Jesus came into the world to save sinners, among whom I am foremost of all. Yet for this reason I found mercy, so that in me as the foremost, Jesus Christ might demonstrate His perfect patience as an example for those who would believe in Him for eternal life. Now to the King eternal, immortal, invisible, the only God, be honor and glory forever and ever. Amen. —1 Timothy 1:12-17

When Paul thought about how he experienced God's abundant grace and mercy, his motivation for ministry was supercharged. He saw the opportunity to serve in God's kingdom as a great blessing. He experienced fulfilment from being an example of God's patience. He rejoiced because God was using his testimony to encourage others to believe in Christ for eternal life. After writing five verses about God's grace in his life, his heart is overflowing with sincere worship for his God and King.

Second, gospel motivation means we are motivated by our love for others and their desperate need for the gospel. "Therefore, we are ambassadors for Christ, as though God were making an appeal through us; we beg you on behalf of Christ, be reconciled to God" (2 Corinthians 5:20). Gospel motivation in ministry means that for the love of all people we do whatever we can short of sin to effectively share the saving message of the gospel with people who are without Christ. It also means that we do whatever we can short of sin to help Christians continue to grow spiritually and become more like Christ through the life-changing message of the gospel. Because of his love for God and his love for others, Paul was constantly looking for the greater progress of the gospel. Consider his comments about ministry motivations in Philippians 1:12-18.

> Now I want you to know, brethren, that my circumstances have turned out for the greater progress of the gospel, so that my imprisonment in the cause of Christ has become well known throughout the whole praetorian guard and to everyone else,

and that most of the brethren, trusting in the Lord because of my imprisonment, have far more courage to speak the word of God without fear. Some, to be sure, are preaching Christ even from envy and strife, but some also from good will; the latter do it out of love, knowing that I am appointed for the defense of the gospel; the former proclaim Christ out of selfish ambition rather than from pure motives, thinking to cause me distress in my imprisonment. What then? Only that in every way, whether in pretense or in truth, Christ is proclaimed; and in this I rejoice. Yes, and I will rejoice,
—Philippians 1:12-18

Paul had very few choices concerning his ministry options at this point in his life. And yet he still chose to look for opportunities "for the greater progress of the gospel," or as the NIV puts it "to advance the gospel." He knew that some people would be preaching the gospel out of selfish ambition rather than from the gospel motivation of love. Such hypocrisy in others would not dampen his spirits or rob him of his joy. His gospel motivation empowered him to rejoice even in prison.

Some bivocational ministers feel like they are in prison, trapped in a situation that is holding them back from a more effective ministry. They feel like they had to get a second job outside of church ministry because they had no other option. When asked, "How has your bivocational ministry been a blessing to the church?" a discouraged bivocational minister said, "Who are we kidding? It has helped financially. That's all. We need me as a full-time minister!"[130]

Believe me, I understand the frustration this preacher is feeling. However, if we really think about it, when it comes to our decisions about work and ministry, we always have more than one option to consider. We might not like the limited options we seem to have. And some options may seem to be so far out in left field that we would never even consider them. But even in those situations when we feel like we have limited options and no real choice in the matter, we can still renew our minds and focus our primary motivation on the gospel.

If we think that we are bivocational primarily for financial reasons, we need to step back and look at the big picture of the gospel. We need to constantly remind ourselves that, like Paul, we are bivocational for the sake of the gospel. The extra

---

130. Kennedy, 119.

income, health insurance, or the retirement package from our "secular" job are not our primary goals in life. They are a means to an end, not the end itself. If it was just about the money, we would quit the ministry altogether and focus on a more lucrative career. And some ministers have done that. But if we know that we have been called to preach the gospel, quitting the ministry is not an option. Regardless of what we get paid, we are motivated and empowered by the gospel to preach the gospel.

Question 17 on the second survey is the question that considers our gospel motivation for bivocational ministry. "How (if at all) did the gospel influence your decision to be bivocational?" Out of the 194 bivocational ministers that participated in the survey, 81 identified the gospel as a factor in their decision to be bivocational. 44 mentioned the example of Paul as a major influence on their decision. 29 left this question blank or said, "Not sure." 23 said, "Not much" or "Not at all." And 17 indicated that some principles of Scripture were a factor but not specifically the gospel. It was encouraging to read the comments of the ministers who were allowing the gospel to influence their decision to be bivocational.

Steven Williams, a minister of the gospel in Bemidji, Minnesota, revealed his gospel motivation for ministry when he gave this response, "The good news about Jesus is what it is all about. At an early age, I committed to "go," (Mark 16:16) no matter where or how."[131] Kenneth Weaver, a bivocational minister in Massillon, Ohio said this about his job outside the church,

> It created a desire for me to spread the "Good News!" Some people have attended services because of my relationship with them through the job. But before they came to church, they had been touched with the gospel outside the church walls.[132]

Lawrence Neargarth is a bivocational preacher in Kingsford, Michigan with a passion for the gospel that empowers his ministry. He gave the following testimony about how the gospel helps him with his bivocational ministry.

> The Gospel has kept me in God's word, kept me tuned into His Spirit and caused me to grow spiritually. Jesus died for me. It's the blessing of mine to work for Him and He has given me the ability.

---

131. Kennedy, 121.
132. Kennedy, 121.

If you don't have the gospel, ministry is a joke. The gospel brings forgiveness, salvation, and eternal life. Bivocational ministry has provided opportunities for me to proclaim the gospel many, many times. In dealing with the public, when you find out a person you're with does not know Jesus, tell them what Jesus has done for you.[133]

In the first survey I conducted, I did not mention the gospel in any of my questions. And yet some of the responses clearly indicated a strong gospel motivation for ministry. A school bus driver in Georgia who is also a gospel preacher said, "I am not dependent on the church's prosperity to support my preaching of the gospel."[134] A bivocational minister in Minnesota, clarified his gospel motivation when he wrote,

From the time I started preaching at the church, the leadership knew that money was not going to be much motivation. They were never going to motivate me or discourage me through my salary. If they fired me, I'd make more at just about any other job. Simply put, I'm not a preacher because I need a job; I'm a preacher because I love the Lord and I love to preach.[135]

That is the same attitude Paul had wherever he went. Regardless of whether he was paid or unpaid, he preached the gospel. Regardless of whether his sermons caused riots or revivals, he preached the gospel. And this was the same attitude he told Timothy to maintain when he said, "preach the word; be ready in season and out of season" (2 Tim. 4:2).

When asked, "What is the main reason you are bivocational?" a gospel preacher who also drives a school bus in Missouri answered, "The extra income is beneficial, but the main reason is outreach. I have interaction every day with our church kids, but I also reach non-church kids as well. And they know who I am."[136]

Another bivocational minister, who chose to remain anonymous, communicated well the gospel motivation we should pursue in bivocational ministry. He wrote,

133. Kennedy, 121.
134. Kennedy, 121.
135. Kennedy, 122.
136. Kennedy, 122.

The Gospel gave me my first love—to work in the Kingdom of God. The message of being a servant is what made me willing to work other jobs so I can do my first love—working in the Kingdom of God. If I didn't love Jesus, if I wasn't grateful for His salvation, I would have stopped working in the church many years ago and switched to laboring in the world and making far more money with far less stress. The Gospel is my reason for getting into other jobs and it is my reason for staying with ministry and other jobs to help supplement our income.[137]

Jesus said that "the mouth speaks out of that which fills the heart" (Matt. 12:34). As I read the words of these preachers, it became obvious that their hearts were filled with gospel motivation. These were the ministers who were eager to share how the gospel was helping them with the challenges of bivocational ministry. However, there were others who never said a word about the gospel, the cross, or what Christ had done for them. They were focused on the more "practical" concerns of bivocational ministry such as finances, time management, and job expectations.

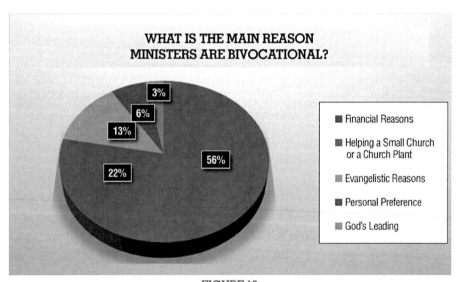

FIGURE 10

---

137. Kennedy, 122.

In the first survey, I asked the question: "What is the main reason you are bivocational?" Of the ministers who answered that question, 56% gave financial reasons, 22% said it was to help a small church or a church plant, 13% gave evangelistic reasons, 6% said it was their personal preference or that they love both of their jobs, and 3% said that it was God's leading.

What is the main motivation that comes to your mind when you think about your ministry? By no means am I claiming to always have a perfect gospel motivation for the things I do in ministry. I need to evaluate my motives and ask God to examine my heart every day. One of the things that helps me with this is a gospel-centered purpose statement. I believe that every preacher should have a gospel-centered purpose statement for their ministry memorized, posted, and reviewed daily. Mine is posted on the wall in my office right below my ordination certificate. It reads, "Mike Kennedy was created to love God with all his heart, soul, mind, and strength and to love every person that God brings into his life. Mike Kennedy was saved by grace to preach the gospel and make disciples for Jesus Christ." What is your purpose statement?

## GOSPEL PROCLAMATION

While the gospel is a powerful life-changing message, it cannot change anyone unless it is proclaimed. The gospel cannot be a *message* of good news unless it is communicated to people in an effective way. The great commission given to all Christians is the command to "preach the gospel" (Mark 16:16). As ministers of the gospel in a post-Christian culture, we need to heed the charge Paul gave to the young evangelist in 2 Timothy 4:1-5.

> I solemnly charge you in the presence of God and of Christ Jesus, who is to judge the living and the dead, and by His appearing and His kingdom: preach the word; be ready in season and out of season; reprove, rebuke, exhort, with great patience and instruction. For the time will come when they will not endure sound doctrine; but wanting to have their ears tickled, they will accumulate for themselves teachers in accordance to their own desires, and will turn away their ears from the truth and will turn aside to myths. But you, be sober in all things, endure hardship, do the work of an evangelist, fulfill your ministry. —2 Timothy 4:1-5

Timothy was commanded to "do the work of an evangelist." The word "evangelist" is a transliteration of the Greek word *euangelistes*. It comes from the same root as the Greek word for "gospel" and it means a "preacher of the gospel."[138]

As preachers of the gospel, we must "be ready in season and out of season" to preach God's word. That means we need to proclaim the gospel not only in those times when a lot of people want to hear it and are willing to pay us for our ministry but also when the message is no longer popular, and we have to get another job just to make a living. That also means that we always need to be ready to share the gospel, not just on Sundays when we are in church standing behind the pulpit but also during the week when we are in the marketplace and working with people in the community (Acts 17:17).

As preachers of the gospel, we must endure hardships and fulfill our ministries even when we are not being paid to proclaim the gospel. The difficult times Paul predicted are here. There are many people in our world who have turned their ears away from the truth and they are refusing to listen to sound doctrine. We must not let that discourage us from preaching God's word. The word of God is powerful, and we must continue to proclaim it with confidence knowing that God is going to work through the preaching of His word. I have the following quote from Crawford Loritts written in the front of my Bible.

> Don't ever dare to stand in front of a group of people with a Bible in your hand and not expect change. We must have a holy confidence—confidence in God and his Word, confidence that God is going to change lives whenever we speak from his book.[139]

As bivocational ministers, we will have unique opportunities to proclaim the gospel that we wouldn't normally have if we didn't have jobs outside of the church. We need to watch for those opportunities, create those opportunities, and consider how we can make the most of them for the sake of the gospel. One of the ways we can create opportunities to proclaim the gospel is by being an active and positive member of the community over a long period of time.

---

138. Bauer and Gingrich, *A Greek-English Lexicon of the New Testament and Other Early Christian Literature*, 318.
139. Haddon Robinson and Craig Brian Larson, eds., *The Art and Craft of Biblical Preaching: A Comprehensive Resource for Today's Communicators* (Grand Rapids, MI: Zondervan, 2005), 36.

A preaching farmer in Missouri described how God is using his dual calling for the sake of the gospel. In his response to the first survey he wrote,

> This small rural church called me to preach 4 years ago. God has blessed us with a growth in attendance. The news of God's faithfulness has spread around the local area and new people have come to hear the gospel preached. I know most of them from some way or another. They are friends and acquaintances from living in this area for 53 years.[140]

J. Paul Tisdel Jr. is a bivocational minister in San Antonio, Texas. He also serves his community as an education consultant. He wrote, "As a bivocational minister I am able to definitely show how the message of Christ applies in real life. I often get to talk to people about Jesus that I would not have met if I were not bivocational."[141]

Jeff Gallup is a bivocational minister in Oakridge, Oregon. He also serves his community as a special education assistant in a public school. He wrote, "As I work and display the love of Jesus and make friends with kids and staff and parents, it leads to people asking me if I'm a Christian. This gives me opportunities to share my faith."[142]

Cameron Bailey is a bivocational minister in Kenbridge, Virginia. He also serves his community as a firefighter and a paramedic. He shared the following testimony:

> Ministry opportunities are everywhere. Whether we are in a church building or a firehouse, we are called to save the lost. I have shared my faith multiple times with coworkers and folks in the community in need. I'm "the preacher man" to tons.[143]

Obviously, in a place of business, we need to know what the boundaries are concerning religious expression. As a bus driver in a public-school district, I am not allowed to invite students to church. We also need to be examples of a good work ethic, which includes being respectful and cooperative to our delegated authorities. If our attempts to proclaim the gospel are done in rebellion to our supervisor or are

---

140. Kennedy, 126.
141. Kennedy, 126.
142. Kennedy, 126.
143. Kennedy, 126.

in any way hindering the quality of our work, we are giving the gospel a bad name. However, if we are serving the community with genuine love and quality work, our message will be far more attractive, and we will have more opportunities to effectively proclaim the gospel (Titus 2:9-10).

Ron Hatley is a bivocational minister in Veedersburg, Indiana. He also serves the community doing heating and air conditioning work. He noted, "I have been able to share Christ with people I have met that I would have never met otherwise. I was a part of a business group that met weekly. This group allowed me opportunities to share 1 on 1 with people and it was great."[144]

Richard Geringswald is a friend of mine in Lakeland, Florida. Before he retired from the monument and grave marker business, he was bivocational for 25 years. Because of the relationships he has developed in the community, he is able to pursue a wide variety of creative opportunities to proclaim the gospel. He wrote,

> You look for opportunities to take Christ into the marketplace and minister to hurting people. We have had opportunities to speak in churches, Rotary Clubs, Veterans Day programs, prayer breakfasts, and archeology clubs to share Bible truths. We have put up 95 faith billboards and sponsored 19,000 TV commercials on God's grace, prayer, and "He is Risen" campaigns. As a result, we have had between 50 to 60 baptisms in 6 years.[145]

As bivocational ministers, we have been entrusted with access and involvement in the community that other ministers simply don't have. We must be good stewards of those opportunities to connect with people outside the church. We must pursue creative, appropriate, and effective ways to proclaim the gospel.

## GOSPEL DEMONSTRATION

While the gospel is a message that must be proclaimed, it is also an event consisting of divine actions and attitudes that must be demonstrated in real life. When asked, "How (if at all) has your bivocational ministry provided opportunities for you to demonstrate or live out the gospel?" one minister responded by saying, "The gospel is a message you proclaim. Christianity is something you live out and

---

144. Kennedy, 127.
145. Kennedy, 127.

demonstrate."[146] The Bible, however, makes no such distinction when it talks about how we are to live out our lives. In fact, the term "Christianity" never appears in the Bible. The word Christian appears three times, but only once with instructions about how we are to live as Christians (1 Peter 4:16). There is a lot of gospel language in the Bible, words and phrases like "put to death," "die," "cross," "crucify," "buried," "rise up," "resurrection," "come to life," and many others. When we read the New Testament, we see that these terms are used dozens of times not just to refer to what Jesus did but also to teach us how to live.

More than any other metaphor, the Bible uses the terminology of the gospel to describe the Christian life. Before Jesus even went to the cross, He told His disciples that if they wanted to follow Him, they would have to take up their cross daily (Luke 9:23). We demonstrate the gospel when we are baptized (Rom. 6:3-4). We demonstrate the gospel when we take the Lord's Supper (1 Cor. 11:26). We demonstrate the gospel when we repent of our sins (Gal. 5:24). In our marriages, we are demonstrating the gospel (Eph. 5:25). In times of suffering, we are demonstrating the gospel (1 Peter 4:13). When we love one another selflessly we are demonstrating the gospel (1 John 3:16).

I mentioned at the beginning of the book that God used Nathan Stewart, a preacher in Jamaica, to show me what it means to be a bivocational minister for the sake of the gospel. Recently, God gave me another demonstration of the gospel in the life of a Jamaican preacher. Rhon Steer is one of my students at Jamaica Bible Seminary. His main source of income comes from farming and raising goats. At this writing, his ministries in the Kingdom of God are voluntary. Every Tuesday, he brings bread and Bibles to people at the local community center and shares a message from God's word.

In the summer of 2019, I asked Rhon to tell me his story. I wanted to know where he gets his relentless drive to pour himself into the ministry of the gospel. In his deep baritone voice he said, "Originally, I was moved by gratitude because of all that God had done for me." Rhon recognized the undeserved kindness of God in the message of the gospel. He was doing well financially running a market. However, when he was baptized into Christ, he made the decision to live for Christ in every area of life including his business. He stopped selling certain products that were not honoring to Christ. As a result, his business took a radical downturn and he had to

---

146. Kennedy, 128.

close the doors. Inspired by the story of Jacob, he decided to take up goat herding. In the church he was attending, opportunities to serve kept pulling at his heart. With each new experience in ministry, Rhon's appreciation for God's grace grew deeper along with his commitment to grow and be better equipped for works of service both in the church and in his community. He visits the elderly in their homes and goes to the community health center to pray with people and encourage them. Rhon said, "He is risen! That is the good news that motivates me and gives me passion and boldness in my ministry." Rhon's life is a demonstration of the gospel in multiple ways.

Back in chapter four, we looked at Paul Miller's diagram of a J-Curve® to illustrate how the gospel can be demonstrated in a Christian's life. Jesus said, "If anyone wishes to come after Me, he must deny himself, and take up his cross and follow Me. For whoever wishes to save his life will lose it, but whoever loses his life for My sake and the gospel's will save it" (Mark 8:34-35). The J-Curve® gives us a picture of this passage and how we are called to live out the sacrificial love that Jesus demonstrated when He went to the cross. Jesus went down the left side of the curve into suffering and death because of His love for us. Then when He rose from the dead, He came up the right side of the curve into power, victory, and life.

In his book, *the J-Curve*, Miller describes five different J-Curves.[147] The death, burial, and resurrection of Jesus is the original J-Curve® of the gospel (fig. 11). However, we are called to demonstrate the gospel in four different ways. First, when we become Christians, we put our faith in Christ, repent of our sins, and are baptized into Christ (fig. 12).[148] That is our initial demonstration of the gospel (Rom. 6:1-11). But then as Christians, we keep on demonstrating the gospel with three different kinds of J-Curves that continue to take place throughout our lives.

Ongoing demonstrations of the gospel can be seen in our repentance, our suffering, and our serving. We can easily see how bivocational ministry for the sake of the gospel gives us unique opportunities to demonstrate each of these J-Curves.

The repentance J-Curve® is part of our ongoing sanctification as we continue to struggle with the selfish attitudes and sinful desires of our fleshly nature (fig. 13). In Colossians 3:5-10, we are commanded to put to death our sinful passions and evil desires. When Rhon made the decision to stop selling those things in his store that

---

147. Paul E. Miller, *The J-Curve: Dying and Rising with Jesus in Everyday Life* (Wheaton, IL: Crossway, 2019), 89.
148. Miller, *The J-Curve*, 89. Paul Miller calls this "the Faith J-Curve." I have chosen to call it "the J-Curve of baptism" because of the visual demonstration of the gospel described in Romans 6:3-5.

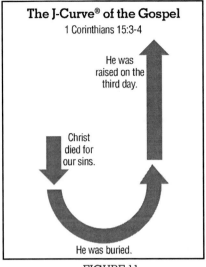

**The J-Curve® of the Gospel**

1 Corinthians 15:3-4

He was raised on the third day.

Christ died for our sins.

He was buried.

FIGURE 11

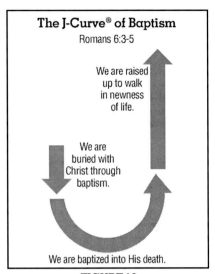

**The J-Curve® of Baptism**

Romans 6:3-5

We are raised up to walk in newness of life.

We are buried with Christ through baptism.

We are baptized into His death.

FIGURE 12

would cause people to sin, he was taking a huge financial risk. He was going down the left side of the curve by denying himself those financial profits. But as a result of his repentance, Rhon developed a deeper faith in Christ and God raised him up the right side of the curve with a renewed spirit.

This is not a one-time event but an ongoing process that continues as long as we are living in these mortal bodies. In Romans 8:9-13, Paul tells us that we can demonstrate the gospel and experience spiritual resurrection

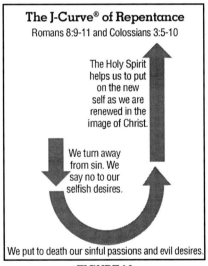

**The J-Curve® of Repentance**

Romans 8:9-11 and Colossians 3:5-10

The Holy Spirit helps us to put on the new self as we are renewed in the image of Christ.

We turn away from sin. We say no to our selfish desires.

We put to death our sinful passions and evil desires.

FIGURE 13

and victory over sin by the power of the same Spirit who raised Jesus from the dead. As ministers of the gospel, we must have the honesty and the humility to demonstrate the gospel through sincere repentance.

131

**The J-Curve® of Suffering**
1 Peter 2:21-23; 4:12-14; & 2 Corinthians 12:7-10

The character traits of Christ grow in us. And His power is perfect in our weakness.

When trials come into our lives, we follow the example of Jesus.

When we go down into suffering we don't seek revenge, but we entrust ourselves "to Him who judges justly."

FIGURE 14

The J-Curve® of suffering is when trials come into our lives (fig. 14). Paul describes his "thorn in the flesh" in 2 Corinthians 12:7-10. He said it was a "messenger of Satan." This was a chronic problem that came into his life and pushed him down the left side of the curve against his will. He prayed for God to remove it three times, but God said, "No. My grace is sufficient for you." Coming up the right side of the suffering curve into new life, victory, and power does not mean that the suffering is taken away. For Paul, coming up the right side of the suffering curve was growing in Christ and sharing in the fellowship of His suffering (Phil. 3:10). Paul saw suffering as an opportunity to depend more on Christ and allow the power of Christ to live in him (2 Cor. 12:9).

Rhon shared how he had been praying for God to take care of a difficult frustration he was struggling with in ministry. Finally, after twelve years of faithfully praying and trusting God, his prayers were answered. Many of us as bivocational ministers are going through difficult times of frustration and suffering. When we are dealing with unreasonable employers or rude customers, when we are frustrated with financial struggles, when we are overwhelmed with busy schedules and not enough time we need to focus on the gospel and see the opportunity God is giving us to demonstrate the gospel. During our times of suffering, people both in the church and in the community are watching us closely. Will they see the message of the gospel displayed in the way that we handle our suffering?

The J-Curve® of serving is the gospel displayed in the way that we make sacrifices to love and serve others (fig. 15).[149] In this curve we willingly move into serving as we sacrifice ourselves in some way because of our love for others. Jesus

---

149. Miller, *The J-Curve*, 89. Paul Miller calls this "the Love J-Curve." I have chosen to call it "the J-Curve of serving" because many people have different ideas about love but everyone understands that serving is going down into humility.

told His disciples that the way to lead in His Kingdom was to be a servant (Mark 10:42-45). In Philippians 2:5-11, Paul shows us how Jesus gave up His glory and honor in heaven to become a slave. Paul exhorts us to have the same attitude that Jesus had that sees others as more important than ourselves.

When Rhon selflessly goes out into the community to serve the elderly, demanding no payment for the bread or the Bibles he gives away, he is demonstrating the message of the gospel. Many bivocational ministers have sacrificed lucrative careers,

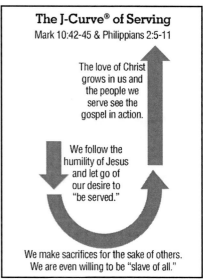

**The J-Curve® of Serving**
Mark 10:42-45 & Philippians 2:5-11

The love of Christ grows in us and the people we serve see the gospel in action.

We follow the humility of Jesus and let go of our desire to "be served."

We make sacrifices for the sake of others. We are even willing to be "slave of all."

FIGURE 15

powerful positions, and financial security to help small struggling churches or to plant new churches. They have given many hours of their lives and worked until they were weary not for any recognition or praise but simply out of their love for God and the people in their community. That is the key that we must keep in mind in all our acts of service and sacrifice. Paul warned us that even the ultimate sacrifice can amount to nothing if it is not an act of sincere love (1 Cor. 13:3). If I am going to effectively demonstrate the gospel as a bivocational minister, I need to sincerely love all those undisciplined middle school students on my bus. I need to serve them in love just like Jesus served me in love.

In several of the survey responses, I saw examples of bivocational ministers living out these different J-Curves and demonstrating the message of the gospel in their lives. A general manager of a landscape company in Illinois has been a bivocational minister for over 13 years. He wrote about his desire to show people the gospel in his actions. He said, "I enjoy being a light in the community of my workplace. It keeps me in touch with people who aren't necessarily Christians. And hopefully, I can show them the gospel each day by my actions."[150]

A construction worker preaching in Illinois wrote, "Through my work, I have

---

150. Kennedy, 132.

come to know a lot of people. When you do work for people, you can relate to them and they to you. And when they see you live out the word in a work environment, it brings validity to your ministry."[151]

A bivocational preacher in Kentucky also serves his community as a custodian at a local elementary school. He testified, "I can be Christ outside of the church to the staff and children at the elementary school."[152]

Jason Murray is a bivocational minister in Mackville, Kentucky. He also works as a motor coach driver. He shared some insightful comments about demonstrating the gospel on the job. He wrote,

> I would say the gospel has always made me willing to be bivocational since there is something incarnational about living both in the church and in the marketplace. However, the marketplace, in my experience, is very sensitive to the perception of religious intolerance. Few bosses allow "proselytizing." At all points, people usually find out quickly that I am a Christian and a preacher, and they watch me closely.[153]

There are many more testimonies I could include as examples of bivocational ministers living out the gospel in ways that demonstrate the love and grace of God. The practical application for us is that we need to make sure that our actions and attitudes both in the church and in the marketplace are telling the same story of love and grace that Jesus demonstrated to us in the gospel. We must also remember that the point of our gospel demonstration is not to build up ourselves but to lead people to Jesus.

## GOSPEL TRANSFORMATION

> Therefore I urge you, brethren, by the mercies of God, to present your bodies a living and holy sacrifice, acceptable to God, which is your spiritual service of worship. And do not be conformed to this world, but be transformed by the renewing of your mind, so that you may prove what the will of God is, that which is good and acceptable and perfect. —Romans 12:1-2

---

151. Kennedy, 132.
152. Kennedy, 132.
153. Kennedy, 133.

Theology is worthless without any practical application. Romans 12:1-2 is the transition passage in the book. It takes us from the theology of the gospel in chapters 1-11 to the practical application of the gospel in chapters 12-16. Because of the "mercies of God" (the theology of the gospel), we must respond as a "living and holy sacrifice" (the practical application of the gospel). This is not something we can do by our own power. Rather it is a transformation we allow God to perform in us as we renew our minds. This is the gospel transformation that we must include in our ministries. But gospel transformation includes much more than changing the heart of an individual. The redemptive purpose of the gospel includes the transformation of all creation (Rom. 8:19-22 and Col. 1:19-20).

Bivocational ministry for the sake of the gospel is a ministry that looks for and encourages gospel transformation both in our churches and in our communities. As we renew our minds with the message of the gospel, God transforms our hearts. As we live out the message of the gospel through sacrifice and serving in our ministries and in our jobs, God causes amazing transformations to take place both in the church and in the community.

Question 18 of the second survey asks, "How (if at all) does the gospel help you as a bivocational minister?" This is a question about gospel transformation because it assumes that we need help as bivocational ministers, and that the gospel will in some way give us the help we need. It is not our power that changes our hearts. It is not our power that causes the church to grow. And it is not our power that transforms a community. However, the power of God will work through us to do those things as we renew our minds with the message of the gospel and demonstrate the message of the gospel in our lives.

Just as personal transformation is a long-term process that does not happen overnight, so also the transformation of a church or a community is a long-term process that requires patience, commitment, and faithfulness. We are far more likely to see a church transform if we are committed to staying there regardless of how green the grass (or the money) seems to be on the other side of the fence (or at some other church). Positive transformation in a community or a place of work will not happen through us unless we are able to develop positive relationships with the people in those environments. If your congregation closed its doors and shut down all its ministries, would it make any difference to the rest of the neighborhood? Would the people in the community miss your church if it was gone?

A preacher who has been bivocational for the over 18 years in Illinois looks for God's leading and allows God to work through him to be a blessing to others even if it requires a sacrifice on his part. In the first survey, he shared the following testimony:

> I have been able to witness, pray with folks, and even do a funeral that I would never have had the opportunity to do and for folks who are unchurched. Most people don't see the blessing that comes in that... I currently work in a Christian bookstore and consult for McDonald's in many areas. Again, it is a blessing one might never know, and one might never have a chance to touch some of these people... I feel like many people think that being bivocational is a failure. I say NO! I have seen God work miracles when they would not have worked under other circumstances.[154]

Another bivocational minister in Illinois says that he has witnessed the transformational power of the gospel in places that are often written off as hopeless. In his response to the first survey he said,

> Forty-two years ago, my wife and I began a prison ministry supported solely by the independent Christian Churches and Churches of Christ. I am an ordained minister and am still working full-time as a volunteer chaplain in three state correctional centers. Three days are spent each week in one or more of the correctional facilities. This year (2017) I will retire from prison ministry but will probably not pursue the full-time position as minister of the church. I absolutely LOVE my job. For me, going into the prisons (sharing, teaching, counseling, etc.) is something I've enjoyed for 42 years. I care about a segment of society that most of us would rather ignore. And when they (inmates) see how much you love and care, well, many respond in a positive way.[155]

Like the Apostle Paul, this bivocational preacher has been allowing God to work through him to transform the hopeless environment of a prison into a place of

---

154. Kennedy, 135.
155. Kennedy, 135.

good news. If the gospel can bring hope and healing to people in a state correctional facility, surely it can transform any of the places where we work. Did you notice the passion and excitement this preacher has for the ministry God has entrusted to him for over four decades? That kind of authentic enthusiasm coupled with genuine faithfulness is evidence of a life transformed by the gospel. When we experience the life-changing power of the gospel we become excited and eager to see that transformation in the lives of others.

Daniel Lutz is an airline captain flying a Boeing 777 internationally. He also preaches at a rural church in Bloomingdale, Indiana. He understands that genuine personal transformation is essential if we are to truly understand and live out the message of the gospel in an effective way. In his response to the second survey, he gave the following advice to bivocational ministers,

> Become a "real world" Christian. I hold a position that God calls people to be ambassadors everywhere, regardless of whether their jobs are "secular" or "in the church." The term "gospel" has been greatly watered down and therefore often misunderstood. Learn the real meaning! The "good news" is I was once spiritually dead and now have been regenerated into eternal life. Now that I'm alive, I can go to work to do the things God has planned for me! I truly believe that churches can thrive with bivocational ministers.[156]

Roger Jarboe has been a bivocational preacher for over 20 years in Lewisport, Kentucky. During that time, he has also served the community as a police officer. From his comments, we can see that Jarboe has a heart for both the church and the community he serves. In his response to the second survey he wrote,

> The gospel gives me the strength to do my job. It has enabled me to fulfill my callings. I have been able to do the two things I have wanted to do the most: enforce the law and preach the gospel. My job keeps me in touch with the real-world conditions. It gives me an opportunity to represent Christ in the secular world. And people have joined our church as a result of my dealings with them on my job.[157]

---

156. Kennedy, 136.
157. Kennedy, 136.

Gospel transformation is not something we do but something we depend on God to do in us and through us. Bivocational ministry provides a great opportunity for gospel transformation to take place not only in us but also in the church we serve and in the community in which we work. Are we allowing God to transform us by renewing our minds daily with the message of the gospel? And are we praying daily for God to work through us to transform our churches and our communities with the message of the gospel?

In this chapter, we have seen specific ways to maintain a gospel perception. We have also explored the applications of principles that can help us focus our ministries on the gospel. These gospel-centered ministry principles include gospel motivation, gospel transformation, gospel proclamation, and gospel demonstration. We have been encouraged both from Scripture and from the testimonies of gospel-centered bivocational preachers. We have heard some of the ways we can apply the gospel to our bivocational ministries. We heard how God is working through bivocational ministers to transform churches and communities. Every time I read these testimonies I am inspired and empowered to look for specific ways to apply the gospel to my ministry. If we are going to be effective as ministers of the gospel, we must be intentional and specific in our application of the gospel.

# DISCUSSION QUESTIONS

1. Why is it especially important to have a gospel perception when we are making decisions about ministry?

2. Why do we tend to focus on the general blessings of the gospel while overlooking the specific applications of the gospel?

3. How can you make a specific application of the gospel to a situation in your life?

4. Do you believe that the gospel needs to be our primary motivation in all ministry decisions? Why or why not?

5. How (if at all) has the gospel influenced your ministry decisions?

6. Write out a personal purpose statement for your life. What can you do to remind yourself of your purpose every day?

7. Do you believe that the gospel is only good news if it is proclaimed? Why or why not? (Support your answer with Scripture.)

8. Read 2 Timothy 4:1-5. What does it look like for a minister to "do the work of an evangelist" in our culture today?

9. How can bivocational ministry provide unique opportunities to proclaim the gospel that other ministers might not have?

10. What are some words or phrases in the Bible that teach us to demonstrate the gospel in the way that we live? (Give Scripture references with your answers.)

11. Describe a time when God caused a transformation in your church or community. Did that transformation surprise you? Why or why not?

12. What can you do to encourage spiritual transformation in your church or community?

# CHAPTER 9

*For Such A Time As This*

"You hypocrites! You know how to analyze the appearance of the earth and the sky, but why do you not analyze this present time?"
—Luke 12:56

As Entrepreneurs of Life, we respond to the call of our great Creator
By seeing all life as an enterprise transformed by his call to "Follow me."
We therefore count the cost, consider the risks,
And set out on each day as a venture to multiply our gifts and opportunities
In order to bring glory to God and add value to this world.[158]

Those visionary words of Os Guinness challenge us to consider the risks and then venture out in our ministries for the glory of God. But how do we know when the risk is too great? We need wisdom and discernment. Like the men if Issachar, we need to understand the times in which we live (1 Chron. 12:32). Many ministry methods seem to be fads that come and go. They seem to work for a while but for whatever reason, the ministry method loses its effectiveness. As a result, many people lose interest, and they want to move on to the next new ministry idea. There is nothing wrong with that. Many ministry decisions are matters of wisdom rather than matters of morality. However, there is a difference between a ministry fad

---

158. Guinness, *The Call*, 234.

and a ministry strategy. A ministry fad is effective for a while simply *because* it is new and different. As soon as it is no longer new, it is no longer effective. A ministry strategy is effective because it is a plan based on an understanding of the culture of the church and the community. A ministry strategy will continue to be effective until the culture changes. Therefore, we need to understand the changes that are taking place in our church and our community and adjust our ministry strategies accordingly. In 1 Chronicles 12:32, we read about the sons of Issachar who understood the times and knew what Israel should do. Jesus rebuked the religious leaders of His day because they could not interpret the signs of the times (Matt. 16:3 and Luke 12:56).

Back in chapter 7, we saw a chart of trends that the Barna Group has written about in the book, *the State of Pastors*.[159]

### 5 CURRENT TRENDS PASTORS NEED TO UNDERSTAND

| 1. Demographic | Not only are Millennials the largest adult generation in terms of sheer numbers, they are also the most ethnically, culturally and spiritually diverse (unlike many of our churches). |
|---|---|
| 2. Social | Young people are generally going through the shaping experiences of adulthood at later ages than did previous generations—yet most of our churches are designed with families in mind. |
| 3. Economic | The economic pressures on middle-class and working families are being passed on to local churches, and the financial and ministry implications are immense. |
| 4. Vocational | The landscape of work is shifting toward a gig-oriented, multi-careering, freelance terrain, and there is profound need for a robust theology of vocational discipleship. |
| 5. Institutional | People get the information they want, when they want, for the price they want to pay. "Disintermediated institutions"—including churches—are no longer the sole mediators of knowledge, and pastors no longer the chief authority. |

TABLE 4

In this chapter, we will consider the first five categories on that chart and how these trends are providing gospel opportunities for bivocational ministers. We will consider what Barna, Pew, and other research organizations are saying about the

---

159. Kinnaman, *The State of Pastors*, 154.

current trends. However, there is no better way for a minister to understand the culture of the community then by being actively engaged in the community. One of the best ways to be actively engaged in the community is through bivocational ministry. Paul was in the marketplace at Athens every day getting to know people and the culture of the city for several days before he got the opportunity to address the Greek philosophers at the Areopagus (Acts 17:17).

As a bus driver, I have become much more familiar with the different neighborhoods of Vancouver, including the geography, as well as the social, economic, and ethnic characteristics of each area. This has helped me to identify and understand the different cultures within Vancouver. As a result, my ability to reach out and minister to people in these different areas has improved. You don't have to be a bus driver to better understand the culture of your community. This principle applies to any vocation where you are meeting and serving people in the community. Charles Battle serves as a financial planner who is also a minister of the gospel in Englewood, Colorado. He made this observation, "Working outside church ministry will give the minister the 'real world' experiences which will increase his empathy and effectiveness."[160]

I did most of the research for this book in 2018. However, a lot has changed since then. None of the reports by Barna or Pew predicted the events of 2020. Things will continue to change in ways that we cannot predict. In order to keep our ministries relevant and effective in uncertain times we must hold firmly to the unchanging message of the gospel and continue to interact with the people in our communities. That being said, a better understanding of the cultural trends will prove to be invaluable.

As we consider some of the current trends in the culture and how they provide opportunities for bivocational ministers to be more effective, we will also consider how to apply the gospel to each of those trends. Before we look at these trends, let's review the five principles we discussed in chapter 8: Gospel Perception, Gospel Motivation, Gospel Transformation, Gospel Proclamation, and Gospel Demonstration.

- **Gospel Perception:** This is the deliberate practice of looking at everything through the lens of the gospel. The gospel is of "first importance" (1 Cor. 15:3). Jesus told His disciples that they must

---

160. Kennedy, 140.

lose their lives for Him and the gospel (Mark 8:35). Paul said he did "all things for the sake of the gospel" (1 Cor. 9:23).

- **Gospel Motivation:** Every effective ministry is driven by *why* we do what we do. We need to examine our motives and make sure that they are all in harmony with the message of the gospel (Phil. 1:16-17). God's love for us at the cross must be our primary motivation for all our ministry decisions. "We love because He first loved us" (1 John 4:19). We should examine the trends of the culture with the same motivation of love for others that God has shown to us in the gospel.

- **Gospel Proclamation:** The gospel is good news that must be proclaimed with words (Rom. 10:17). The gospel is the message of the death, burial, and resurrection of Jesus for our salvation. But people cannot be saved by this message unless they hear it and believe it. We need to examine the current trends in order to find ways to be more effective in our proclamation of the gospel.

- **Gospel Demonstration:** We are called to not only proclaim the gospel but also demonstrate the gospel in the way that we live (Mark 8:34-35). We demonstrate the gospel in repentance (Gal. 5:22-24), acts of service and self-sacrificing love (1 John 3:16-17), and suffering afflictions (2 Cor. 12:9-10). We should examine current trends in order to find opportunities to demonstrate the gospel more effectively.

- **Gospel Transformation:** The gospel is a message of redemption and transformation for all creation (Rom. 8:19-21). While the gospel is a message of salvation for the lost it is also a message of continual transformation for the saved. The gospel is a message of both justification and sanctification. In addition to transforming the lives of individuals, the gospel can also transform our communities and cultures for the common good.

As bivocational ministers reaching out to people in a world that is constantly changing, let's consider how we can put into practice these principles of gospel application.

## DEMOGRAPHIC TRENDS

The Barna chart gives a lot of attention to the Millennial generation. It seems like everyone these days has an opinion about Millennials. I have always been somewhat skeptical of the descriptions made by the "experts" who do these generational studies. When I hear descriptions of people, based on the generation they are a part of and compare that to the people I know in those generations I often see more differences than similarities. However, the recent studies on the Millennial generation are valid and helpful. They give us a general idea of how this generation is changing the culture.

In the category of "Demographic Trends," the Barna chart says, "Not only are Millennials the largest adult generation in terms of sheer numbers, they are also the most ethnically, culturally and spiritually diverse (unlike many of our churches)."[161] The Barna Group also reported that "one in three Millennials believe the Bible is not divinely inspired."[162] Millennials tend to be skeptical of organized religion but they want to be a part of something that is making a positive difference in the world. Unchurched millennials tend to have a negative perception of Christian ministers in general, but they describe the pastors they know personally in more positive terms.[163]

These observations are important for bivocational ministers to keep in mind when we have opportunities to work with Millennials. This is an opportunity for gospel application. God may be using our jobs outside the church to clear a path for the gospel to come into the lives of unchurched Millennials. These young adults can get to know bivocational pastors personally outside of organized religion as they work together in the marketplace. This strategy is true for people of any age in our culture. 48% of American adults have an opinion of Christian pastors that is only "somewhat positive."[164] However, their view of the ministers they know personally is much more positive. The Barna report states,

> The news is somewhat better when it comes to pastors whom
> people know personally, rather than "pastors" as a general idea.
> More than half of U.S. adults say they personally are "very"

---

161. Kinnaman, *The State of Pastors*, 154.
162. David Kinnaman, *The Bible in America: The Changing Landscape of Bible Perceptions and Engagement* (Ventura, CA: Barna Group, 2016), 91.
163. Kinnaman, *The State of Pastors*, 115.
164. Kinnaman, *The State of Pastors*, 115.

(32%) or "somewhat familiar" (26%) with a Christian minister, and nearly two-thirds of these respondents say their opinion of the pastor they know is "very positive" (64%).[165]

Mike Stewart is a preacher in Ohio who also works in a funeral home. He says,

> I am continually exposed to people younger than me who don't know the Lord. I have co-workers at the Funeral Home who ask lots of questions about God and the church. My coworkers say, "You're not like any preacher or priest we have ever known. You're just a normal person like us."[166]

We can't change the negative spin the liberal news media tends to put on religious leaders. We can't change the typical portrayal of preachers in Hollywood movies and TV shows. But if the statistics show that many non-Christians have a negative view of Christian pastors in general while at the same time holding a more positive view of the pastors they know personally, there is something we can do in response to that. We can get to know more non-Christians. Through personal interaction and gospel demonstration, we can produce a more positive perception of Christian leaders in the communities where we serve. One of the best ways to get to know more non-Christians is to go to work with them.

In the first survey, I discovered that many (34) of the bivocational ministers who participated are also working as college professors. Being a college professor is a great opportunity for bivocational ministers to get to know young adults and allow them to gain a more positive and accurate perception of Christian leaders. Rob O'Lynn is a college professor who is also serving as a bivocational minister. He notes that "Being bivocational breaks down some of the stigmas associated with religious leaders, which opens doors for evangelism. It puts me in front of non-Christian persons more often than when I was in full-time ministry."[167]

I also discovered that many (37) bivocational ministers are school teachers and many (32) are school bus drivers. I mentioned before, that as an employee of a public school district, I have to be very careful about what I say to students when I am at work. However, even when we don't have current opportunities for gospel

---

165. Kinnaman, *The State of Pastors*, 115.
166. Kennedy, 143.
167. Kennedy, 144.

proclamation, we always have opportunities for gospel demonstration and gospel transformation. Public school students are not going to be children forever. If you work as a teacher or a bus driver, you have a great opportunity to be a blessing to students, to love them, and create a positive and safe environment for them where they can grow and flourish. Even if they don't know that you are also a preacher, they will never forget the positive impact you had on their lives. Later, in their adult years, when they visit your church or meet someone from your congregation, they will find out that one of their favorite teachers or bus drivers was also a Christian minister and it will be a powerful witness for the gospel. It will greatly reduce any negative perceptions they had of Christian leaders.

## SOCIAL TRENDS

Concerning social trends, the Barna chart says, "Young people are generally going through the shaping experiences of adulthood at later ages than did previous generations—yet most of our churches are designed with families in mind."[168] This is not to say that Millennials are slow to learn or lazy when it comes to their preparation for adult life. It is often just the opposite. Millennials are taking longer to "grow up" because they have a higher value for the process and experiences of personal growth. Larry Alton makes the following observations,

> More than any other generation, millennials consider themselves politically independent, religiously unaffiliated, and interested in a wide variety of different nations, cultures, ideas, and beliefs. They want to travel, and be exposed to new things…Speaking of growth, millennial workers are demanding it—both in corporate and individual contexts. In general, millennials want more feedback on their performances, in part because they want affirmation, and in part because they want to keep learning and improving.[169]

As bivocational ministers, we should see these social trends as opportunities for gospel proclamation and gospel transformation. We can give Millennials the benefit of the doubt and assume that they are interested in growing, learning, and

---

168. Kinnaman, *The State of Pastors*, 154.
169. Larry Alton, "How Millennials Are Reshaping What's Important In Corporate Culture," *Forbes*, last modified June 20, 2017, accessed May 18, 2018, https://www.forbes.com/sites/larryalton/2017/06/20/how-millennials-are-reshaping-whats-important-in-corporate-culture/.

improving. We can offer them constructive feedback on how they are doing in their job performance. Unless they tell us otherwise, we should never assume that young adults are intolerant of our beliefs. It could very well be that they are interested in learning about what we believe and why we believe it. The gospel is a message of good news, redemption, and transformation. We need to look for opportunities to show people how the gospel can have a positive effect on communities, workplace environments, as well as individuals.

As the comment by Barna suggests, we can make sure that our churches offer opportunities for Millennials to grow and experience life in practical and positive ways. I have taken dozens of young adults on short-term mission trips where they experience many different forms of serving together with others as well as the experience of living, for a time, with difficulties in an unfamiliar culture. If your church doesn't do short-term mission trips, consider local community care projects. You can use these projects as an invitation for young adults to experience serving together in the local community. These are great opportunities for the church to partner with local businesses for the common good of the community. Most Millennials support corporate social responsibility (CSR) programs. 70% of Millennials are willing to spend more money on goods and services when they know that part of their money is going to help social causes.[170]

A few years ago, I shared some of these ideas with the Millennials attending my church. They, in turn, took them to their places of work. Four of these young adults were employed at Kohl's department store. Kohl's has a community service program called "Kohl's Cares." In this program, employees volunteer to help out the community with some kind of service project. That year those young adults signed up for every "Kohl's Cares" project that was put on the calendar at their store.

Another social trend we should be aware of concerns the growing number of multigenerational homes. More young adults are living at home with mom and dad longer into their adult years. In addition to this, more grandparents are moving in with their adult children. Pew Research writers D'Vera Cohn and Jeffrey Passel note that "In 2016, a record 64 million people, or 20% of the U.S. population, lived with multiple generations under one roof."[171] The report shows that this trend of multigenerational homes is growing in every ethnic group. This indicates that many

---

170. Alton.
171. D'Vera Cohn and Jeffrey S. Passel, "A Record 64 Million Americans Live in Multigenerational Households," *Pew Research Center*, April 5, 2018, http://www.pewresearch.org, accessed May 18, 2018.

Millennials still have regular interaction with members of their families who are not Millennials. While, in many ways, society is becoming more individualized, families are still coming together geographically for practical and economic reasons. In the book of Acts, we see several passages where the whole household was converted to Christ. The multi-generational home was a common characteristic of the first-century Mediterranean culture. The early Church took advantage of that by looking for opportunities to bring the gospel into multigenerational households. As bivocational ministers, we need to reach out to all people and be ready to share the gospel with anyone regardless of their ethnicity or age because Jesus died for the sins of all people. In addition to that, we should remember that sharing the gospel with one individual may lead to a whole household of conversions.

In my case, driving a school bus has provided some unique opportunities. This vocation makes it possible for me to develop connections with people of all ages in the community. As a school bus driver, I work with over a hundred fellow bus drivers in addition to school employees, students, parents, and grandparents. Occasionally, I have opportunities to minister to my non-Christian co-workers. I have performed weddings and funerals for family members of fellow bus drivers simply because I was the only minister they knew.

Prayer is also a great way to strengthen your connections with co-workers. When someone tells you about a problem in their life, ask them how you can pray for them. One of my co-workers asked for prayer for her daughter and grandson who were living with her. She told me that her grandson was required to do several hours of community service, but he was having a hard time finding things to do that would qualify. Of course, I prayed about the situation, but I also offered to help. I gave the grandson some basic jobs to do around the church building that would qualify as community service. The grandmother, her daughter, and her grandson were all very grateful.

## ECONOMIC TRENDS

The Barna chart reports that "The economic pressures on middle-class and working families are being passed on to local churches, and the financial and ministry implications are immense."[172] Back in chapter 2. we saw another chart by the Barna Group that shows how the older generations are far more generous in

---

172. Kinnaman, *The State of Pastors*, 154.

their giving to a church than the younger generations (table 1).[173]

Many churches are struggling with low attendance and a decline in charitable giving. Many churches are finding it difficult to pay a full-time preacher, support missionary works, and still provide benevolence to meet the needs of church members and people in the local community. This problem will continue to grow as more of our senior saints pass away. This economic trend will continue to force more and more churches to look for bivocational and volunteer ministers.

Michael Robertson is a school bus driver in West Virginia. He is also a minister of the gospel. For ministry students who are considering bivocational ministry, Robertson gives the following advice:

> Most of our churches do not pay a living wage. That is a fact. Try to cultivate skills that will enable you to be bivocational. The days of a one skill person are largely gone in our society. In most of our congregations, you as a minister (and your family) will suffer financially unless you are bivocational or your wife has a good skill. In my understanding, bivocational ministers are the future of ministry in our churches with less than 150 in average attendance.[174]

However, this economic trend is an opportunity for bivocational ministry to help the church continue to proclaim and demonstrate the message of the gospel. Bivocational ministry is an answer to this trend that helps the local church reach out and serve people in the community in practical ways.

The social gospel and the gospel of salvation should never be separated and pitted against each other. Jesus sent out the twelve to preach the gospel *and* heal the sick (Luke 9:6). The first Christians boldly proclaimed the resurrection of Jesus while generously giving to those in need (Acts 4:33-34). When the Apostles in Jerusalem reaffirmed Paul's calling to preach the gospel to the Gentiles, they specifically asked him to include benevolence in his gospel ministry (Gal. 2:10). Bivocational ministry gives us a unique opportunity to demonstrate the message of the gospel by serving people in the community and providing more financial resources for the church to meet the needs of those who are struggling.

---

173. Kinnaman, *The Generosity Gap,* 9.
174. Kennedy, 148.

Bivocational ministers are in a better position to invite millennials and the organizations that employ them into partnerships and projects to meet the needs of the community. Bivocational ministry has made it possible for people in my congregation to work together with my fellow bus drivers on projects for the common good. There is a group of bus drivers who call themselves the "Sunshine Committee." They put together fundraisers for people who are struggling with financial needs. My congregation has teamed up with the Sunshine Committee to help them with different projects. One was a yard sale we had at the church to raise money to help a bus driver who was battling cancer. Another was just a special offering we took up to help a struggling family. Even though these small projects did not require a lot of time or effort they accomplished something much deeper than their intended goal. When the congregation teamed up with bus drivers in the local school district, they experienced God working through them for the common good of the community. These partnerships in gospel demonstration would not have happened if I was not connected to the community through my job as a bus driver.

## VOCATIONAL TRENDS

The observation of the Barna Group in the area of vocational trends is that "The landscape of work is shifting toward a gig-oriented, multi-careering, freelance terrain, and there is profound need for a robust theology of vocational discipleship."[175] Bivocational ministry fits like a glove in this vocational environment. The term "gig-oriented" means that it is normal for people to have more than one job at a time. Many people are intentionally learning more than one marketable skill for that reason. The 2018 Deloitte Millennial Survey found that most Millennials and Generation Z workers are already "gig-oriented."

> The recent rise of the gig economy has seen large numbers of people leave full-time employment or supplement their income by taking on short-term contracts or freelance work. Therefore, we asked our respondents whether they would consider taking on such roles either instead of or in addition to existing full-time employment. In both cases, a clear majority said they had already taken on such roles or would consider doing so; fewer than two in

---

175. Kinnaman, *The State of Pastors*, 154.

10 millennials (17 percent) and Gen Z respondents (13 percent) rejected the idea outright.[176]

Bivocational ministers need to see this trend as an opportunity for us to be more effective in gospel proclamation and gospel demonstration. This trend gives bivocational ministers more credibility in our culture. It helps us to relate to people and form connections based on similar life experiences.

"And is your husband working now... or is he still in the ministry?"[177]

A small business owner in Nebraska who also serves as a minister of the gospel described how his work outside the church has been an opportunity to relate to people and make connections that he would not have made otherwise. He said,

I have real opportunities to meet, work, and interact with people in the community without some artificial reason. I am in a serving vocation and people appreciate that. I work to earn a living just as they do. People appreciate someone who can identify with them as far as being a "working" person, one who experiences the same

---

176. Deloitte, "2018 Deloitte Millennial Survey: Millennials Disappointed in Business, Unprepared for Industry 4.0," *Deloitte*, last modified 2018, accessed May 18, 2018, https://www2.deloitte.com/global/en/pages/about-deloitte/articles/millennialsurvey.html.

177. Mary Chambers, *Church Is Stranger Than Fiction* (Downers Grove, IL: InterVarsity Press, 1990), 11.

situations they do because of their "work."[178]

Another vocational trend is the fact that there are more Millennials in the workforce now than any other generation. A report by Pew states that,

As of 2017 – the most recent year for which data are available – 56 million Millennials (those ages 21 to 36 in 2017) were working or looking for work. That was more than the 53 million Generation Xers, who accounted for a third of the labor force. And it was well ahead of the 41 million Baby Boomers, who represented a quarter of the total. Millennials surpassed Gen Xers in 2016.[179]

Again, this is an opportunity for bivocational ministers to reach out to Millennials with gospel proclamation and gospel demonstration. Many bivocational ministers are in the marketplace working shoulder to shoulder with Millennials who need to know that the gospel can make a positive difference in the workplace. In this setting, it is important for bivocational ministers to be aware of the vocational values of Millennials. The first observation Larry Alton made in his 2017 article about Millennials was concerning their value for a healthy work environment.

First, millennials value company culture more than any other generation that's come before them. Even though the idea of "corporate culture" has been around since the 1970s, only recently has it started to become a bigger priority for workers. On average, millennials would be willing to give up $7,600 in salary every year to work at a job that provided a better environment for them.[180]

The vocational trend statement on the Barna chart said that "there is profound need for a robust theology of vocational discipleship." The gospel is redemptive and transforming both of individuals and communities. This vocational trend is an opportunity for bivocational ministers to demonstrate self-sacrificing love and service in the workplace and create an environment where people can flourish.

---

178. Kennedy, 150.
179. Richard Fry, "Millennials Are the Largest Generation in the U.S. Labor Force," *Pew Research Center*, April 11, 2018, accessed May 18, 2018, http://www.pewresearch.org/fact-tank/2018/04/11/millennials-largest-generation-us-labor-force/.
180. Alton, "How Millennials Are Reshaping What's Important In Corporate Culture."

In another study, Barna looked at the way Christians make connections between their faith and their work and how many Christians intentionally live out their faith in the workplace.[181] In their report, Barna found that 34% of Christians are "compartmentalizers." These are people who see their faith and their work as separate compartments of life. Barna identified 38% of Christian workers as "onlookers." These are Christians who see and even appreciate connections between their faith and their work when they happen, but they are passive in the process. The last 28% of Christian workers Barna identified as "integrators." These are Christian workers who intentionally and enthusiastically integrate their faith and their work. The report did not comment on the unique position bivocational ministers are in to model a Christian work ethic and encourage the "compartmentalizers" and "onlookers" to be "integrators."

Bivocational ministry for the sake of the gospel assumes that both non-Christians and Christians can and should be blessed by ministers with second jobs. Christians need on-the-job reminders that their work can be a demonstration of the gospel of grace. Many people have accepted the false doctrine that "secular" jobs are not spiritual. "The faith at work movement—a loose global network of scholars, clergy, students, and marketplace leaders—has sought to reverse this trend by encouraging and equipping Christians to see their work as part of God's purposes in and for the world."[182]

Bivocational ministry for the sake of the gospel assumes that believers need to see and experience practical examples of vocational stewardship in the lives of their spiritual leaders. Vocational stewardship is seeing the calling that God has given us as a precious gift of His grace. It is making the most of every opportunity to use our vocation to exemplify the gospel of grace and create a culture of grace in the workplace. This is far more likely to be effective and contagious among Christians when they see it exemplified by their spiritual leaders.

In her book, *Kingdom Calling*, Amy Sherman encourages pastors to inspire Christians with living examples of faith at work.

> A final aspect of inspiring the congregation involves searching for people in the church who are modeling vocational stewardship and telling their stories. A pastor can preach all day about the call

---

181. David Kinnaman, Tod Brown, and Bill Denzel, *Christians at Work: Examining the Intersection of Calling and Career* (Ventura, CA: Barna Group, 2018), 50.
182. John Terrill, "The Faith at Work Movement," *Response*, (Autumn 2012), 19.

to integrate faith and work, and to see our work in a God-centered, service-centered way. But without living, breathing examples of this, church members may have difficulty putting that teaching into practice.[183]

While many pastors preach and teach what the Bible says about having a good work ethic, they also need to practice and exemplify vocational stewardship for the common good. Many Christians feel like they are trapped in a "secular" job that drains their faith. For some of them, the work environment is hostile to Christian values. When Christians—who are struggling during the week at work—hear a sermon on Sunday telling them to be salt and light in the workplace, it will mean a lot more to them if they know that the preacher is also going to clock in on Monday morning.

A bivocational preacher in Ohio shared with me his journey into vocational stewardship for the sake of the gospel. In the first survey when he was asked why he was bivocational, he said,

Initially, it was in order to meet requirements to be vested in Medicare—after opting out of social security. Having met that requirement, I continue to work outside the church in order to share Christ, stay in touch with my community, and avoid hyperfocus... People in my congregation get to hear and see that I am modeling and doing what I encourage and teach them to do.[184]

## INSTITUTIONAL TRENDS

The Barna Group notes that "People get the information they want, when they want, for the price they want to pay. 'Disintermediated institutions'—including churches—are no longer the sole mediators of knowledge, and pastors no longer the chief authority." However, bivocational ministry for the sake of the gospel makes it possible for pastors to preach and teach about gospel transformation with greater authority and effectiveness.

In his book *Desiring the Kingdom*, James Smith identifies a weakness in

---

183. Amy Sherman, *Kingdom Calling: Vocational Stewardship for the Common Good*, (Downers Grove, IL: InterVarsity Press, 2011), 113.
184. Kennedy, 153.

our typical approach to Christian education. In our attempts to equip Christians and encourage spiritual transformation we tend to focus on communicating information in the classroom or the church service. However, a much deeper level of transformation takes place when we experience these ideas in action.

> ...the distorted understanding of worldview that dominates current models assumes a rationalist, intellectualist, cognitivist model of the human person; as a result, it fails to honor the fact that we are embodied, material, fundamentally desiring animals who are, whether we recognize it or not (and perhaps most when we don't recognize it), every day being formed by the material liturgies of other pedagogies—at the mall, at the stadium, on television, and so forth.[185]

Our efforts to encourage spiritual transformation through preaching and teaching are important but they cannot compete with the ongoing experiences Christians have in the workplace throughout the week. Listening to a sermon is usually a passive experience that requires little or no response. Work is an active experience that requires us to use more than just our sense of hearing. Typically, workers are involved in routines that form complex patterns consisting of both actions and thoughts. In addition to this there is a huge difference between the amount of time people spend in church and the amount of time they spend at work. Most Americans spend over 1,900 hours at work each year.[186] Most Christians do not attend church every Sunday. But even if a Christian faithfully attended a one-hour church service every week, that would only amount to 52 hours a year.

Another institutional trend that has been gaining momentum for several years is the way people view the organized church. Many Christians have stopped attending church for various reasons, but they continue to believe in Jesus. Many unchurched Americans have never been members of an organized church, but they believe in Jesus. The Barna Group reports that

> Today, nearly half of America is unchurched. But even though more and more Americans are abandoning the institutional church

---

185. James K. A. Smith, *Desiring the Kingdom: Worship, Worldview, and Cultural Formation*, (Grand Rapids, MI: Baker Academic, 2009), 33.
186. Jennifer Johnson Gilnett, "Work and the Whole Christian Life," *Response*, (Autumn 2012), 4.

and its defined boundary markers of religious identity, many still believe in God and practice faith outside its walls.[187]

Bivocational ministers can effectively reach out to those who have an aversion to attending an institutional church by forming non-traditional faith communities with them at work or in their homes. We need to recall the simplicity of the early church. They met in their homes. They didn't have the expensive and time-consuming theatrical productions and professional concerts that many churches today have every Sunday. Wolfgang Simson observes that,

> Before they were called Christians, followers of Christ were called "the Way." One of the reasons for this title was that these believers had literally found the way to live. The nature of church is not reflected in a constant series of religious meetings led by professional clergy in holy places especially reserved to experience Jesus. Rather, it is mirrored in the prophetic way followers of Christ live their everyday lives in spiritual extended families, as vivid answers to the questions that society asks, and in the place where it counts most—in their homes.[188]

The church in the New Testament grew because Christians were living out their faith in everyday life and forming simple communities of faith in their homes. The common structure of most churches in America looks and feels more like a business than a home. As such, many people today are not interested in being a part of the typical organized church.

Hugh Halter in his book *Bivo: A Modern-Day Guide for Bivocational Saints* notes that in the current culture the typical business model of church is not sustainable. He writes,

> As we've said, the world will continue to change and most likely the church under its present business model and discipleship model will collapse, or at least be altered beyond recognition. The

---

187. Roxanne Stone, "Meet Those Who 'Love Jesus but Not the Church,'" *Barna Group*, accessed May 28, 2018, https://www.barna.com/research/meet-love-jesus-not-church/.
188. Wolfgang Simson and George Barna, *The House Church Book: Rediscover the Dynamic, Organic, Relational, Viral Community Jesus Started* (Carol Stream, IL: BarnaBooks, 2009), xiii-xiv.

ones who get ahead of the curve now or skate to where the puck is going will be the best positioned to not only survive through the tremors, but also thrive![189]

Halter is not suggesting that we should only have small house churches. In the book *AND: The Gathered and Scattered Church*, he and his coauthor argue that both mega churches and micro churches can be effective in gathering Christians together in fellowship to worship as well as scattering Christians into the world to share the gospel.[190] However, many bivocational and volunteer ministers are effectively preaching and demonstrating the message of the gospel through simple non-traditional communities of faith. My friend, Jon Schuller is a bivocational minister in Spokane, Washington. When he was working with me in ministry, I saw him develop a passion for the gospel and a desire to bring people to Christ in unconventional ways. God blessed him with an amazing ability to think outside the box. For a while he was leading a network of house churches called Antioch.

> Each Sunday, throughout the city, we have house churches meeting to eat, pray, remember, disciple, and share their lives with one another. The house churches are led by ordinary people - mechanics, construction workers, accountants, etc. According to the example of the early church, these gatherings center around prayer, Bible teaching, and sharing a meal together…We want to teach ordinary people - even those who are new in their faith - to start to think and act like missionaries in their communities. That way we can help build God's Kingdom - together.[191]

There are many other trends in the culture that we should be aware of in order to make our ministries more effective for the sake of the gospel. The trends we have considered in this chapter present both challenges and opportunities for all ministers of the gospel. Again, these are general trends for the nation. Things may be different in the specific communities your congregation is trying to reach with the gospel. *Percept Group* is an excellent resource that every church should take advantage

---

189   Halter, *Bivo*, 134.
190   Hugh Halter and Matt Smay, *AND: The Gathered and Scattered Church* (Grand Rapids, MI: Zondervan, 2010), 26.
191   Jon Schuler, "Antioch," *Antioch Church*, accessed May 28, 2018, http://antiochspokane.com/.

of in order to better understand the demographics of their community. Their basic six-page report will cost you $85 or if you want to spend $219 you can get a more comprehensive 27-page report.

However, none of the reports published by the Barna, Pew, Percept, or anyone else were able to predict the global pandemic of 2020. Perhaps God is using the unprecedented events of 2020 to wake up His church and pull her out of the traditional methods of ministry. Because of COVID-19, many congregations have been forced to be more flexible in the way they do church. Ministers have learned how to do church online and in small groups at various locations. Church members have stepped up and learned how to host small groups in their homes and lead Bible studies and prayer groups. 2020 has taught us that we can't always predict the changes that are going to take place in our culture, so we have to be flexible in our methods of ministry. We must be ready and willing to change our methods of ministry for the sake of the gospel. The best way to understand how to minister to the people in your community right now is to get out of the church office and interact with the people in your community, talk to them, work together with them, pray for them, and serve them.

In this chapter, we have seen how bivocational ministers can take advantage of the current trends and put into practice the principles of Gospel Perception, Gospel Motivation, Gospel Proclamation, Gospel Demonstration, and Gospel Transformation. In the next two chapters, we will consider some of the common challenges in bivocational ministry.

## DISCUSSION QUESTIONS

1. Why is it important for ministers to be aware of the current changes taking place in the culture? (Support your answer with Scripture.)

2. What can ministers do to stay current and engaged in the culture they are reaching out to?

3. What are some observations researchers have made about the millennial generation that you think are important for ministers to be aware of? Why?

4. What can bivocational ministers do to effectively reach out to millennials with the gospel?

5. What can bivocational ministers do to give non-Christians a more positive perception of Christian ministers?

6. How can you use one of the current social trends to proclaim or demonstrate the gospel?

7. How have you seen economic trends affecting the churches and ministries?

8. What vocational trends do you think are especially important for bivocational ministers to be aware of? Why?

9. How can bivocational ministers use these vocational trends to proclaim and demonstrate the gospel?

10. Give an example of something Christians could do in the workplace to demonstrate the redemptive message of the gospel and help to create an environment where people can flourish?

11. How can bivocational ministry help to improve the effectiveness of the preaching and teaching in the church?

12. How can bivocational ministers be more effective in reaching out to those who have an aversion to an "institutional" church?

# CHAPTER 10

THE
CHALLENGE
OF TIME
MANAGEMENT

"Therefore be careful how you walk,
not as unwise men but as wise,
making the most of your time,
because the days are evil."
—Ephesians 5:15-16

"You must therefore zealously guard in his mind the curious
assumption 'My time is my own.' Let him have the feeling
that he starts each day as the lawful possessor of twenty-
four hours. Let him feel as a grievous tax that portion of this
property which he has to make over to his employers, and
as a generous donation that further portion which he allows
to religious duties. But what he must never be permitted
to doubt is that the total from which these deductions
have been made was, in some mysterious sense, his own
personal birthright."

Your affectionate uncle,
SCREWTAPE[192]

Time management is a universal concern. As mortals we are all bound by time
regardless of how many jobs we have or what kind of ministries are demanding our

---

192. Lewis, *The Screwtape Letters,* 112.

attention. Whether we work 40 hours a week or 80 hours a week we still only have 168 hours in each week. Whether we are approaching the first day of retirement or the first day of a new career, we still only have 24 hours in each day. Regardless of whether we are "full-time," bivocational, or volunteer ministers, we all have a limited amount of time every day and every week to do all the things we need to do. The Bible commands us to "make the most of our time" (Eph. 5:16) so time management is a concern for all of us.

Time management is especially critical for the bivocational minister. Almost every book on bivocational ministry has a chapter on time management. This seems to be the primary struggle that preachers and congregations have when they are considering bivocational ministry. When "full-time" ministers have to shift to bivocational ministry, they think, "If it was so hard to manage my time when I only had one job, how on earth am I going to do it with two jobs?"

Dennis Bickers has written more about bivocational ministry than anyone else. Among all the bivocational ministers he has talked to; he sees time management as the most prevalent concern. He writes,

> At every bivocational conference I lead, the attendees are given index cards and asked to write down their biggest challenges as bivocational ministers. Without exception, every card returned to me includes the problem of time. They want to know how to find the time to lead the church, work their second jobs, spend time with their families, and have some time for themselves. These ministers understand that their effectiveness as leaders depends upon their ability to manage their time.[193]

In this chapter, we will consider how the gospel can help us with time management in the busy life of bivocational ministry. We will apply some biblical principles concerning time and priorities to bivocational ministry. And we will also explore some time management tips and strategies suggested by various authors and bivocational ministers.

---

193. Dennis Bickers, *The Bivocational Pastor: Two Jobs, One Ministry* (Kansas City, MO: Beacon Hill Press of Kansas City, 2004), 127.

## TIME FOR THE GOSPEL

In previous chapters, I have underscored the importance of putting into practice the principles of gospel perception, motivation, transformation, proclamation, and demonstration. As bivocational ministers of the gospel with busy schedules, we will have struggles with time management. However, these gospel principles will not only help us to stay focused, but they will also lift the weight of unnecessary time constraints and burdens we often try to carry by ourselves.

To apply these gospel principles to time management, we must consider how our time and the gospel are connected. Here are three important connections between our time and the gospel.

### 1. Time is a Gift of God's Grace.

Both our creation and our salvation are by the grace of God. Every day of your existence is a gift from God that you did nothing to earn or deserve. The quote from Screwtape at the beginning of this chapter, shows how we typically think of our time as a very personal thing belonging to us as an entitlement. Such is not the case. But when we acknowledge that it is a gift generously given to us by the God who created us and redeemed us, it empowers us with great confidence and freedom.

Leland Ryken writes,

> The practical implications of viewing time as God's gift are far-reaching. An obvious response is for people to accept time as God's gift with gratitude. Time is not a curse but a gift. Applied to work and leisure, we have a reason to accept every moment of them as something sent from God. They may be wearisome or delightful, but in either case they are something that God has designed for us.[194]

### 2. The Gospel is Both Urgent and Important.

In the classic time management book, *The 7 Habits of Highly Effective People*, Stephen Covey gives us a time management matrix that shows us the four quadrants where we spend our time.[195]

---

194. Leland Ryken, *Redeeming the Time: A Christian Approach to Work and Leisure* (Grand Rapids, MI: Baker Books, 1995), 275.
195. Stephen R. Covey, *The 7 Habits of Highly Effective People: Powerful Lessons in Personal Change*, Anniversary edition. (New York: Simon & Schuster, 2013), 160.

## COVEY'S TIME MANAGEMENT MATRIX

| | URGENT | NOT URGENT |
|---|---|---|
| IMPORTANT | **Quadrant 1**<br>Activities:<br>Crises<br>Emergencies<br>Deadline-driven projects<br>Some phone calls | **Quadrant 2**<br>Activities:<br>Prevention and planning<br>Relationship building<br>Family time<br>Exercise |
| NOT IMPORTANT | **Quadrant 3**<br>Activities:<br>Interruptions<br>Some phone calls<br>Some emails<br>Some text messages<br>Some meetings | **Quadrant 4**<br>Activities:<br>Trivia<br>Most email<br>Social media<br>Video games<br>Television |

TABLE 5

This matrix is designed to help us evaluate and prioritize the way we spend our time. The left side of the chart are urgent things that demand our time, but we should only give our *immediate* attention to those urgent things that are truly important in quadrant 1. The urgent things that are not that important in quadrant 3 should be delegated. The big time wasters are the activities in quadrant 4. These are the things we should try to avoid. The time savers are in quadrant 2. Many of the things in quadrant 2 prevent a lot of the urgent things that pop up in quadrants 1 and 3.

Time management books and seminars often present this matrix as an effective tool to help us evaluate our schedules. However, they usually present it from a business perspective with the aim of becoming more efficient and productive. There is nothing wrong with that, but I would suggest that we should use this matrix for the sake of the gospel. If we are looking through the "gospel glasses" we talked about in chapter 4, we will see all our activities in the light of the gospel. Everything we do will be in some way a response to the gospel and for the sake of the gospel. Some of our gospel opportunities will be in quadrant 1 because they are both urgent and important. Evangelism will often be in quadrant 1 while discipleship will usually be in quadrant 2. While all opportunities to proclaim and demonstrate the gospel are important, we must still exercise wisdom and discernment and determine when we should take action and when we should train and delegate others to take action.

Richard Schimansky, a bivocational minister in Point Marion, Pennsylvania, gave some good advice about this in one of his responses to the second survey. He wrote,

> For all ministers, but especially for bi-vocational ministers; recognize that your ability to prioritize will impact both your effectiveness and your longevity as a minister. In our culture in particular, we allow the "urgent" to take precedence over the "important." To the minister, this is a dangerous practice. You can't build healthy relationships in discipleship if you neglect your relationships at home. You can't wield the Word of God in public if you are not digesting the Word of God in private. And you absolutely cannot be everything to everybody. Sometimes, to keep your priorities in order, you have to say "no." Learn how to do this.[196]

**3. The Gospel Helps Us to Redeem the Time.**

> Therefore He says: "Awake, you who sleep, Arise from the dead, And Christ will give you light." See then that you walk circumspectly, not as fools but as wise, redeeming the time, because the days are evil. (Eph. 5:14-16 NKJV)

The ESV says, "making the best use of the time" instead of "redeeming the time" but both ideas are implied in the context. When we live in the light of the gospel, allowing the message of the gospel to renew our minds and transform our hearts, we experience a spiritual resurrection. We come to life spiritually and Christ gives us light. The Holy Spirit within us motivates us and empowers us to make the best use of our time for the sake of the gospel.

However, there are some active imperatives in this passage that we are required to obey. The message of the gospel and indwelling of the Holy Spirit will empower us but we must take action. We must wake up, get up, and start walking in wisdom, making the most of our time. In the following verses, Paul describes the active partnership we share with the Holy Spirit in this process of redeeming the time.

---

196. Kennedy, 162.

> So then do not be foolish, but understand what the will of the Lord is. And do not get drunk with wine, for that is dissipation, but be filled with the Spirit, speaking to one another in psalms and hymns and spiritual songs, singing and making melody with your heart to the Lord; always giving thanks for all things in the name of our Lord Jesus Christ to God, even the Father; and be subject to one another in the fear of Christ. —Ephesians 5:17-21

Walking in wisdom and making the best use of our time means that we are constantly seeking to understand what the will of the Lord is for us at any given time. To do that, we must be filled with the Holy Spirit and we must avoid those things that impair our judgment, like drugs and alcohol.

"Be filled with the Spirit" is a passive imperative. Imperative means that it is a command and as such we have a responsibility to obey it. But since it is passive it is not an action we do, but an action we allow to be done to us. The Holy Spirit wants to fill us and accomplish His work of sanctification in our lives but there are things we can do to resist, grieve, and quench the work of the Holy Spirit. However, there are other things we can do to cooperate with the work of the Holy Spirit. Following the passive imperative verb "be filled" there are five present participles in this passage that describe our part in the work of being filled with the Holy Spirit: addressing one another, singing, making melody, giving thanks, and submitting to one another. These are all relational activities that we do to and with one another.

The typical business model of time management places the emphasis on efficiency and productivity. The biblical model of time management places the emphasis on our relationships with God and one another. The participles in Ephesians 5:19-21 are not a foolish waste of time. In fact, they are an essential part of redeeming the time.

## TIME FOR PRIORITIES

Another connection between our time and the gospel is that of priorities. In the gospel, we see God's priorities, values, and love. In a similar way, when we look at our schedules and how we spend our time, we see our priorities, values, and love. All the time management books emphasize the importance of putting first things first. If we are going to make the most of our time for the sake of the gospel, we need to get our priorities straight. Here are three important principles to remember as we evaluate our priorities and the way we spend our time:

**1. How You Spend Your Time Reflects Your Priorities.**

Even if we don't plan out our schedules and set priorities, people will notice how we spend our time and from those observations they will know what is most important to us. Paul said that the gospel is of "first importance" (1 Cor. 15:3). When you look at your schedule, is it obvious that the gospel is of "first importance"?

At a certain point in His ministry, Jesus began to focus His attention on going to Jerusalem to die for our sins. "As the time approached for him to be taken up to heaven, Jesus resolutely set out for Jerusalem" (Luke 9:51, NIV). We need to have the same resolute focus on the gospel as we evaluate our priorities and plan out our schedules (Heb. 12:2).

**2. How You Spend Your Time Will Shape Your Values.**

Those things that you invest your life into will naturally become more important to you. Jesus said, "For where your treasure is, there your heart will be also" (Matt. 6:21). Notice that He put the treasure first in this formula. While it is true that people will spend their time and money on the things that are close to their heart, it is also true that our hearts grow fonder for those things in which we are investing our treasure. Charles Crane notes that,

> Love grows by sacrifice. As a Christian sacrifices for the Lord, and invests time and effort in the building of the local church, its calling program, its teaching program, and the various aspects of outreach and mission work, that person will grow to love Christ and the church.[197]

When you spend time watching a certain television show, that show becomes more important to you. When you spend time playing a certain video game that video game becomes more important to you. When you spend time reading a certain book that book becomes more important to you. When you spend time with certain people, those people become more important to you. How do you want to adjust or

---

197. Charles Arthur Crane, *A Practical Guide to Soul Winning* (Joplin, MO: College Press Publishing Company, 1987), 21.

strengthen your values? What parts of your life do you want to become even more important to you than they already are?

### 3. How You Spend Your Time Communicates Your Love.

In the book, *The Five Love Languages* Gary Chapman identifies "quality time" as one of the important expressions of love in a relationship.[198] The gospel is a demonstration of God's love for us (Rom. 5:8). And the gospel is demonstrated in our lives by our love for God and other people (1 John 3:16). Both the quality and the quantity of time you spend with people are expressions of your love and potentially demonstrations of the gospel.

Most time management books speak of priorities in terms of the activities we do, the tasks that need to be completed, and the efficiency and productivity of those activities. However, I would suggest that our priorities should be evaluated and adjusted in terms of the relationships we have with the people in our lives. Robert Randall wisely observes that,

> Time management, therefore, is not ultimately about time; it is about people. Time management has to do with affecting the lives of others. How we deal with time in ministry does not incidentally or secondarily affect people; how we deal with time *is* dealing with people.[199]

Here are the four main relationship categories we need to consider as we prioritize the way we spend our time:

**God** — Your number one priority must be your relationship with God. If you are not putting this relationship first and giving it both the quantity and the quality time it needs to flourish, then every other relationship you have will suffer as well. And don't try to fool yourself into thinking that your time preparing sermons and lessons can serve as your personal devotion time. Bickers warns us against that tendency when he writes,

> We can easily slip into the mindset that doing God's work is the same as developing one's relationship with God. They are two

---

198. Gary Chapman, *The 5 Love Languages: The Secret to Love That Lasts* (Chicago, IL: Northfield Publishing, 2015).
199. Robert L. Randall, *The Time of Your Life: Self/Time Management for Pastors* (Nashville, TN: Abingdon Press, 1994), 44.

different things, though. We must not allow the busy schedule of ministry to substitute for spending time with God and growing deeper in our walk with him.[200]

Your relationship with God is an opportunity for both gospel proclamation and gospel demonstration. We need to preach the gospel to ourselves every day for our own spiritual growth and sanctification. The gospel is demonstrated to the people in our lives as they watch us and see the development of our relationship with God. Do the people in your life see you depending on God's grace in your times of weakness and failure? Do people see you model humility before God in honest confession and sincere repentance? Remember that repentance is a demonstration of the gospel (fig. 8).

Jerry Bridges provides an encouraging observation about how the gospel must be a source of personal daily revival and restoration for every minister when he writes,

> We need to put ourselves up against the gospel every day. By this frequent and intentional application of its truth, we build a continual realization of God's grace and its transforming effect on our character. We need to review every day whether we're living in that power and grace. And when we do such a daily reassessment, we get excited about the gospel at work in us and become so aware of the grace of God that we want to live an effective life—and it continually transforms us...Think of highly visible pastors and Christian leaders whose lives are filled to the brim. How do they travel, speak, write, administer a church, and still allow adequate time for the Lord to do for them and to them what we've just been discussing? Though the details differ in every ministry, the pressures to bypass daily renewing are real for every pastor regardless of the size of his church.[201]

**Family** — Your first congregation is your immediate family. Before God established the church, He established the family. The first social institution established for mankind was marriage. And one of the main reasons God designed marriage the way He did was to proclaim and demonstrate the message of the gospel (Eph. 5:22-33). God also designed the relationship between parents and children to be a

---

200. Dennis Bickers, *The Art and Practice of Bivocational Ministry: A Pastor's Guide* (Kansas City, MO: Beacon Hill Press, 2013), 32.
201. H.B. London Jr., ed., *Refresh, Renew, Revive: How to Encourage Your Spirit, Strengthen Your Family, and Energize Your Ministry* (Colorado Springs, CO: Focus on the Family Publishing, 1996), 36.

demonstration of His relationship with us (Matt. 7:9-11). The time we spend with our families is a time for intentional gospel application.

As bivocational ministers with families, we must be careful to give our families the time and attention they need. Paul did not have this responsibility to balance with his ministry. In 1 Corinthians 7:32-35 he advises single Christians to remain single so they can focus their attention on pleasing the Lord and not have their interests divided. This was not a command, but advice given in response to the questions the Corinthians asked him about marriage. It was wisdom based on the culture of the times (1 Cor. 7:26).

This does not mean that ministers with families cannot be bivocational. It is possible with God's help to be an effective bivocational minister with a spiritually healthy thriving family. The key, however, is to focus and depend on the gospel. Your spouse must be on board as a supportive partner who truly believes in ministry for the sake of the gospel. Likewise, you need to instill in your children a value for the gospel and a growing understanding of what Christ has done for us. My father found creative ways to do this for me and my siblings when we were very young.

My dad was a bivocational preacher in a small church of about 20 members. He also owned and operated a small janitorial business. He never sacrificed his time with his family for either of his jobs. He found creative ways to include his children in both his janitorial work and his church ministry. One of the contracts he had for his janitorial business was Timberline Lodge on Mount Hood. Almost every night he would make the two-hour drive from Portland to Mount Hood to clean the lodge. He would often take us kids to work with him. When we were very young (grade school age), he taught us how to sweep and mop floors and clean toilets. And we loved it!

My brother and sister are 5 and 4 years older than me, so they started going to work a few years before me. I remember crying at night because I had to stay at home while my big brother and sister got to go to work and clean toilets. The reason we enjoyed mopping floors and cleaning toilets was not because of the work itself; it was because we got to work with our dad.

I was only nine when my dad taught me how to play chess and reach out to the lost at the same time. In the small community of Bonny Slope where our church was located, there was an elderly couple named Mr. and Mrs. Schable. Mrs. Schable attended church faithfully every Sunday by herself. Mr. Schable, on the other hand, wanted nothing to do with church. He didn't like church, but he liked to play chess. So, upon my father's request, Mr. Schable agreed to allow me and my dad to come to his house once a week for a game of chess. Our time with Mr. Schable developed into a warm friendship, however, he still wasn't interested in coming back to church. He had been a Christian in the past, but something happened that made him bitter and angry and as a result, he walked away from Christ.

About a year later Mrs. Schable passed away. That's when Mr. Schable's hard heart finally softened and opened back up to Christ. God used that experience in my life not only to develop a love for the lost but also a growing sense of amazement for the power of the gospel. Every Sunday since Mrs. Schable passed away, Mr. Schable would be in church sitting right where Mrs. Schable used to sit. And whenever we sang "The Old Rugged Cross" Mr. Schable would weep uncontrollably. That was a powerful, life-changing lesson for a ten-year-old to take in and process. And frankly, I'm still being shaped by the experience.

I am thankful for the way my dad spent time with me, developing my relationship with him and my relationship with Christ. His example taught me the importance of making my family a priority and finding creative ways to include them in my busy schedule.

In response to the second survey I conducted, Donald Ray Miller gave practical advice about making sure we faithfully schedule time for our families. He said,

> Develop a great support system and remember to always take care of the family first. Keep a calendar of everything that is in planning. If they have a family, have a centralized calendar with all events on it. I have google calendar and I send my wife invites all the time so she will know if I have something going on. I also do this to make sure I'm not double booking myself.[202]

**Congregation** — The main reason God calls us to church leadership is to equip Christians for "the work of service to the building up of the body of Christ" (Eph. 4:11-12). In most churches, pastors and ministers are doing a lot of busy work that is not equipping Christians to build up the body of Christ. We need to evaluate and identify the most time-consuming responsibilities we have in ministry. Why do those jobs need to be accomplished? Are those jobs equipping Christians to

---

202. Kennedy, 170.

proclaim or demonstrate the gospel in some way? If you are spending a lot of time doing something in ministry that is not equipping Christians to build up the church, but it is still a job that needs to get done, train and delegate someone else to do it. Turn it into an opportunity to equip a Christian to serve and build up the church by helping you with that task.

Make sure that you are giving yourself the time you need to adequately prepare for the preaching and teaching of God's word. At the age of 22, Bob Russell became the minister of a small congregation of 120 members. He was not a bivocational minister, but he was committed to taking the time he needed to prepare a solid gospel message every week. Russell believes that one of the reasons that church grew from 120 members to over 18,000 was because of the time he spent preparing his sermons. He writes,

> You have to be convinced that study for preaching must take priority. It's one thing to say preaching is a priority, but until it is a regular part of your weekly routine, study will inevitably be shoved aside as the pressure of the immediate takes precedence over the most important. It's my observation that most guys fail in ministry due to a lack of discipline of time than because of talent. I'm convinced my rigid discipline of studying the same time every week was a huge factor in my lengthy stay and the growth of Southeast Christian.[203]

We also need to equip Christians to serve and build up the church in the way that they live throughout the week. The most effective demonstration of the gospel happens in everyday life with the people we work with and interact with Monday through Friday. Many of the members of your congregation are probably very busy with packed schedules and no time to get involved in ministries like vacation Bible school, calling night, drama ministry, choir, worship team, summer camp, small group Bible study, etc. But we need to remember that if we have members who are busy doing a lot of other things in life, they are probably doing those things with people who need the gospel. Christians need to be taught, equipped, and motivated to demonstrate the gospel and share their faith every day with the people they know at work, at the gym, at their kids' soccer games, at the stores where they shop, and

---

203. Bob Russell, *After 50 Years of Ministry: 7 Things I'd Do Differently and 7 Things I'd Do the Same* (Chicago, IL: Moody Publishers, 2016), 120-21.

at the restaurants where they eat. Hugh Halter observes,

> Whenever I train people or pastors on incarnational/missional living, the biggest questions I get are about time. How do we add incarnational life to our already jammed schedules?... Missional life isn't adding anything, but it is seeing everywhere you are as a possible mission field.
>
> Now, if we can give our people vision for their mission field, it exposes the fact that we may not need to hire anyone full time to do the work of ministry. The synergy of God's inexpensive mission happens when you, as a part-time or even unpaid pro, spend the majority of your time equipping the people of God for the mission of God.[204]

The first command of the Great Commission in Matthew 28:19, "go" is actually a temporal participle modifying the main verb "make disciples." It could be translated "as you go." The idea is that we are commanded to make disciples as we go through all our activities in life. The same principle was taught to the Israelites in the *Shema* (Deut. 6:7). Parents were commanded to teach and demonstrate to their children how to love the LORD their God in all their daily activities.

**Community** — Do you love the sinners in your community? One of the common complaints the religious leaders had concerning Jesus was that He would eat with sinners (Matt. 9:11 and Luke 15:1-2). In the Great Commission, Jesus commanded us to "go into all the world and preach the gospel" (Mark 16:16). We are commanded to "make disciples of all the nations" (Matt. 18:19). Jesus gave the early church a simple strategy of sharing the gospel where they were in Jerusalem and then continue to expand the proclamation of the gospel into the communities throughout Judea and then Samaria and then throughout the rest of the world (Acts 1:8). The reason Jesus died on the cross is that "God so loved the world" (John 3:16) and He doesn't want anyone to perish (2 Peter 3:9).

Does your schedule communicate that Christ-like love for the unsaved people in your world? Are you spending time every week making connections and building relationships with the lost people in your community? Take the following challenge that Doug Black gives us when he writes,

---

204. Halter, *Bivo*, 78-79.

I encourage you to try an exercise to determine whether you are on mission with Christ. Create a schedule, and breakdown how you spent each hour of your ministry this past week. Be brutally honest, and don't skip anything. How many of those hours were with those far from God?[205]

## TIME FOR A PLAN

Organizing our priorities is essential, not just for time management but also to maintain a clear vision of our values. The gospel and all these important relationships with God, our family, our congregation, and our community should be placed in quadrant 2 on Covey's Time Management Matrix. As bivocational ministers, we will have many things on our "to do" list that are directly related to these important values and we won't always have the time we need to get them all done when we want to get them done. Leland Ryken notes that,

> The whole time management movement, while no doubt helping some people get a handle on their lives, has also been the cause of a great deal of heartache because it misleads people into thinking that they can find enough time for everything.[206]

We will never be "all caught up" with all the important things we need to do. We need to remember that God's strength is perfected in our weaknesses and His grace is sufficient for us. God is still with us and working through our ministries even if we don't finish all those "important" projects by a certain deadline.

Recognizing our need for grace in time management should motivate us to seek God's help in the process. Recognizing the abundant grace God has given to us in Christ should give us the confidence that He wants to help us with our plans. Getting organized and making plans is not a lack of faith; it is practicing good stewardship with what God has entrusted to us. As ministers of the gospel, we have been entrusted with a limited amount of time to proclaim and demonstrate the gospel in our world. Here are three habits we can develop to make sure we are being good stewards of that time:

---

205. Doug Black, *Marathon: A Manual for Bivocational Ministry* (Philadelphia, PA: CreateSpace Independent Publishing Platform, 2014), 64.
206. Ryken, *Redeeming the Time, 271.*

## 1. Plan Out Every Week.

Many pastors live from Sunday to Sunday struggling to get everything done during the week so that everything that needs to happen on Sunday is ready to go. Many jobs in the world are set up on a weekly schedule with five workdays and a two-day weekend. The very first work schedule that God established in Genesis was one week with six workdays and one day of rest.

For the bivocational minister, it is especially important to set aside a time Saturday or Sunday to plan out the next week. We need to look at our two work schedules and bring them together in a way that they complement each other. We need to fill in our calendar with specific devotion times, family times, sermon preparation times, meetings, appointments, and other ministry duties as well as the specific hours we will be at our other job. There are several time management phone apps that have a week-to-week schedule. I use one called "Time Tune" that works well for me. In my planning sessions, I always write it out on paper first before I program it into my phone. There is something about writing things out that helps me to cement it into my memory.

The most important thing about weekly planning is that it helps us to remember to take a day for our Sabbath rest. Searcy and Jarman emphasize the necessity of this practice.

> What is a Sabbath? It's a weekly twenty-four-hour period dedicated exclusively to resting and recharging. This can be any twenty-four hours during the week. During your Sabbath day you should intentionally stay away from anything work-related and use your time to reconnect with God and your family and do things that refresh your soul. In order for you to remain effective in the long term, you *must* take a Sabbath day of rest. It's non-negotiable, and it isn't an indulgence.[207]

## 2. Plan Out Every Day.

In the book, *Eat That Frog*, Brian Tracy notes that many times the most difficult responsibilities that we are tempted to procrastinate are often the most rewarding and the most important things we need to do. He writes,

---

207. Dr. Nelson Searcy and Richard Jarman, *The Renegade Pastor's Guide to Time Management* (Boca Raton, FL: Church Leader Insights, 2017).

It has been said that if the first thing you do each morning is to eat a live frog, you can go through the day with the satisfaction of knowing that that is probably the worst thing that is going to happen to you all day long. Your "frog" is the biggest, most important task, the one you are most likely to procrastinate on if you don't do something about it. It is also the one task that can have the greatest positive impact on your life and results at the moment.[208]

Over the years I have put into practice various strategies of daily planning. By no means am I claiming to have found the perfect system that always works. In fact, for me, things seem to work better when I try something different each year. When I wrote this chapter in 2018, I had a huge project in my life with this book that I was trying to complete. I developed a daily routine that helped tremendously. Each night before I went to bed, I took a sticky note and wrote down the top three to five things I wanted to accomplish on the following day. I prayed about the list and circled the frog. I would then put the sticky note on my smartphone which is also my alarm clock. The first thing I did in the morning when the alarm went off was pray about my list and get started on eating the frog.

### 3. Pray Out Every Plan.

Nelson Searcy and Richard Jarmen encourage busy pastors to take time to pray the time management prayer, "God, what is the best use of my time right now?"[209] This may seem like a simple and obvious thing to do, but how often do we actually pray this prayer in contrast to how often we find ourselves wasting time. This prayer is basically a more specific version of the prayer for wisdom in James 1:5. If we pray this prayer in faith, we have the promise that God will give us the wisdom we need to decide how we should use our time. We should pray this prayer often but Searcy and Jarmen suggests that we get into the habit of praying this prayer at these specific times:

- *At the beginning of every day.* Start your day meditating on God's Word and talking with him in prayer. Make the Time Management Prayer part of this morning devotion.

---

208. Brian Tracy, *Eat That Frog! 21 Great Ways to Stop Procrastinating and Get More Done in Less Time* (Oakland, CA: Berrett-Koehler Publishers, 2017), 2.
209. Searcy and Jarman, *The Renegade Pastor's Guide to Time Management*, 41-42.

- *During natural transitions throughout the day.* Every day has natural transition points—breaks, meals, a few minutes of down time after an appointment, etc. During these times ask God to lead and direct you.

- *When planning your calendar for the week ahead.* Make planning your calendar an exercise of faith by praying for wisdom with regard to every activity.

- *During interruptions.* Interruptions can be huge time-wasters. Ask God to show you which interruptions are unnecessary— and which are divine appointments.[210]

Ephesians 5:15-16 says, "Therefore be careful how you walk, not as unwise men but as wise, making the most of your time, because the days are evil." I have these verses printed out on a piece of card stock and taped to the computer monitor in my office. Every time I sit down at my desk and turn on my computer, this passage reminds me to pray the time management prayer.

In this chapter we have seen how the gospel helps us to be good stewards of our time. While time management strategies like daily planning are important, we must always remember to bring it back to the gospel. Be careful not to get so caught up in time management that it becomes an idol or the main goal in ministry. Time management is a means to an end, not the end itself. Robert Randall gives pastors a relevant warning against a common tendency in our culture when he writes,

> Time management strategies can be symptomatic of a pastor or congregation having moved away from a ministry by faithfulness to a ministry by objective. Establishing yearly goals becomes more important than caring for persons. We must be alert to the character of time management techniques in the church. They may create problems rather than resolve them.[211]

When ministers are primarily focused on time management and efficiency, people get the impression that the church is more like a business than a family. The main goal seems to be effective productivity rather than reconciliation and spiritual

---

210. Searcy and Jarman, 36.
211. Randall, *The Time of Your Life*, 15-16.

growth. Remember that the gospel is effectively proclaimed and demonstrated in the context of relationships. Your relationships with God, your family, your congregation, and your community are all opportunities to proclaim and demonstrate the gospel with the sincere motivation of your love for God and your love for others.

**THE GOSPEL MATRIX**

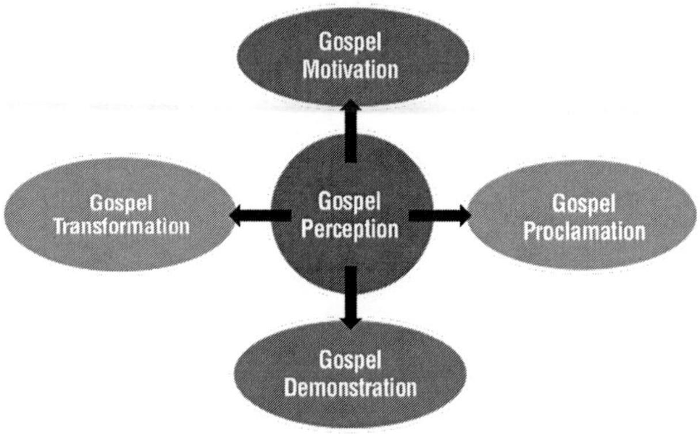

FIGURE 16

As ministers of the gospel, we need to use a gospel matrix to evaluate our priorities and plan out our schedules. We must start with a gospel perception (see fig. 16). We need to put on our "gospel glasses" and maintain a gospel perception of everything on our calendar. When we are trying to decide if a certain activity is making the most of our time, we can evaluate it in the light of gospel motivation, proclamation, demonstration, and transformation. Does the gospel motivate us to do this activity? How could this activity provide us or others an opportunity to proclaim the gospel? How could this activity provide us or others an opportunity to demonstrate the gospel? How could this activity provide us or others an opportunity to experience gospel transformation?

# DISCUSSION QUESTIONS

1. Read the quote by Screwtape at the beginning of the chapter. Why do so many people (even Christians) think that their time is something they deserve?

2. What could you do to remind yourself that every day of your life is a gift from God?

3. Have you ever used Covey's Time Management Matrix? If you have, how was it helpful? If you haven't, do you think it would be helpful to you in some way? Why, or why not?

4. How does the Holy Spirit help us to manage our time wisely? What is His part and what is our part in the process of "redeeming the time"?

5. Keep track of how you spend your time this week. At the end of each day, fill out the column for that day on the chart at the end of this chapter. Give a one- or two-word summary for how you spent each hour. What did you learn about how you spend your time?

6. How has your investment of time in certain people or activities shaped your values?

7. How much of your time each day is usually devoted to your relationship with God?

8. Look at the time chart you filled out at the end of the week. How much of your time was spent interacting with members of your family? How much of your time was spent interacting with other Christians?

9. What do you think pastors and ministers should keep at the top of their priority list of ministry responsibilities that require their time?

10. Look at the time chart you filled out at the end of the week. How much of your time was spent interacting with non-Christians?

11. When do you usually plan out and pray about your week? If you hardly ever plan out your week, when could you set aside a time each week to start?

## WEEKLY TIME CHART

|  | SUNDAY | MONDAY | TUESDAY | WEDNESDAY | THURSDAY | FRIDAY | SATURDAY |
|---|---|---|---|---|---|---|---|
| 12 AM |  |  |  |  |  |  |  |
| 1 AM |  |  |  |  |  |  |  |
| 2 AM |  |  |  |  |  |  |  |
| 3 AM |  |  |  |  |  |  |  |
| 4 AM |  |  |  |  |  |  |  |
| 5 AM |  |  |  |  |  |  |  |
| 6 AM |  |  |  |  |  |  |  |
| 7 AM |  |  |  |  |  |  |  |
| 8 AM |  |  |  |  |  |  |  |
| 9 AM |  |  |  |  |  |  |  |
| 10 AM |  |  |  |  |  |  |  |
| 11 AM |  |  |  |  |  |  |  |
| 12 AM |  |  |  |  |  |  |  |
| 1 PM |  |  |  |  |  |  |  |
| 2 PM |  |  |  |  |  |  |  |
| 3 PM |  |  |  |  |  |  |  |
| 4 PM |  |  |  |  |  |  |  |
| 5 PM |  |  |  |  |  |  |  |
| 6 PM |  |  |  |  |  |  |  |
| 7 PM |  |  |  |  |  |  |  |
| 8 PM |  |  |  |  |  |  |  |
| 9 PM |  |  |  |  |  |  |  |
| 10 PM |  |  |  |  |  |  |  |
| 11 PM |  |  |  |  |  |  |  |
| 12 PM |  |  |  |  |  |  |  |

TABLE 6

# CHAPTER 11

OTHER
CHALLENGES
TO
BIVOCATIONAL
MINISTRY

"Apart from such external things, there is the
daily pressure on me of concern for all the churches."
—2 Corinthians 11:28

Those who are engaged in a spiritual ministry such as
preachers and pastors must likewise remain steadfast
before the peril of death. We have a plain command from
Christ, "A good shepherd lays down his life for the sheep
but the hireling sees the wolf coming and flees." For when
people are dying, they most need a spiritual ministry which
strengthens and comforts their consciences by word and
sacrament and in faith overcomes death.
—Martin Luther[212]

Besides time management, there are many other challenges that bivocational ministers struggle with every week. The above quote from Martin Luther was originally written at a time when a pandemic was sweeping through parts of Europe. In his pamphlet, *Whether One May Flee from a Deadly Plague*, Martin Luther exhorts pastors to stay in those towns where there was a fatal pestilence and care for the sick and dying. It was a deadly risk that Luther, himself was willing to take for

---

212. Mary Jane Haemig, *The Annotated Luther, Volume 4: Pastoral Writings* (Minneapolis, MN: Fortress Press, 2016), 392-93.

the sake of the gospel. At times, the frustrations of ministry will seem like a deadly plague and we will be tempted to give up and get out while we are still alive.

Any pastor who has been in ministry for any number of years can probably write down a long list of ministry struggles that would cause anyone to question why they're still doing it. However, when we read the list of ministry troubles that Paul faced in 2 Corinthians 11:23-29, we quickly realize that we have nothing to complain about. Earlier in the same book, he calls them "light and momentary troubles" (2 Cor. 4:17). I have experienced some difficult struggles in ministry, but I would never describe prison time, beatings, whippings, shipwrecks, and having rocks thrown at me as "light and momentary troubles." Paul did not have his head in the sand. He was not ignoring the difficulties of his ministry. Paul had a gospel-centered perspective that allowed him to face those challenges with both faith and wisdom. In this chapter, we will consider some of the common struggles that bivocational ministers are going through and what we can do to prepare for them. We will see how a gospel perspective is the best way to approach these challenges.

## FINANCES

One of the most difficult challenges of many ministers is the financial struggle. Often it is both the church and the pastor who are having to make difficult financial decisions. Many of the ministers who responded to my first survey specifically mentioned the recession of 2008 as one of the reasons they had to find secondary sources of income. Over a decade later, there is still an increasing number of smaller churches looking for ways to cut back on payroll expenses.

While having a gospel-centered perspective will not remove our financial problems, it must be the starting point when we need to make difficult financial decisions. Paul started with the conviction to do all things for the sake of the gospel and then after analyzing the culture and evaluating what would work best to advance the gospel, he then decided to either accept wages for his ministry or supplement his income by making tents. So, we too must start with a conviction to do all things for the sake of the gospel. Bivocational minister, Thaddeus Hinkle, wisely observes,

> Ministry to others in the name of Jesus—not self-service—is our purpose as Christians. Enter a second vocation as a way to extend and add another venue to your ministry. Make sure your motive is

not merely to augment your income just so you can live closer to "the American dream."[213]

Jeff Blaine, another bivocational minister, gives the following gospel-centered advice to those who are considering bivocational ministry:

> Give it time. Don't seek out bivocation as a necessity (because of debt or poor spending habits) but as an opportunity to walk with Jesus throughout your community. Be patient. Jesus will naturally share with you the best place for you and Him to be together. And those around you will experience your relationship.[214]

A bivocational minister in Michigan, notes how being bivocational has made it possible for his congregation to be more effective in benevolence and mission work. He writes,

> Being bivocational is a personal preference. Since our church has chosen not to buy a building and because I don't need to earn my livelihood from the church, our church gives around 60% of our church income to missions and benevolence. We like being generous.[215]

When asked, "What is the one thing that has helped your bivocational ministry to be more effective?" he responded by saying, "My commitment to the gospel and to preaching the word of God. We have a congregation of mature believers that make a significant impact on our community—the priesthood of all believers."[216]

Steven Williams is a bivocational minister I know who preaches in Bemidji, Minnesota. He makes a similar observation about the finances in his congregation. When he was asked if it was his goal to eventually be fully funded by the church, he said, "No, we think our current system is functioning very well. It allows more funds to go to missions and outreach."[217]

Another preacher in Minnesota sees his bivocational ministry as a blessing to

---

213. Kennedy, 180.
214. Kennedy, 180.
215. Kennedy, 180.
216. Kennedy, 180.
217. Kennedy, 181.

the church. When he and his wife were asked what has helped them to be more effective in ministry, they said,

> The church has a different kind of freedom by not having to supply the preacher's salary. We are free to support more mission work—local and abroad. We laugh at men's/church meetings whenever it comes to "salary increases" or "vacation time." We have nothing to fret or fight over. Our needs are met and we serve freely from our own means. As a result, we have more joy in serving one another.[218]

These testimonies are encouraging and inspiring. However, financial needs are a matter of reality that require wisdom and a careful examination of our options. Having faith and a gospel-centered perspective will not remove our responsibility to make difficult financial decisions. However, we must start with a gospel perspective because it gives us the values we need to make those difficult decisions. God expects us to exercise both faith and wisdom with our finances. Churches and ministers are all dealing with unique financial situations that require wisdom and open communication. Pastors should humbly and honestly let the congregation know what their needs are without being demanding or greedy (1 Tim. 3:3 and 1 Peter 5:2). And congregations should generously provide for the needs of their spiritual leaders (Gal. 6:6 and 1 Tim. 5:17-18).

This can be a tricky problem because we tend to camp on those verses that are addressing other people while avoiding the passages that call us to change. We are like the husband and wife who come into the pastor's office for marriage counseling. The husband has a list of verses telling the wife what she needs to do. And the wife has a list of verses telling the husband what he needs to do. But neither one wants to follow the other person's list. Sometimes pastors and congregations are acting like that husband and wife. We need to focus on what the Bible is saying to us instead of camping on what the Bible says to others.

## ISOLATION

Another challenge that many bivocational preachers struggle with is isolation. Often bivocational ministers will feel like they are all alone and disconnected

---

218. Kennedy, 181.

from the "full-time" ministers in other churches. In 1999 the Brethren Academy conducted a survey of bivocational ministers in the Brethren churches. Steve Clapp, Ron Finney, and Angela Zimmerman noted this problem of isolation among bivocational ministers at that time. They report,

> The bivocational ministers who responded to our survey also indicated that they felt less supportiveness in their ministry from other clergy than they did from the members of the church they served. These references were not to other clergy who might be on a free ministry team with them but rather their colleagues in neighboring congregations. Some felt that those who were full-time pastors with graduate seminary degrees looked down on people serving in part-time capacities without graduate degrees.[219]

These perceptions that full-time ministers look down on bivocational ministers may be based more on the subjective feelings rather than reality. Or it may be that perceptions have changed since that survey was taken. In the surveys I conducted, there were very few (11) bivocational ministers that said anything about negative impressions from other ministers. Back in 1996, Doran McCarty noted that sometimes the isolation problem is because many bivocational ministers tend to be "loners" and as a result, they may develop negative attitudes toward the "full-time" pastors. McCarty writes,

> The bivocational minister often serves a church with little contact with other ministers. Part of this is a time issue and part of this is a tendency of the bivocational ministers to be "loners." Other ministers are your colleagues. They are also leaders in the kingdom of God. They should not be objects of jealousy. Nor should they be objects of attacks. You may not understand what they do or why they do it. Neither do they understand you. Neither knows the other's situation. Attacks on others only raises the hysteria and paranoia about ministry.[220]

---

219. Steve Clapp, Ron Finney, and Angela Zimmerman, *Preaching, Planning & Plumbing: The Implications of Bivocational Ministry for the Church and for You: Discovering God's Call to Service and Joy* (Fort Wayne, IN: Christian Community, 1999), 59.

220  McCarty, *Meeting the Challenge of Bivocational Ministry*, 223.

I don't think that bivocational ministers tend to be "loners" as such. In fact, many of the bivocational ministers that responded to my surveys seemed to be extroverts, enjoying the multiple connections they had because of their work in the community. However, I think there are several bivocational ministers who have very little interest in making and maintaining connections with "full-time" ministers. As McCarty notes, a big part of this is because of their busy schedules. Often when I receive information about conventions or conferences for ministers, I can't go because they are scheduled at a time when I am working. If there is an organization that sponsors conventions or conferences for church leaders that you would like to go to, but you usually can't because of your work schedule, let them know what would work better for you.

In the Restoration Movement, there is a tendency for some ministers to be isolated simply because of our heritage and our emphasis on local autonomy. Some leaders shy away from any kind of structure or organized connection between congregations that might resemble "denominationalism." I know ministers who refuse to list their church in *the Directory of the Ministry* for this reason. If you are a bivocational minister and you don't have any interaction with other ministers at least once a month, get to know some of the ministers in your area. Find two or three ministers that you can get together with once a month and encourage each other and pray for each other. You don't have to agree with each other on every doctrine in order to be a blessing to each other. I owe a debt of gratitude to Kyle Davies, a church planter in Vancouver Washington. At a difficult time in my ministry, he encouraged me and several other ministers in the area to get together once a month and pray for each other.

In most of his letters, Paul mentions by name some of his fellow workers in the ministry of the gospel. When you put them all together along with the individuals in Acts who worked with Paul in ministry, you have a list of over 75 names! And Paul didn't have Facebook or Twitter. Do you personally know at least 75 fellow workers in God's Kingdom who have worked with you, prayed for you, and encouraged you in your ministry? Many of these individuals are specifically identified as "fellow workers." Some of them Paul describes as "servants" or "working hard." Consider the comments Paul makes about Eudia and Syntyche in Philippians 4:2-3.

> I entreat Euodia and I entreat Syntyche to agree in the Lord. Yes, I ask you also, true companion, help these women, who have labored side by side with me in the gospel together with Clement

and the rest of my fellow workers, whose names are in the book
of life. —Philippians 4:2-3

Obviously, these two women had a sharp disagreement about something, but
Paul still considered them his fellow workers for the cause of the gospel. And he
said that their names are in the book of life.

A bivocational minister in Missouri wrote about the help he gets from other
ministers. When asked what has helped him to be more effective in his ministry, he
said, "The help of the former pastor and other pastors who are bivocational."[221]

The first survey I conducted was mainly for quantitative data. Looking back, I
think that the letter I sent with it was a little too formal and impersonal. However,
that didn't prevent John Frey from reaching out to me and encouraging me in prayer.
John Frey is a bivocational minister at the New Life Christian Church in Hutchinson,
Kansas. At the end of the survey, he added these words, "I have added your letter
to my prayer journal. I will pray for the successful completion of your dissertation
and ministry."[222] That encouraging note motivated me to go back and pray for every
minister who filled out the survey. It also inspired me to add a question to the second
survey: "How can I pray for you?" John Frey, thank you for your encouragement
and your prayers!

## SELF-IMAGE

Sometimes isolation is caused by feelings of insecurity or low self-esteem.
Bivocational ministers in smaller congregations often struggle with their identity
and self-worth. When a bivocational preacher compares his ministry in a small
church to several different growing churches with fully funded ministers, he may
isolate himself from those ministers as a defense mechanism.

I remember when I was a young man in Bible college, a larger church in
Portland Oregon hosted a "Church Growth Clinic" every year. One year I asked a
bivocational preacher if he would like to go the Church Growth Clinic with me. He
said he didn't have time to go listen to "experts" and megachurch pastors brag about
their ministries. At the time, I didn't understand what he was feeling, but I knew that
his criticism was probably unwarranted.

---

221. Kennedy, 184.
222. Kennedy, 184.

Ray Gilder notes that,

A number of bivocational pastors struggle with identity crises. They are unsure about their roles as bivocational pastors, preachers in the workplace, and husbands and fathers who are gone a lot of the time. Some think that because they are not fully funded they are not as successful.[223]

We need to be careful to avoid the comparison game. The value of our ministry and our effectiveness in God's kingdom is not determined by a comparison to other churches. Paul did not evaluate the worth of his ministry by comparing it to others. Writing to the Christians in Corinth, he said, "For we are not bold to class or compare ourselves with some of those who commend themselves; but when they measure themselves by themselves and compare themselves with themselves, they are without understanding" (2 Cor. 10:12). We also see that Paul's sense of identity and his motivation to work hard was based firmly on God's grace. Paul said, "But by the grace of God I am what I am, and His grace toward me did not prove vain; but I labored even more than all of them, yet not I, but the grace of God with me" (1 Cor. 15:10).

A preacher who responded to the first survey said that he is retired after working 41 years in public education. He has also been a minister of the gospel for over three decades. He is currently living off his public-school retirement and receiving a small payment from the church to cover gas and phone expenses. In the last 12 years, he has seen God grow the congregation from 20 to 100. When he was asked what has helped him be effective in his ministry he said, "I am very healthy, energetic, and I feel that my service for the Lord is my witness for the gospel."[224] This preacher is not worried about what other people think of him or how his ministry compares to anyone else's ministry. He finds his sense of worth and purpose in his calling as a minister of the gospel.

Mark Wright, a bivocational minister in Mandeville, Louisiana shares these words of encouragement with his fellow bivocational gospel preachers:

Be patient with it. Do not measure your worthiness based on the size of the church where you serve. Be faithful with the assignment God has given you. Be content. I have become completely

---

223. Gilder, *Uniquely Bivocational-Understanding the Life of a Pastor Who Has a Second Job*, 63.
224. Kennedy, 186.

content as a bivocational pastor. I do not wish to be a full-time pastor. I was full-time for 20 years but now I am very happy to be bivocational.[225]

Dennis Bickers reminds us of how God wants us to view the value of the ministry entrusted to us when he writes,

> View the church God has given you to serve as a significant ministry. Regardless of its size, your church is made up of people for whom Jesus died. They need a shepherd who will minister to their needs and lead them in paths God has laid out. The community in which your church is located is a mission field that needs your church to be a lighthouse that can help guide them into a relationship with God. The exciting thing about this is that God has called you, a bivocational minister, to be the person who will be used to provide this ministry and this leadership![226]

If you are a minister of the gospel, thank you for your faithful service in God's kingdom. Remember that God has entrusted you with your present ministry for a reason. He believes in you. And no one has been entrusted with the exact same ministry that you are serving in right now. You cannot evaluate your present ministry accurately by comparing it to someone else's ministry. The only thing you should compare present ministry to is your past ministry. Certainly, we should evaluate ourselves, and we should strive to improve in the effectiveness of our ministries. But like Paul, we should also remember that we are in ministry by the grace of God. It is God who causes the growth (1 Cor. 3:6). As we meditate on God's grace, like Paul, we will be motivated and empowered in our ministries.

## BURNOUT

Many Christians believe that the ideal scenario for a congregation would be to have their pastor working full-time for the church. Bivocational ministry makes it impossible (or at least very difficult) for the pastor to give as much time and attention to the church as a full-time pastor would. Usually, when a bivocational

---

225. Kennedy, 186.
226. Bickers, *The Work of the Bivocational Minister*, 57-58.

minister is trying to do all the work that a full-time pastor typically does in addition to the responsibilities of his other job, he feels overwhelmed and overworked. He becomes frustrated because he can't do everything everyone is expecting him to do. This leads to burnout. As Terry Dorsett observes,

> Pastors who feel ineffective in their ministries have increased negative emotions, which in turn increase the likelihood of burn-out. Therefore, systems must be put in place to help pastors overcome feelings of depression so they can be healthier individuals and more effective in their ministries. When such systems are not in place, pastors become trapped in a downward spiral that feeds upon itself until they become emotionally paralyzed in ministry and in their personal lives.[227]

This difficult situation can serve as an opportunity to promote a much more biblical model of ministry than what we often see in churches today. The system or safeguard that Dorsett talks about in his book is a program of training and delegation for church members to take on more of the ministry responsibilities that typically fall on the minister. If bivocational pastors can delegate responsibilities to other members in the church and if church members can get onboard with the New Testament model of every member being a minister, the church will grow stronger. All ministers and elders need to practice Ephesians 4:12 and equip the members of their congregations for works of service. Some church members will be glad to help their bivocational pastor by taking on extra responsibilities. Dorsett notes that this problem gives bivocational ministry the potential to make congregations healthier.

> Bivocational pastors feel they are better able to encourage the churches they serve to create a culture whereby the laity use their gifts and devote more time for ministry, since there were no fully funded pastors "paid" to "do everything" for congregations. Most bivocational pastors feel this creates healthy churches over the long term, though it sometimes creates more stress in the short term.[228]

---

227. Terry W. Dorsett, *Developing Leadership Teams in the Bivocational Church* (Bloomington, IN: Crossbooks, 2010), 18.
228. Terry Dorsett, "8 Benefits to Bivocational Ministry," *Baptist Press*, (Sunday, May 15, 2011), http://www.crosswalk.com/church/pastors-or-leadership/8-benefits-to-bi-vocational-ministry.html?ps=0, accessed 10/9/2018.

The plan that Dorsett lays out in his book, *Developing Leadership Teams in the Bivocational Church*, is a great idea, a biblical idea, and I highly recommend it. However, it assumes that members will have the level of commitment and spiritual maturity to step up and give the time it will take to be trained for ministry. In our culture today, the number one frustration pastors are having in their ministries is a lack of commitment among members. The Barna Group reports that,

> Given an opportunity to identify the one or two biggest downsides of their job, the top five frustrations reported by pastors are:
> 1. Lack of commitment among laypeople (35%)
> 2. Low level of spiritual maturity among churchgoers (27%)
> 3. Financial and/or administrative duties (19%)
> 4. Church politics (18%)
> 5. Implementing change in the church (16%)[229]

The lack of commitment among church members is the natural result of the business model that so many churches have been following. We have created a church culture of consumerism where Christians think of choosing a church the same way they think of going to a restaurant. No one goes to a restaurant because they want to serve. No one goes to a restaurant because they want to learn how to set a table or cook a meal. People go to a restaurant because they want to be served. Most people in our culture who are looking for a church are not looking for opportunities to serve others. They are looking for a church where they will be served by paid professionals. They are looking for a church where the service is high quality with the best music and the most comfortable environment. In this culture, many Christians are comfortable with the business model of doing church and they haven't been told about the joy and fulfillment that comes from the biblical model of doing church. As a result, bivocational ministers have difficult time training members to be ministers actively serving in God's Kingdom.

To avoid burnout, bivocational ministers must have a church leadership and membership that is onboard with the biblical model of equipping every member to be a minister. However, in order to do that, we must also simplify the way we do church so that we are not overwhelmed with all the projects and programs in the typical American church that have nothing to do with discipleship. A lot of people in

---

229. Kinnaman, *The State of Pastors*, 100.

our fast-paced culture are far more interested in being a part of a simple church that is focused on spiritual growth rather than being a part of a busy church with a lot of high-quality programs and the most attractional Sunday morning show in town. Thom Rainer and Eric Geiger write,

> The busyness and complexity of life makes simple a great commodity, something desired. Simple churches intuitively know this. And because they are consumed with the call to make disciples, they have implemented a simple design for church ministry. They have designed a simple process to reach and mature people. Thus, these churches are getting people's attention and commitment.[230]

Ultimately the simplest ministry of the church is the ministry of the gospel, both for evangelism and discipleship. The best way to guard against burnout is to focus on the simple ministry of the gospel. Proclaim the gospel to lead people to Christ. Teach and demonstrate the gospel to help Christians grow in their commitment and spiritual maturity. Then train them and equip them for works of service in the church and in the community.

## "SECULAR" EMPLOYMENT

Another set of difficulties that develop in many bivocational ministries is in how we view our "other job." If you are a ministry student preparing for bivocational ministry or a fully funded minister who needs to switch over to a bivocational role, you may be asking, "What kind of job would work best for someone who is also a minister?" If you are already bivocational you may be struggling with questions about how to live out and share your faith in an appropriate way when you're on the job. These may not seem like serious problems, but they are challenges that we need to consider.

### CHOOSING A SECOND JOB

Survey results revealed that there is a wide variety of occupations that bivocational ministers have pursued. Here are the top ten most common jobs among the bivocational ministers who responded to the first survey along with the number

---

230 .    Thom S. Rainer and Eric Geiger, *Simple Church: Returning to God's Process for Making Disciples* (Nashville, TN: B&H Books, 2011), 15.

of ministers in each field.[231]

1. School Teacher (37)
2. College Professor (34)
3. Bus Driver (32)
4. Small Business Owner (31)
5. Chaplain (27)
6. Insurance Agent and/or Sales (22)
7. Counselor (21)
8. Construction Worker (16)
9. Retail Sales (15)
10. House Rentals and/or Property Manager (14)

There are several factors that will go into your decision about the kind of career you are going to pursue outside of ministry. The most significant factor is your starting point when you decide to prepare for bivocational ministry. Obviously, if you start that preparation early while you are still preparing for ministry you will be ahead of the game. However, most bivocational ministers did not prepare for bivocational ministry when they were in Bible college. They had to shift over to a bivocational situation after they were already in a fully funded ministry for several years and they had little time to prepare for the transition.

If that's your story and you haven't had a job in the real world for several years, you never trained for a career other than ministry, and you're not sure how to get started on this journey, I would recommend that you get Doug Black's book, *Marathon: A Manual for Bivocational Ministry*. The last section of the book is a goldmine of information, tips, and advice for ministers who want to find the best job possible for their situation. Black writes,

> As I've looked over and over again at the amount of books on bivocational ministry, the thing that is usually missing is the practical day-to-day manual on how to move into a marketplace job, how to keep said job, keep your ministry, keep your family, and keep your sanity. Lots of advocates, not a lot of advice.[232]

---

231. Question 8 on the 1st survey asked, "What is your current job or career outside of your ministry in the local church?" A more complete list of the jobs held by bivocational ministers is recorded in Appendix A.
232. Black, *Marathon*, 145.

I think a lot of the other books on bivocational ministry have good advice on keeping your job, keeping your ministry, keeping your family, and keeping your sanity. However, he is right about the first thing on his list: there are very few resources out there with detailed advice on how a minister can move into a marketplace job. In that section of his book, Black gives specific instructions about preparing and adjusting your résumés, selling your ministry skills as marketplace skills, networking to find better options, and evaluating your job options to find what will harmonize best with your present ministry.

The Barna Group notes that ministry training and experience can actually be a great asset in today's job market because of the social skills and character development that take place in ministry. Barna reports,

> As technical skills become increasingly specialized, it's likely that more employers will view training in "hard skills" as a process most effectively done in-house, so that new hires learn how to do things "our way." The soft skills associated with character, however, are much harder to teach in a two-week crash course.[233]

In job interviews, cover letters, and résumés, include your track record of good character. Let your potential employers know that as a minister it is your job to exemplify and teach good character to others. Give them personal references of people who will testify to your honesty, dependability, integrity, teamwork, and diligence. Character is not something that can be learned in a two-week training course. Many organizations are desperately looking for trustworthy employees with a good work ethic.

If you are still preparing for ministry be careful how much you go into debt paying for higher education. David Wheeler notes that,

> Of the seminary students who graduated in 2011 with a Master of Divinity degree (the typical degree for a full-time pastor), more than 25 percent accrued more than $40,000 in educational debt, and five percent accumulated more than $80,000 in debt. Those lucky enough to get a full-time job as a pastor will join a profession whose median wage is $43,800, according to the U.S.

---

233. David Kinnaman, *What's Next for Biblical Higher Education* (Ventura, CA: Barna Group, 2017), 34.

Department of Labor.[234]

Unless you have a full scholarship or wealthy parents who are going to pay for your education, avoid going to an expensive university all four years for a bachelor's degree. If the career you are considering absolutely requires an accredited bachelor's degree, take as many classes as possible from a community college and then transfer the credits over to the university. If you are pursuing a ministry degree, remember that churches a far more concerned about your track record in volunteer ministry and how well they know you than about whether you have an accredited degree from an expensive university.

Donnie Collins, a bivocational minister in Owenton, Kentucky shares his advice about a legitimate alternative to going into debt to get a ministry degree. He writes,

> Don't go and acquire $40,000-$50,000 in student loans in pursuit of a career that generally pays $25,000-$38,000. Understand that accredited degrees are for governmental purposes (military chaplains, professorships at universities, etc.) If a church wants your degree to be accredited they'll tell you so in their job vacancy posting.
>
> Understand that this advice is an exception to the rule of post-secondary education. If you're a high school kid, your guidance counselor will tell you not to even consider non-accredited schools, and in every other instance they'd be right. In going this route— you won't have FASFA, governmental grants, scholarships, or in many cases employer-related tuition reimbursement funds available to you. But in the long run it's still cheaper to get the un-accredited degree and pay as you go. Many of these schools have payment plans, scholarships of their own, or your church may be willing to pay for bible college. Many equate non-accredited degrees as a "scam" or "diploma-mill" where you'll get your degree as long as you pay—whether you've actually done the work or learned anything. These are out there, but the churches who seek to employ a solid minister know the good schools and

---

234. David R. Wheeler, "Higher Calling, Lower Wages: The Vanishing of the Middle-Class Clergy," *The Atlantic*, last modified July 22, 2014, accessed June 12, 2018, https://www.theatlantic.com/business/archive/2014/07/higher-calling-lower-wages-the-collapse-of-the-middle-class-clergy/374786/.

the not-so-good ones—regardless of their accreditation status. I don't intend to "tear down" the bigger schools, but many who aspire to ministry go and get the degree—and then can't afford to go into the field because of student loan debt. I'll go ahead and plug the two best un-accredited schools I'm aware of— Louisville Bible College of Louisville, Kentucky and Summit Theological Seminary of Peru, Indiana. These are two of the finest conservative schools around.[235]

At the risk of revealing my personal bias, I would also recommend Northwest College of the Bible in Portland, Oregon which is where I received a bachelor's in theology degree. With that non-accredited degree, I was still able to continue my education at an accredited seminary to complete my post-graduate work. And now I am one of the volunteer professors at Northwest College of the Bible.

Gary Farley gives good advice to ministry students concerning the preparation and training for a secondary career when he writes,

The wisest counsel for today's ministerial student is to learn a marketable, portable skill while in preparation for the ministry. Many can do this while in college by majoring in social work, computers, or in education and obtaining a teacher's certificate. Others might train for business administration, farm management, or a health occupation. The keys are to identify growth occupations that call for skills and aptitudes that the student possesses and which can complement the skills needed in ministry.[236]

Ministry students should also consider trade schools and trade unions with training programs. Currently, our economy is desperately in need of more skilled laborers in high paying trades like electricians, plumbers, welders, etc. In a recent article, Ashley Gross and Jon Marcus reported that,

While a shortage of workers is pushing wages higher in the skilled trades, the financial return from a bachelor's degree is softening, even as the price — and the average debt into which it plunges

---

235. Kennedy, 193.
236. McCarty, *Meeting the Challenge of Bivocational Ministry*, 185.

students — keeps going up. But high school graduates have been so effectively encouraged to get a bachelor's that high-paid jobs requiring shorter and less expensive training are going unfilled.[237]

In the second survey I conducted, I asked bivocational ministers what advice they would give to ministry students who were considering bivocational ministry as an option. Here are some of their responses:

Jeff Dalrymple said, "Aim for a self-employed occupation to have greater flexibility. Let prospective employers know that you are a Christian first. Let them know your priorities up front and work to earn respect."[238]

Dr. Richard Geringswald said, "Get a job that gives you a flexible schedule to do God's work."[239]

Vinton Richey said, "Get a teaching certificate."[240]

A fellow bus driving preacher I know here in the Northwest said, "Do not take a job that will tempt you to leave the ministry."[241]

Paul Funk said, "Be prepared to work hard and possibly work for free. I worked in ministry without pay for years before I was hired, but I never took my eyes off the goal. Remember, Paul worked hard as a tentmaker and a preacher (Acts 20:35)."[242]

Ronnie Bruce Gregory said, "DO IT! There are so many small churches who can't afford a full-time minister, but they need a preacher too. JUST DO IT!"[243]

## WORKPLACE EVANGELISM

Many places of business will not tolerate Christian employees who are evangelistic in the workplace. Robert LaRochelle believes that bivocational ministers should avoid being evangelistic in the workplace.

With due respect to those of a more conservative, evangelical approach, I caution that the workplace should not become the arena for trying to convert or "save" one's fellow workers. The primary

---

237. Ashley Gross and Jon Marcus, "High-Paying Trade Jobs Sit Empty, While High School Grads Line Up for University," *NPR.Org*, last modified April 25, 2018, accessed April 27, 2018, https://www.npr.org/sections/ed/2018/04/25/605092520/high-paying-trade-jobs-sit-empty-while-high-school-grads-line-up-for-university.
238. Kennedy, 194.
239. Kennedy, 194.
240. Kennedy, 194.
241. Kennedy, 194.
242. Kennedy, 194.
243. Kennedy, 195.

responsibility of working in the workplace is to do the job that is required there. In fact, the minister in this situation has to work through various scenarios in which his or her pastoral inclination and the responsibilities of the job may be in tension.[244]

This seems to be a false choice where Christians, according to LaRochelle, cannot try to convert fellow workers and do the job their work requires at the same time. Paul did not seem to have this attitude in Acts 17:17. Certainly, different situations will require wisdom to determine how much we can say about our beliefs in the workplace. However, if we are going to be bivocational for the sake of the gospel, should we not have the same purpose in going into the world that Jesus had for coming into our world? Jesus said, "For the Son of Man has come to seek and to save that which was lost" (Luke 19:10).

If you have the option, choose a job that gives you more freedom in this regard. If you can be self-employed, there is nothing that can prevent you from proclaiming the gospel at work. However, we still need to remember the advice Paul gives us in Colossians, "Conduct yourselves with wisdom toward outsiders, making the most of the opportunity. Let your speech always be with grace, as though seasoned with salt, so that you will know how you should respond to each person" (Col. 4:5-6). Another good strategy is to look for service jobs that put you in the community serving people in need like hospice care, social workers, funeral home workers, EMTs, firefighters, counseling, chaplain work, etc. These roles show people the love of Christ in us. They display the message of the gospel through humble acts of service.

Question 23 on the second survey asked, "For 'full-time' ministers who, for the first time, need to switch over to bivocational ministry, what advice or encouragement would you give them?" Here are some of the responses that provide us with wisdom to know how to effectively use our secondary employment for the sake of the gospel:

> Donnie Collins said,
> Try to pick a vocation in your community that puts you in position to talk to people you have a potential of reaching out to—substitute teach, work at the local coffee shop, maybe get some hours at a

---

244. Robert LaRochelle, *Part-Time Pastor, Full-Time Church* (Cleveland, OH: The Pilgrim Press, 2010), 57.

local mom and pop shop where things tend to be less formal and conversation with customers is allowed, and so forth.[245]

Thaddeus Hinkle said,
Most of the people you work with outside the church these days have no exposure to Christianity nor to the Church. They live lifestyles that are outside the life of Christ. You must serve them anyway, and serve them in love. Your job may also not allow you to be overt with your Christianity, so the love and service you show them will be your best gospel presentation. Additionally, I would advise them to look for a secondary vocation that fits their gifts and experience. Public schools are always looking for good, patient, paras and substitute teachers, for example.[246]

Neil Larimore said,
You will have many opportunities to serve that you may never have had as a full-time minister. Watch for them. I have been able to be known in the community and by the people outside and have been able to share with many over the years. Both managing a camp and driving a school bus have helped me to make many contacts with youth and their parents.[247]

Daniel Brown said, "In many cases, you will have to make sure you do not bring your 'Bible talk' into work but you must bring your 'Bible walk' into the secular workplace. They can shut down your talk but not your walk."[248]

In 2 Corinthians 11, Paul listed over two dozen different kinds of trials and challenges he faced in his ministry, but he saw them all as opportunities to join with Jesus in a fellowship of suffering that would draw him into a closer more intimate union with Christ (Phil. 3:10). In 2 Timothy 1:8, Paul invites Timothy to "join with me in suffering for the gospel." The challenges we face today in ministry have changed since the time of Paul and Timothy. The challenges that ministers will face in the future will no doubt be different from the challenges we face today. However, one thing will never change: regardless of the challenges we face, the gospel will

245. Kennedy, 196.
246. Kennedy, 196.
247. Kennedy, 196.
248. Kennedy, 197.

always be the good news and the power of God to get us through even the most difficult trials.

In this chapter, we have looked at some of the common struggles that bivocational ministers face. We have also considered how the gospel can help us maintain effective and fulfilling ministries even during those struggles. There are many more challenges we could probably add to our list, just as Paul could have added more difficulties to his list. However, the gospel will continue to be the same message of salvation and restoration that helps us through every challenge we face in ministry.

# DISCUSSION QUESTIONS

1. Make a list of the struggles you or a preacher you know has gone through in ministry. How do those struggles compare to the difficulties described in 2 Corinthians 11:23-29?

2. What kept Paul going in his ministry regardless of all the struggles he faced?

3. How were the financial responsibilities of Paul different from the financial responsibilities of most ministers today?

4. What are some of the reasons bivocational ministers often feel isolated and disconnected from other ministers?

5. Who are the fellow workers in God's Kingdom who encourage you and pray for you on a regular basis? How often do you contact them, encourage them, and pray for them?

6. What are some things that might cause ministers to struggle with thoughts of insecurity or low self-esteem?

7. How do you guard yourself against the negative thoughts and feelings in your life?

8. When have you (or a minister you know) suffered from burnout? What do you think caused the burnout? How (if at all) was the problem corrected?

9. What can bivocational ministers do when most of the members are too busy or just not interested in volunteer ministry?

10. Read the quote by Rainer and Geiger from their book *Simple Church*. How could the churches you're familiar with simplify their activities and focus more on making disciples?

11. How can we demonstrate the message of the gospel in the workplace when we don't have the freedom to speak openly about our faith?

# CHAPTER 12

Preparing a Church for Bivocational Ministry

"Therefore do not be ashamed of the testimony of our Lord
or of me His prisoner, but join with me in suffering
for the gospel according to the power of God."
—2 Timothy 1:8

"The church Jesus said He would build was a suffering
church. Its founder was crucified...What will our children
think of us 100 years from now if we let this heavenly
message die, refusing to suffer for it?"
—Archie Word, 1960[249]

In this chapter, we will consider how to prepare a congregation to transition into a bivocational ministry for the sake of the gospel. Ray Gilder writes, "There is no such thing as a bivocational church. There are churches which are led by bivocational pastors, but no church has two vocations."[250] I understand what he is saying, and this may just be an issue of semantics, but both the leaders and the members of a congregation with a bivocational preacher must see themselves as a bivocational church. As one body, the leadership and the congregation must have a

---

249. Victor Knowles, ed., *Repent or Perish: Selected Sermons & Essays of Archie Word* (Joplin, MO: College Press, 1994), 195.
250. Gilder, *Uniquely Bivocational-Understanding the Life of a Pastor Who Has a Second Job*, 4.

unified perspective of their strategy for ministry. All Christians are bivocational in a general sense. We are all called to be ministers to one another and ambassadors in the world. More specifically, a bivocational minister needs to know that the members and leaders of his congregation are united with him and supportive of him in his bivocational ministry.

Mark Edington emphasizes the importance of this principle when he writes,

> The successful implementation of a bivocational model of ministry *is a work of the entire faith community*, and not just the ordained member (or members) of that community. "Bivocational ministry" is much more than a shorthand description of the working life of the pastor of a church. It's a way of describing a different way of thinking about how the ministry of the whole faith community works.[251]

When a minister is switching over from being "full-time" to being bivocational, the church needs to be prepared for the transition. The other leaders and influential members need to be brought onboard as co-workers with the minister.

## CHURCH MODELS

There are a lot of different church models out there that the church growth "experts" write about and either advocate or critique. Some churches follow the attractional "seeker-friendly" model where the aim is to have a church service that is high quality and attractive to a certain segment of the unchurched community. Some churches follow a "missional" model where they focus on going out to the world and drawing people to Christ through acts of service in the community.[252] Other churches follow an attractional evangelistic model where the focus is on inviting people to a church service that is so good, they will keep coming back for more. There is the house church model,[253] the purpose-driven church model,[254] the

---

251. Mark D. W. Edington, *Bivocational: Returning to the Roots of Ministry* (New York, NY: Church Publishing, 2018), 26.
252. Alan Hirsch, *The Forgotten Ways: Reactivating Apostolic Movements* (Gard Rapids, MI: Brazos Press, 2016).
253. Simson and Barna, *The House Church Book.*
254. Rick Warren, *The Purpose-Driven Church: Growth Without Compromising Your Message and Mission* (Grand Rapids, MI: Zondervan, 1995).

lay-driven church model,[255] the servant-driven church model,[256] the organic church model,[257] and a dozen other church models, all of which have their strengths and weaknesses. In a sense, bivocational ministry is a model of ministry. However, it is usually a model within a model. If a full-time pastor in a "purpose-driven" church becomes a bivocational pastor, that doesn't mean that the church is no longer purpose-driven.

Models are helpful; however, they must be a means to an end and not the end itself. Many times, churches get so wrapped up in the model of ministry they are following that it seems like the model is the most important thing. Whatever model or method of ministry your church is using, it must not take center stage in front of the gospel. Whether you are a fully funded minister, a bivocational minister, or a volunteer minister, you must first determine to be a minister of the gospel and then choose a model for the sake of the gospel.

When Redeemer Presbyterian Church in New York City began making headlines, church leaders from other parts of the country came out to visit the church and see what the new church model was that was so successful in the "big apple." Timothy Keller recalls what these pastors were looking for when he writes,

> They wanted instructions for specific programs and techniques that appealed to urban people. One pastor said, "I've tried the Willow Creek model. Now I'm ready to try the Redeemer model." People came to us because they knew we were thriving in one of the least churched, most secular cities in the U.S. But when visitors first started coming to Redeemer in the early and mid-1990s, they were disappointed because they did not discern a new "model"—at least not in the form of unique, new programs. That's because the real "secret" of Redeemer's fruitfulness does not lie in its ministry programs but in something that functions at a deeper level.[258]

The "secret" Keller was referring to was being gospel-centered regardless of the specific programs and techniques commonly seen in the various models of

---

255. Melvin Steinbron, *The Lay Driven Church: How to Empower the People in Your Church to Share the Tasks of Ministry* (Ventura, CA: Regal Books, 1997).
256. Ray Fulenwider, *The Servant-Driven Church: Releasing Every Member for Ministry* (Joplin, Mo: College Press Publishing Company, 1998).
257. Neil Cole, *Organic Church: Growing Faith Where Life Happens* (San Francisco, CA: Jossey-Bass, 2005).
258. Keller, Horton, and Ortlund, *Shaped by the Gospel,* 12.

ministry. Granted some models are closer to the church we see described in the New Testament like the house church model. And other models (like the attractional model) seem to have within them a tendency to become the main thing so that members are converted to the model more than they are to Christ. Don't get me wrong, I'm sure God is using the big expensive attractional model churches to bring a lot of people in to hear the gospel. And that is great! But those attractional churches must constantly emphasize that Jesus is the One we must be attracted to with a sincere and sacrificial love. Otherwise, many people will be attending those churches simply because of the great facilities, the amazing programs, and the professional performances each Sunday. Bivocational minister, Bob Crowder, wisely points out,

> We are a consumer culture. This is just as true in the church as in the local stores. It's mostly not a good thing. Ministry is for each believer. The church is not the place where your desires for the right music, the right preaching, and the right programs are to be sought out and then found. In these things, we are merely shoppers looking for the satisfaction of our superficial preferences and wants and desires.[259]

Mark Dever warns us of the dangers of putting our faith in a modern church model rather than in the gospel and the model God provided for His church in the New Testament. He writes,

> A clear understanding of the gospel is foundational for any genuine renewal in evangelical churches. Solutions treated as normative but which are not found in Scripture must be rejected as latter-day tradition that lacks the authority of the apostles.[260]

The early church was persecuted severely for the first three centuries. At times it had to go underground and meet in secret. Even amid such persecution, the church continued to grow. It grew because Christians had a clear gospel perception. They were motivated by the gospel. They boldly proclaimed the gospel even in the face of suffering and death. They were committed to demonstrating the gospel in real life

---

259. Kennedy, 201.
260. Mark Dever, *The Church: The Gospel Made Visible* (Nashville, TN: B&H Academic, 2012), 163.

through sacrificial acts of service. They were truly transformed by the gospel and as a result, they were willing to live and die for the sake of the gospel.

In his book, *The Forgotten Ways*, Alan Hirsch compares the phenomenal growth of the early church to the underground church in China. Because of severe persecution neither the early Christians nor the Christians in China had all the expensive things we typically think are necessary to have a growing church. Hirsch writes,

> Persecution drove both the early Christian movement and the Chinese church to discover their truest nature as an apostolic people. Persecution forced them away from any possible reliance on any centralized religious institution and caused them to live closer to, and more consistently with, their primal message—namely the gospel. We have to assume that if one is willing to die for being a follower of Jesus, then in all likelihood that person is a real believer. This persecution, under the sovereignty of God, acted as a means to keep these movements true to their faith and reliant on God—it purified them from the dross of nonessential churchly paraphernalia.[261]

I'm not suggesting that we should pray for persecution. I believe all Christians can and must be focused on the gospel in both good times and bad times. And Christian leaders must be committed to the New Testament model of church growth described in Ephesians 4:12. When we as bivocational ministers willingly accept a difficult calling that requires a greater sacrifice of our time and energy we need the support and encouragement of our fellow leaders, elders, deacons, and other ministry leaders. We also need the support and involvement of the members of the church. The more a congregation buys into the New Testament model of church leaders equipping all members to be ministers, the more effective bivocational ministry will be. But this requires members to have a gospel perception and a gospel transformation in them that develops a sincere desire to proclaim and demonstrate the gospel in their lives. How can we, like Paul, invite and encourage other Christians to join with us in suffering for the gospel?

---

261. Alan Hirsch, *The Forgotten Ways: Reactivating Apostolic Movements* (Gard Rapids, MI: Brazos Press, 2016), 7.

## ELDERS

In the first survey, several bivocational ministers indicated that the ministry of their elders was a major factor in their effectiveness. If you are a bivocational minister in a church without elders I would strongly suggest that you put together a plan to train and appoint elders in the church. This was the main reason Paul left Titus in Crete (Titus 1:5). We need to preach and teach about the importance of every congregation having a plurality of elders leading it. Approach the men you think are qualified or could be qualified with some training and see if they are interested in becoming elders. Set up an "elders in training" class where you help men to develop the leadership skills and Christian character essential for healthy church leadership. Jim Estep, David Roadcup, and Gary Johnson have written a four-part series on eldership that would serve as an excellent resource for such a class. This series includes: *Answer His Call*,[262] *Reflect His Character*,[263] *Lead His Church*,[264] and *Enjoy His People*.[265]

If you are a bivocational minister in a church that has elders, but they are not sharing the workload of preaching, teaching, and pastoral counseling, I would encourage you to take your elders through a course that would give them the knowledge and skills to do those things with confidence. The book *Developing Leadership Teams in the Bivocational Church* by Terry Dorsett would be an excellent resource for such a class. In this book, Dorsett emphasizes the importance of helping all the leaders come together as a team. He writes,

Only in working in partnership together can pastoral leadership teams help develop healthier churches and healthier pastors. By developing these teams, bivocational pastors will not be as prone to burn-out. Churches will also benefit from the development of these teams because they will have a multiple leadership approach instead of a single leader approach.[266]

---

262. Estep, Roadcup, and Johnson, *Answer His Call*.
263. David Roadcup, Gary Johnson, and Jim Estep, *Reflect His Character* (Joplin, MO: College Press, 2009).
264. Jim Estep, Gary Johnson, and David Roadcup, *Lead His Church* (Joplin, MO: College Press, 2010).
265. Jim Estep, Gary Johnson, and David Roadcup, *Enjoy His People* (Joplin, MO: College Press, 2011).
266. Dorsett, *Developing Leadership Teams in the Bivocational Church*, 5.

James Highland stresses the importance of having a leadership with a *team* mentality when he writes about the concept of "shared leadership." He notes that a healthy shared leadership will develop when four important characteristics are present.

> Such leadership includes the understanding that leadership is a selfless act of service. It is not about self-gratification or acts of ego, but a servant heart. A second characteristic of shared leadership is embracing the Lordship of Christ. This includes the natural question, "Who is in charge here?" Lordship means the surrender of ourselves to the Lord Jesus and allow Him to lead us. "Shared Leadership" is also accepting "partnership" with others and with God to work as valued partners. The fourth characteristic of "Shared Leadership" is embracing a stewardship attitude. Stewardship, the reality of holding God's resources in our trust and accountable for their use, divides the responsibilities and the blessings of serving.[267]

This brings up a commonly asked question about authority in local church government. Many people are confused about the relationship between the elders and the preacher. In some Christian Churches and Churches of Christ, there is a power struggle between the elders and the preacher. One solution is to have preaching elders or at least one of the elders as the preacher (1 Tim. 5:17). This helps the members and all the leaders to see the leadership as one team.

But how does a preacher who is not an elder work together with an established eldership? In 1 and 2 Timothy we see a young evangelist ministering at a church with an established eldership. Paul commanded Timothy to "do the work of an evangelist and discharge all the duties of your ministry" (2 Tim. 4:5, NIV). When we look at all the commands Paul gave Timothy in those two letters, we see a lot of duties that overlap with the duties of the elders. For Timothy, teaching and preaching God's word seemed to be among the most urgent tasks that he was to accomplish together with the elders (1 Tim. 4:13 and 5:17). The elders and the evangelists are leaders on the same team, with the same Lord as their head, with the same spiritual vision and goals for the Lord's church. Both the elders and the evangelists are to

---

267. James W. Highland, *Serving as a Bivocational Pastor* (Newburgh, IN: Newburgh Press, 2013), 123-124.

have high standards and live their Christian lives above reproach. Both are held responsible for the spiritual health of the church. Both are expected to lead the church by their example, their teaching, and exhortation. Both are involved in the spiritual discipline of church members. So, what's the difference? Well, perhaps in looking so hard for the differences we've missed the importance of the similarities and having a unified team of leaders working together in the Lord's church.

One practical difference between the evangelist and the pastor can be seen in the meaning of the titles. If the preacher is an evangelist, it would seem that his responsibilities would be focused more on the evangelistic work of the church and pastors would be focused more on the pastoral work of the church. Certainly, these leadership roles will overlap in their responsibilities depending on the gifts, skills, and abilities of each individual leader. However, James Estep makes a great observation when he writes,

> Many of our congregations do not appreciate or agree with the term "pastor" when applied to the preacher, but when elders do not actively shepherd the congregation, we create a *de facto* pastor by our own omission of this ministry. As elders, you lead through shepherding God's flock. The ministry of shepherding is *not* optional in Scripture, but a fundamental expectation for those who would lead God's people.[268]

## DEACONS AND OTHER MINISTRY LEADERS

The word for "deacon" (*diakonos*) in the New Testament is the same word for minister and servant. Jesus taught us that leadership in the church must be different from the typical leadership we see in the world. Leaders in the church must lead by serving (Mark 10:42-45 and John 13:12-17). When deacons and ministry leaders serve with sacrificial love putting the needs of the church above their own personal preferences, they are demonstrating the gospel (Phil. 2:3-8). Jesus had equality with God and He willingly humbled Himself taking the form of not just a servant (*diakonos*) (Mark 10:43), but a slave (*doulos*) (Phil. 2:7). While Paul describes the central message of the gospel as the death, burial, and resurrection of Jesus in 1 Corinthians 15, we see from Philippians 2 and other passages that an important

---

268. Estep, Johnson, and Roadcup, *Lead His Church*, 86.

part of the gospel was also the incarnation and ministry of Jesus. While elders do not need to be selected from among a group of ordained deacons, all leaders in the church must be people who have learned how to serve before they can be put into positions of leadership.

As bivocational ministers, we must preach, teach, and model servant leadership. We must help the congregation develop a value and a joy for serving. Ephesians 4:12 tells us that one of the main reasons God established the leadership roles of evangelists and pastors was "for the equipping of the saints for the work of service, to the building up of the body of Christ." Bivocational ministry cannot work effectively unless this biblical model is taught and caught in the congregation. Most churches have ministry leaders even if they don't have people officially ordained as "deacons." The essential biblical principle that I want to emphasize here is equipping and delegating spiritually mature members to serve in a visible capacity. I say "spiritually mature members" because while deacons are not in roles of authority in the same way as elders, they are still leading by example.

Deacons are servants who have been appointed to serve the church in a way that not only accomplishes a task but also provides a godly example for others to follow. The qualifications Paul gives Timothy for selecting and delegating deacons places a strong emphasis on spiritual maturity and godly character (1 Tim. 3:8-13). The men selected to serve the Greek-speaking widows in Acts 6 may not have been the first "deacons" of the church in the same way that Paul describes the role in 1 Timothy 3, however, they were to be men who were "full of the Spirit and of wisdom." The role of deacon did not include the responsibility of establishing policies for the local church. The emphasis was on serving. However, they may have had roles of teaching that was a part of their serving ministry as Mark Moore suggests when he writes, "Perhaps the ministry of benevolence included the ministry of the word. It may well be that the Apostles intended for the seven Greek-speaking servants to deliver the meals and then sit down with the widows and instruct them in the faith."[269] We know that in Acts 7 and 8, Luke describes two of these servants (Stephen and Philip) engaging in gospel proclamation.

The New Testament describes the elders as the leaders and policymakers in the local congregation and deacons as servants conducting their ministries under the oversight of the elders. Jack Cottrell warns us about a common problem in many

---

269. Moore, *The College Press NIV Commentary: Acts*, 126.

churches where there is little or no distinction between the responsibilities of elders and deacons. He writes,

> A long-standing tradition in many Christian churches and churches of Christ is for elders and deacons to form one governing body for the congregation, with deacons having authority equal to that of the elders. In this kind of situation, in practice, the deacons actually "run the church," since they usually outnumber the elders. This seems to be in direct violation of NT teaching, however, which portrays the elders alone as the ones in authority. A better arrangement, then, is to have a board of elders (always more than one) appointed by the congregation to be the church's spiritual overseers and policymakers, and a board of deacons appointed to assist the elders in carrying out their work.[270]

There are many different models of church structure that may be working for various congregations today. I am convinced that the New Testament provides the best pattern for how a local congregation should organize its leadership and ministries. However, the New Testament principle that I want to emphasize here as essential for bivocational ministers to be effective is the equipping principle in Ephesians 4:12. Charles Crane warns against the danger of a preacher neglecting the Ephesians 4:12 principle. He writes,

> Today a hard-working preacher trying to do everything that is needed in the church is a serious mistake. He may fall into the rut of mowing the lawn, cleaning the toilets, doing all the calling on the sick, and the end result is that he becomes tired and disenchanted with ministry. Burnout is the inevitable result. The wiser minister accepts the true commission God has given him of being an equipper and assigner of duties. He will learn to give jobs to people. He will help them to prepare to do these jobs. He will give them advice when it is needed, but then entrust them to go on with the work they have been appointed to do.[271]

---

270. Jack Cottrell, *The Faith Once for All: Bible Doctrine for Today* (Joplin, MO: College Press, 2002), 430.
271. Crane, *A Practical Guide to Soul Winning*, 76-77.

Bivocational ministry cannot work unless the elders, deacons, and ministry leaders believe and practice this biblical model of equipping every member to be a minister. However, in those cases when a church has not bought into the Ephesians 4:12 model, bivocational ministry often helps a church see the need for this biblical model. When members of a congregation see their minister working a "regular" job Monday through Friday as well as serving in ministry for the sake of the gospel, it inspires them and motivates them to do more for the sake of the gospel. Glen Layfield, a bivocational minister in Scio, New York, observes that in a bivocational ministry, "more members are aware of congregational needs and concerns and other leaders are quicker to help."[272] Henry Kott, a bivocational minister in De Tour Village, Michigan said that as a result of being bivocational, "more people step up and fill in the gaps. And God blesses their ministry."[273] Jeff Gallup, a bivocational minister in Oakridge, Oregon said that when he took a second job, "The congregation had to pick up the slack and get more involved for the sake of the whole church."[274]

For the ministries of any church to be effective and healthy all of the deacons, and ministry leaders have to be on the same page when it comes to their philosophy of ministry. It must be a team effort with a unity in the whole leadership that the congregation can see. Several bivocational ministers indicated that the teamwork of the leaders and ministers in their congregation was one of the main reasons they were effective in ministry. A bivocational minister in Montana stated that "Cultivating and using the leading, teaching, and administrative talents of others in the church have helped greatly. We are a small church, but ministry here is a team effort."[275]

Some churches have elders and ministry leaders who are unified in the idea of seeing bivocational ministry as a strategy for the church. They have bought into the concept and instead of growing with the goal of making the bivocational minister a fully funded minister they are growing with the goal of adding more bivocational staff. A bivocational minister in Oklahoma reported, "The church had only 25 in attendance when I started. Since then, our numbers have come up and we hired a bivo youth minister."[276]

Donald Hart was a friend who used to live in the Northwest. Before he passed away in 2020, he was a bivocational minister at the Antioch Christian Church in

---

272. Kennedy, 208.
273. Kennedy, 208.
274. Kennedy, 208.
275. Kennedy, 209.
276. Kennedy, 209.

Pittsburg, Missouri. He said, "Although I give a lot of hours to the congregation, they have allowed me to be flexible with my schedule. This is a very old congregation (est. 1843) and has always had part-time ministers."[277] The Antioch Christian Church has a rich heritage with connections to all three branches of the Restoration Movement. You can read about their story on their website at www.antioch-christian.org.

Some churches have chosen to have all their leaders and ministers working as volunteers for the church. The Saint James Christian Church in Saint James, Missouri responded to the first survey, saying, "We do not have a vocational minister. Several of the men preach and work other jobs. We believe that is the New Testament pattern for ministry."[278]

## MEMBERS

As Bivocational ministers we must also equip and delegate members who are not as mature as we would like them to be. There are many jobs that members can be involved in that do not require them to have the same level of maturity that we require of deacons and ministry leaders. One of the best ways to help people grow spiritually is to equip them to serve in some way and then entrust them with a responsibility. This is also an opportunity to create an atmosphere of grace. Church leaders who intentionally proclaim and demonstrate the gospel will also show grace and patience as they equip members to serve in various ways. Doran McCarty explains the importance of delegating with grace when he writes,

> Perfectionism may be a problem in delegation. Others may not do as well as you, especially at first. They will do well only when they have responsibilities. A good delegator is a person mature enough to be receptive of ideas from others. Also to realize the costs of other's mistakes is a valuable investment in the most important resource—people. A good delegator has patience and tolerance.[279]

Creating and cultivating an atmosphere of grace in the church is not only essential for getting people involved in ministry; it is essential for the church to be a

---

277. Kennedy, 209.
278. Kennedy, 210.
279. McCarty, *Meeting the Challenge of Bivocational Ministry*, 199.

convincing witness for Jesus Christ and the message of the gospel. We should look for ways to get members thinking and talking about the grace of God in their lives and in their church. Mark Dever shares some of the ways we can cultivate a culture of grace in our congregations when he writes,

> Churches receive God's grace, relish it, and reflect it to others. Congregations should note and repeat evidences of God's grace in one another's lives through testimonies and other public encouragements. Baptismal testimonies, thoughtful prayer requests, interviews during members meetings—these and many other ways can encourage the church in discipleship and make the atmosphere helpfully provocative for Christian growth.[280]

Another way to create and cultivate an atmosphere of grace is to publicly appreciate and celebrate the work members are doing. If you have been in ministry for a while, you probably know what it is like to pour your heart into a project that took a lot of your time, hard work, and energy, only to have it criticized or ignored. You know what it is like to work hard and not be appreciated or celebrated. We need to remember that most of the volunteers in our churches are also busy people pouring their hearts into the work they are doing for the church. We need to thank them and celebrate their service. Leith Anderson and Jill Fox give the following advice,

> Decide ahead of time when celebrations will happen to ensure they will get done. Put them on your calendar and announce them so volunteers can also get them into their plans. Here are a few practical ideas to consider:
>
> - Write birthday cards with a personal note for your volunteers at the start of each month and make sure they get sent.
> - After a retreat or large event, send a thank you email highlighting all the great things your volunteers accomplished.
> - Add "celebration" to the agenda, so each week you and your team can have a conversation about who or what needs to be celebrated.[281]

---

280. Dever, *The Church*, 158-159.
281. Leith Anderson and Jill Fox, *The Volunteer Church: Mobilizing Your Congregation for Growth and Effectiveness* (Grand Rapids, MI: Zondervan, 2015), 51-52.

When the members of a congregation catch a vision for New Testament Christianity and experience God working through them as a priesthood of believers ministering to one another, it creates an atmosphere of joy and excitement in the church. Many of the bivocational ministers who responded to the first survey said that the involvement of the members is what makes their ministry effective. A bivocational preacher in Oklahoma said, "The lay people who do the work I can't, have helped me to be more effective in ministry."[282] A bivocational minister in Oregon writes, "The thing that has helped me the most is the support of my church to fill in the gaps and come to my defense if a ball is dropped. I also feel like God set this up."[283]

The best way for the members of a church to help their bivocational minister to be effective is simply to live out the message of the gospel through their love for one another. A bivocational minister in North Carolina has been blessed by the members of his congregation. He writes, "These are the most loving and kind people I've ever met. They work hard to keep this very rural church alive. I've done little more than just preach the gospel and love them."[284]

Love is the primary motivation of the gospel (John 3:16). When the gospel is intentionally proclaimed and demonstrated in the life and ministries of a church, the members develop a clearer gospel perception and a deeper gospel motivation. As a result, they learn to love each other more. "We love because He first loved us" (1 John 4:19).

Cultivating a culture of grace and love in the ministries of the members is a powerful and essential aspect of effective church growth. Sincere love is contagious. When church members and visitors see leaders consistently demonstrating sincere love through humble acts of service, it transforms the culture of the congregation. Actions of sincere love inspire people to get involved in ministry.

This was one of the final leadership lessons that Jesus gave His disciples before He was crucified. Jesus demonstrated "the full extent of His love" (John 13:1 NIV) by washing the feet of His disciples. He commanded them to follow His example of serving (John 13:15). Soon after that, He gave them a "new" commandment to "love one another" (John 13:34). But "love one another" was not, in and of itself, a new commandment. The new aspect of this commandment was in the next phrase,

---

282. Kennedy, 212.
283. Kennedy, 212.
284. Kennedy, 212.

"as I have loved you." Now they had a living example of God in the flesh showing them what love looks like in real life. Jesus just demonstrated the "full extent of his love" through His humble acts of service.

As we demonstrate our sincere love through humble acts of service, the Holy Spirit will continue to transform hearts and create a culture of love in the congregation. This in turn will draw people in the community to Christ. In the very next verse, Jesus tells His disciples that their love for one another is the key to effective evangelism. He says, "By this all men will know that you are My disciples, if you have love for one another" (John 13:35). Bob Russell observes,

> People assume that smaller churches must have better fellowship and stronger relationships because everybody knows everybody. But churches that genuinely love each other don't stay small very long. If you want your church to grow—if you want to attract people to Jesus Christ and to your church—then learn how to love one another.[285]

In this chapter, we have considered the challenge of getting the whole church onboard with the biblical concept of equipping every member to be a minister. Bivocational ministers need the support of elders, deacons, ministry leaders, and members. This support comes in the form of serving one another in love. Love is the motivation of the gospel. When a church comes together with a unified vision of serving in love, the result is that a culture of grace and love develops, and the gospel is demonstrated in the ministries of the church.

---

285. Bob Russell and Rusty Russell, *When God Builds a Church: 10 Principles for Growing a Dynamic Church* (West Monroe, LA: Howard Books, 2000), 199.

# DISCUSSION QUESTIONS

1. What model of ministry do you think is most effective in the culture and community where you live? Why?

2. When a congregation adopts a model of ministry, how can church leaders make sure that the model does not become more important than the gospel?

3. Why did the early church experience healthy growth even in times of severe persecution?

4. In our culture today, how can we encourage Christians to join with us in suffering for the gospel? (2 Tim. 1:8)

5. Why do you think some preachers are reluctant to train and appoint elders to lead the church?

6. How important do you think it is for a local congregation to be led by a plurality of elders? Why?

7. What can a preacher do when he is working in a church with elders, but the elders don't want to share the ministry responsibilities of preaching, teaching, and pastoral counseling?

8. Do you think it is better if a preacher is also one of the elders in a congregation? Why or why not?

9. What did Jesus teach His disciples about servant-leadership in Mark 10:42-45? How can this help ministers and elders to work together more effectively?

10. What does the New Testament emphasize when it talks about the role of deacons?

11. In those congregations where the members want the minister to do most of the work of ministry, what can we do to help them buy into the model of ministry described in Ephesians 4:12?

12. How can the gospel help us to equip immature Christians for works of service?

# CHAPTER 13

"Now I want you to know, brethren, that my circumstances
have turned out for the greater progress of the gospel."
—Philippians 1:12

"Discipleship means allegiance to the suffering
Christ, and it is therefore not at all surprising
that Christians should be called upon to suffer.
In fact it is a joy and a token of his grace."
—Dietrich Bonhoeffer[286]

God has used my experience as a school bus driver and a minister of the gospel to draw me into the message of the cross in a deep and personal way. The research and writing I have done on bivocational ministry have helped me to see how God has been using my life as a demonstration of the gospel and a proclamation of God's love and grace. At the beginning of this journey, I was thinking of myself as a baseball player up to bat with the bases loaded. I thought about my decision to become bivocational as an opportunity for me to either hit a grand slam or strike out in failure. But that was a poor analogy because it was putting all the focus on me and my performance. That me-centered mindset is the very thing that had to

---

286. Dietrich Bonhoeffer, *The Cost of Discipleship* (New York, NY: Touchstone, 1995), 91.

change. I needed to have a gospel-centered mindset. I needed to call on Jesus to be my designated hitter.

The grace we have in Christ does not mean that we just sit on the bench and let God do all the work. God is at work in us, and we cooperate with Him trusting in His grace and empowered by His Spirit. As I allowed God to change my perspective, He helped me to gain a gospel perception of the difficulties I was going through in ministry. I began to see my bivocational situation not as a trial to endure but as an opportunity for the greater progress of the gospel. I began to see gospel transformation taking place in the community, in the church, and in my own personal life.

## THIS IS MY SONG

One of the most important things God has taught me as a bivocational minister is that my story is not really my story and my song is not really my song. My story must be His story and my song must be His song.

The famous hymn writer, Fanny Crosby has an amazing story. The first year of her life was marked by a devastating illness and the loss of her father. The suffering she went through from her sickness was almost as bad as the treatment which left her blind for the rest of her life. After her father died, her mother went to work as a maid and Fanny was raised primarily by her grandmother. Despite her struggles (or perhaps because of them), Fanny wrote over 8,000 gospel songs and hymns. Kenneth Osbeck notes,

> It is truly amazing that anyone, and especially a blind person, could write on this variety of spiritual truths and experiences with such proliferation. For a considerable period during her life, while under contract to a music publisher, she wrote three new hymns each week.[287]

However, in the chorus of the hymn, "Blessed Assurance," Crosby humbly recognizes that her story is really His story and her song is really His song. She found her greatest joy and fulfillment in life not from singing her own praises but from singing the praises of her Lord and Savior Jesus Christ.

This is my story, this is my song
Praising my Savior all the day long

---

287. Kenneth W. Osbeck, *101 Hymn Stories* (Grand Rapids, MI: Kregel Publications, 1982), 43.

The New Testament church began composing songs about Jesus very early in church history. One of those early hymns is believed to be recorded in Philippians 2:5-11.

> Have this attitude in yourselves which was also in Christ Jesus, who, although He existed in the form of God, did not regard equality with God a thing to be grasped, but emptied Himself, taking the form of a bond-servant, and being made in the likeness of men. Being found in appearance as a man, He humbled Himself by becoming obedient to the point of death, even death on a cross. For this reason also, God highly exalted Him, and bestowed on Him the name which is above every name, so that at the name of Jesus every knee will bow, of those who are in heaven and on earth and under the earth, and that every tongue will confess that Jesus Christ is Lord, to the glory of God the Father.—Philippians 2:5-11

This early hymn tells the gospel story and Paul includes it in this letter with an exhortation to have the same attitude of humility and service in us that we see in Jesus. God has used the gospel and my experience as a bivocational minister to teach me and help me to imitate the attitudes of Jesus seen in this passage.

## SELFLESSNESS

In the verses right before this hymn, Paul exhorts the Philippians to consider others as more important than themselves and to demonstrate the same selfless love that we see in Jesus. For all eternity Jesus, as the Word, was with God and was God. He was equal with the Father and the Holy Spirit. And yet, Jesus did not consider equality with God something to be grasped and held on to tightly. He was willing to let go of His glory, power, and majesty in heaven for the sake of others. In his commentary on this passage, Anthony Ash observes, "The more one meditates on the reality expressed by these words, the richer the divine care for man appears. Any reader sensing the power of this exhortation should surely be moved to humility and service."[288]

As I meditate on the reality expressed by these words and as I sense the power of

---

288. Anthony Lee Ash, *The College Press NIV Commentary: Philippians, Colossians, and Philemon* (Joplin, MO: College Press, 1995), 65.

the exhortation, I am compelled to view my bivocational ministry not as something I have to do for myself but as something I must do regardless of myself. My ministry must be in response to the selfless love and sacrifice that Jesus gave for me.

## SERVICE

In the NIV, verse 7 says that Jesus "made himself nothing, taking the very nature of a servant, being made in human likeness." The Greek word here for "servant" is *doulos*, the word that is usually translated as "slave." Jesus, the Lord of lords, willingly became a slave for us. The phrase "made himself nothing" clearly indicates that it was the choice and desire of Jesus to come to earth as a human and serve others. "Being made in human likeness" indicates His willingness to become something completely different in order to relate to the people He came to serve. As I meditate on these words I am inspired and motivated to see my bivocational ministry as an opportunity to serve others as Jesus served me. I also see my job as a school bus driver as an opportunity to become something completely different in order to better relate to the people God has called me to serve.

## HUMILITY

Verse 8 says, "Being found in appearance as a man, He humbled Himself." It is humbling to be demoted by your superiors or to be forced into a situation that lowers your status and position in the eyes of others. It is humbling to make a major mistake that ruins your reputation or accidentally do something that damages your credibility and influence. But Jesus intentionally humbled Himself. He was not demoted by the Father and the Holy Spirit. He did not accidentally fall into humanity. R. Kent Hughes states,

> So at every level, his humbling was his own doing.
> His not holding tightly to his equality with God—
> his emptying—
> his becoming a servant in body and soul—
> his full entrance into humanity—
> his humbling—were all of his own doing.[289]

---

289   R. Kent Hughes, *Philippians, Colossians, and Philemon: The Fellowship of the Gospel and The Supremacy of Christ* (Wheaton, IL: Crossway, 2013), 86-87.

As I continue to consider the humility of Jesus in His incarnation, I am convicted to sacrifice my pride and serve both as a bus driver and as a minister with the same humility that Jesus exemplified, a humility that considers others, even that disrespectful middle school student who cussed me out last week, as more important than myself. That doesn't mean that I just ignore the students when they violate the rules. I wrote a referral and reported the violation to the student's parents and the school principal. However, I didn't write the referral to "get even" with the student. I wrote the referral because I love all the students on the bus, and I want to help them develop the character traits that will continue to bless their lives.

## OBEDIENCE

The second part of verse 8 says, "He humbled Himself by becoming obedient to the point of death, even death on a cross." When I think about the level of obedience described in this verse, I am reminded of the evaluation the author of Hebrews invites us to consider. "You have not yet resisted to the point of shedding blood in your striving against sin" (Heb. 12:4). But what could motivate this level of obedience? What could empower a person to willingly suffer such a cruel and agonizing death? Certainly not fear. While many people obey God out of fear, that is not the motivation Jesus displayed in His obedience. The motivation that empowered Jesus to obey even to the point of death was the love of God. And the love of God is the same motivation that can empower us to obey and even suffer for the sake of the gospel.

## BIVOCATIONAL MINISTRY FOR THE COMMON GOOD

Another important lesson this bivocational journey has taught me is that the gospel is a message of good news that should create and cultivate a culture of love and grace wherever it is shared. As Christians, we are the salt of the earth and the light of the world. Our presence in any community should have a positive effect that gives people hope. The way we share and live out the message of the gospel at work should create and cultivate a culture for the common good of everyone there.

Andy Crouch suggests that when we are trying to create or cultivate culture for the common good, we should form partnerships with God, with people who are empowered, and with people who are disempowered. He writes, "God's basic work is to build partnerships between the powerful and the powerless."[290] God does not need us to preach the gospel. God does not need us to lead people to Christ. God does not need us to accomplish anything He wants to do. And yet He invites us to partner with Him in His great plan of redemption. God enjoys working together with His children. By God's grace, the gospel empowers us with significance and purpose inviting us to work together with God.

When we build partnerships between the powerful and the powerless and invite them to work together for the common good, we are demonstrating the message of the gospel and creating a culture of grace. In one sense we are all powerless and dependent on God. But God in His wisdom has given different strengths and weaknesses to different people requiring them to come together and depend on each other in relationships of grace and love. When God gives us power in some way, we need to recognize it as a stewardship. We need to put on our gospel glasses and look for the opportunities God is giving us to use that power to bring His grace and love into the lives of others.

As a school bus driver, I have the opportunity to create an envirnment on the bus that will help students feel safe and encouraged. For most students, the bus driver is the first and the last school employee they will see each day. Many times, the bus ride to school each morning will establish the attitudes that the students will take with them into the classroom. Likewise, the bus ride home in the afternoon has the potential to send children into their families either broken or blessed.

There are several things that, by God's grace, I am doing to create an environment on the bus where students will flourish. I try to remember the names of every student. I greet each of them when they get on the bus. I talk to them as they leave. I look for good behavior and good attitudes to appreciate and celebrate. I emphasize the fact that we are all on the same team going in the same direction. When there is a behavior problem, I try to empower the students by asking them to help me out with it. At least once a week, I come in early and before I do my pre-trip safety inspection, I imagine specific students sitting in their seats. As I walk down the aisle in the bus, I pray for God to help me exemplify the fruit of the Spirit to these students. I pray for character traits like kindness, patience, gentleness, and self-control to be produced, practiced, developed, and displayed. As a result, I have seen remarkable improvements in the attitudes and behaviors of the students.

---

290. Andy Crouch, *Culture Making: Recovering Our Creative Calling*, (Downers Grove, IL: InterVarsity Press, 2008), 234.

Students on the bus often feel like they are disempowered. One time I kept the students on the bus for a few minutes after we got to school in the morning. I usually do this once a month to go over some guidelines and expectations. However, this time I told them I needed their help coming up with some rules for riding the bus. I emphasized that it was my goal for all of us to work together to create an environment on the bus where everyone would feel safe and encouraged. I gave them the day to think of some rules that would help us accomplish this goal. That afternoon after all the students got on the bus, I kept the bus parked at the school for a few minutes while I listened to their ideas. This worked out well. I did have to add a few details, but they came up with almost every rule that I would have given them without their help. This not only gave them a sense of power, but it also helped them to take ownership of the bus environment and accept responsibility for the whole group. After that day, the students were constantly encouraging each other to respect the rules they made.

Occasionally, a group of students will push the boundaries and try to display their power in a negative way. In those situations, I will identify the "ring leaders" and keep them on the bus for a few minutes in the morning after the other students leave. While talking with them I acknowledge their influence among their peers. I tell them they are natural leaders with a lot of potential. I also tell them that the other students are going to follow their examples and I need their help to create an environment on the bus that is safe and encouraging for everyone. I found that I get much better results from this approach than from writing referrals. Writing referrals is leadership by authority and title. Empowerment is leadership by influence and testimony. I still write referrals when I need to, but I always try to empower students first.

There are several good things that are taking place among the employees of the Vancouver School District. I see God working through my situation as a bivocational minister to encourage and cultivate an environment of grace and love. At the beginning of each school year, all the bus drivers are required to participate in some state-mandated training sessions. Some of these classes are designed to help workers pursue and develop a work environment that is positive and encouraging.

When I first started driving for the school district, I went to the training sessions because they were required. I listened and learned from the presentations. But I didn't go out of my way to encourage and promote the healthy work environment they were trying to create. I wasn't seeing the bigger picture. God was giving me

231

an opportunity to develop a culture of grace in the workplace. However, now I make it a point to encourage or thank at least one coworker each day. I watch for examples of the workplace principles we talk about in our training sessions. When I see someone doing something that we talked about in our training, I bring it to their attention and compliment them for it.

We exemplify the gospel and create an atmosphere of grace when we bring together the empowered and the disempowered and help them to work together for the common good. In my specific example of driving for the Vancouver School District, the empowered would be the administration, those who work in the office as supervisors and safety officers. I know some of them are Christians. They occasionally ask me how things are going at my church and they will tell me about special events at their congregations. Others are suspicious of me as a pastor. During my first year of driving for the district, I wore a shirt with an American flag on it that said, "In God We Trust." It was September 11, so I thought it would be fine. One of my supervisors told me I couldn't wear it because of the "separation of church and state." I thought that was ridiculous since our currency, which is issued by the government, says, "In God we trust." However, I resisted the temptation to complain about it. I kept reminding myself of Colossians 4:6 "Let your speech always be with grace, as though seasoned with salt, so that you will know how you should respond to each person."

I am by no means a perfect bus driver. There have been several times when my mistakes have been rightfully brought to my attention. However, all the supervisors and safety officers have expressed appreciation for my work ethic and my attempts to create a positive work environment in the way that I interact with them and other employees. All the administrators recognize the value of having bus drivers who are trustworthy, dependable, safe, kind, and patient. They know that these are character traits that Christians are trying to maintain and develop in their lives.

Some of my fellow employees feel disempowered. They are the bus drivers who are frustrated with their jobs for various reasons. They may be Christians who are having a hard time living out their faith at work. Or they may be non-Christians who just can't find any fulfillment in what they are doing. A vision for what they can do to be a blessing to others and contribute to the common good will give them hope and a sense of purpose in their work. When they are expressing frustration with difficulties in other areas of life such as family matters or health concerns, I ask them how I can pray for them. I then write down the prayer request on a card and I make a commitment to pray about it. Later, I tell them I have been praying about the situation and I ask them how things are going.

When we offer to help the disempowered, it is easy to imply that we have power, and they don't. Crouch reminds us of how we should partner with those who may seem to have less power than us. He writes "We do not approach the relatively powerless as recipients of our charity but as sources of a power that we who are relatively powerful may not even know."[291] Typically I have always tried to solve my own problems. In the past, I would only ask for help if I knew that I could not take care of the problem myself. I have changed my thinking on this subject. Now I look for opportunities to ask disempowered people for help. When I am doing my pre-trip safety inspection, I will ask one of the newer bus drivers to check my brake lights for me. When I am frustrated with a student who is being difficult, I will ask for advice from a substitute bus driver who has driven my route. When I am having a hard time living out my faith at work, I will ask one of the Christians who works with me to pray for me.

In this bivocational journey, God has taught me to lean on Him in prayer. He has taught me to humbly ask for others to pray for me. By no means do I think that I have it all figured out. I know that I am completely inadequate for the tasks that God has entrusted to me. But I also know that His grace is more than adequate to make up for all my weaknesses. That motivates me and empowers me to work even harder in my job and in my ministry for the sake of the gospel.

I'm sure that as I continue to go through the various stages of life my ministry opportunities will continue to change. I will continue to evaluate those opportunities for the sake of the gospel. In the future, I may have opportunities to be a fully-funded minister or a volunteer minister. But whether I am a fully-funded, bivocational, or volunteer minister, I will always be a minister for the sake of the gospel.

> "But by the grace of God I am what I am, and His grace toward me did not prove vain; but I labored even more than all of them, yet not I, but the grace of God with me." —1 Corinthians 15:10

---

291. Andy Crouch, *Culture Making: Recovering Our Creative Calling*, (Downers Grove, IL: InterVarsity Press, 2008), 230.

## DISCUSSION QUESTIONS

1. Read Philippians 2:5-11. Write a list of the Christ-like attitudes that are demonstrated in this passage. What are the top three attitudes that you need to cultivate in your life?

2. What example of Christ-like selflessness have you seen in a minister?

3. When is it especially difficult for you to maintain an attitude of selflessness?

4. What example of Christ-like service have you seen in a minister?

5. Why is it important for church members and people in the community to see that church leaders are committed to serving others?

6. What example of Christ-like humility have you seen in a minister?

7. How can the gospel help us to be humble as leaders even in those times when we know we are right, and others are wrong?

8. What example of Christ-like obedience have you seen in a minister?

9. What motivates you to obey in those times when you don't want to obey?

10. How is submission a character trait of strength rather than a sign of weakness?

11. How have you seen a church working for the common good in your community?

12. How could you invite someone in your community or place of work to partner with you for the common good?

# APPENDIX A

In this appendix, I will present the results of the first survey I conducted as part of my research for my dissertation on bivocational ministry. The *2016 Directory of the Ministry*[292] is a listing of all the instrumental Churches of Christ and Christian churches in America. During the spring of 2017, I sent out surveys to all 5,032 churches listed in the directory. The following is the survey letter and the survey questions I sent out to all the churches.

Dear Minister,

I am a preacher at the Minnehaha Church of Christ in Vancouver Washington and a student at Western Seminary. I am currently working on a dissertation on "Effective Bivocational Ministry in the Churches of Christ and Christian Churches." I am studying bivocational ministers in the Restoration Movement because I want to find out why they are either successful or struggling in order to help ministers and ministry students to better prepare for effective bivocational ministry.

As an essential part of my research, I am conducting a survey

---

292   Judy Noll, *2016 Directory of the Ministry: A Yearbook of Christian Churches and Churches of Christ* (Springfield, IL.), 2016.

of all the churches in the United States listed in *the Directory of the Ministry*. Please take a few minutes to fill out this brief survey and return it in the self-addressed envelope. The more congregations that participate in this survey the more helpful the results will be. I would greatly appreciate your willingness to support this research project through your participation.

This initial survey is mainly for quantitative information. After I get the raw data, I will be conducting personal interviews with some bivocational ministers to better understand the factors and strategies that make for an effective bivocational ministry. If you are enjoying a productive bivocational ministry or you have some ideas that you think will help me in my research, please let me know.

In His Service,
Michael Kennedy
bivocationalpreacher@gmail.com

## BIVOCATIONAL MINISTRY SURVEY

For this survey I am defining "bivocational" as having two or more jobs at the same time, one job being employed as a minister of a local congregation and the other job being employed by some other organization.

1. What is your name and the name of the church?

2. How long have you been employed in your current position?

3. What is the approximate weekly attendance of the congregation?

4. Have you ever been bivocational while employed as a minister?

5. Are you currently a bivocational minister?

    If your answer to question 5 is "no," thank you for your participation. Please use the self-addressed envelope to return this survey or e-mail your answers to bivocationalpreacher@gmail.com.

    If your answer to question 5 is "yes," please answer the following questions.

6. How long have you been bivocational at the church where you are currently working?

7. What is the main reason you are bivocational?

8. What is your current job or career outside of your ministry in the local church?

9. Is it your goal to be fully funded by the church and quit your other job?

10. What is one thing that has helped your bivocational ministry to be more effective?

Thank you for your participation. Please use the self-addressed envelope to return this survey or e-mail your answers to bivocationalpreacher@gmail.com.

Here are the results of the survey:

- 1,264 churches responded to the survey.

- In the **NM** category (No Minister), there were 29 churches (2.3%) that had no minister and they were in need of a minister.

- In the **VM** category (Volunteer Minister) there were 39 churches (3%) that intentionally had volunteer ministers and they were not looking to hire a minister.

- In the **BVM** category (Bivocational Minister), there were 393 churches (31%) that had bivocational ministers. Of those bivocational ministers, 167 have a goal to be fully funded by the church. 261 said that they do not have a goal of being fully funded by the church. And 14 of those 261 bivocational ministers actually said that it is their goal to eventually receive no funding from the church and to have a completely volunteer ministry.

- In the **FFM** category (Fully Funded Minister), there were 803 churches (64%) that had ministers who are not bivocational.

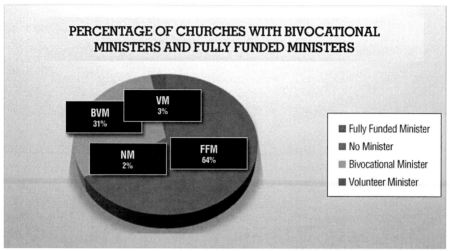

FIGURE 17

Most of the 432 bivocational and volunteer ministers are serving in small churches. However, there were several of these ministers serving in medium and large congregations who also responded to the survey. 178 bivocational ministers are preaching in congregations with fewer than 50 members in attendance each week. 151 bivocational ministers are serving in congregations with an average attendance of 50-99. 77 bivocational ministers are serving in churches with an average attendance of 100-199. 19 bivocational ministers are serving in churches with an average attendance of 200-499. And 7 bivocational ministers are serving in churches with an average attendance that is over 500. Figure 10 is a graph showing the attendance in congregations where the minister is bivocational.

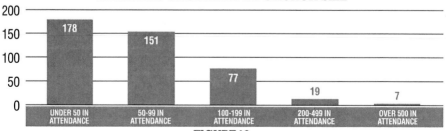

FIGURE 18

238

Of the 803 fully funded ministers who responded to the survey, 99 are serving in churches with an average attendance under 50. 186 are serving in congregations with an average attendance of 50-99. 244 are serving in churches with an average attendance of 100-199. 178 are serving in churches with an average attendance of 200-499. And 96 are serving in churches with an average attendance of over 500. Figure 11 is a graph showing the attendance of congregations where the minister is fully funded.

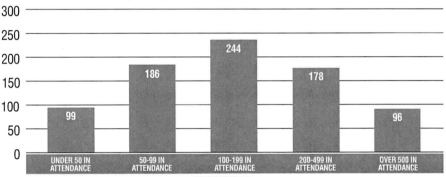

**NUMBER OF CHURCHES WITH FULLY-FUNDED MINISTERS ORGANIZED BY CHURCH SIZE**

FIGURE 19

Of all the ministers who responded to the survey, 795 (64%) are or were at some point bivocational. There were also 47 ministers who are not technically bivocational, but they have retired from a career outside of the church. They are now working full-time as volunteer ministers or ministers receiving a small stipend to cover their expenses.

Question 7 asked, "What is the main reason you are bivocational?" There were a variety of answers but most of them could be placed in one of five categories as follows:

- 56% said that the main reason for being bivocational was financial.

- 22% said that they were bivocational to help a small church or a church plant.

- 13% gave evangelistic reasons and/or a desire to be involved in the community.

- 6% said it was their personal preference or that they loved both of their jobs.
- 3% said that it was God's leading.

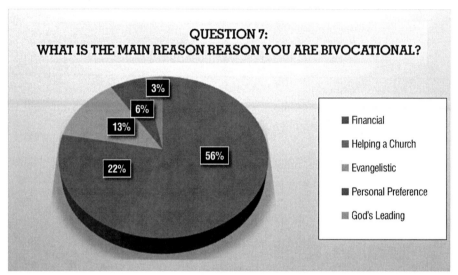

**QUESTION 7:**
**WHAT IS THE MAIN REASON REASON YOU ARE BIVOCATIONAL?**

- Financial
- Helping a Church
- Evangelistic
- Personal Preference
- God's Leading

FIGURE 20

For question 8 I asked, "What is your current job or career outside of your ministry in the local church?" There is a wide variety of occupations that bivocational ministers have pursued. Here are the top twenty most common jobs among bivocational ministers along with the number of bivocational ministers in each field.

1. School Teacher (37)
2. College Professor (34)
3. Bus Driver (32)
4. Small Business Owner (31)
5. Chaplain (27)
6. Insurance Agent and/or Sales (22)
7. Counselor (21)
8. Construction Worker (16)
9. Retail Sales (15)
10. House Rentals and/or Property Manager (14)

11. Funeral Home Director or Assistant (12)
12. Adult Care or Hospice Worker (11)
13. Landscaping (9)
14. Truck Driver (8)
15. Sports Coach (7)
16. Farmer (7)
17. Fire Fighter and/or EMT (6)
18. Law Enforcement (5)
19. Postal Worker (5)
20. Nurse (4)

In addition to these occupations, there were also some bivocational ministers who had jobs that surprised me. I'm not sure why I was surprised. However, it was a refreshing reminder that Jesus calls men from all walks of life to preach the gospel. There is an airline pilot preaching the gospel in Indiana. There is dance instructor preaching the gospel in California. There is Department of Defense administrator preaching the gospel in Arizona. There is a Disney World employee preaching the gospel in Florida. There is a professional musician preaching the gospel in Kentucky. There is a 911 dispatcher preaching the gospel in Missouri. There is a dentist preaching the gospel in Ohio. There is a commercial fisherman preaching the gospel in North Carolina. There is an attorney preaching the gospel in Texas. There is a knife maker preaching the gospel in Montana. There is a sports reporter preaching the gospel in Illinois. And there is a doctor preaching the gospel in West Virginia.

In the survey, I gave each church the option of either responding by e-mail or by snail mail. I included a self-addressed return envelope but I did not include postage. It was interesting to me that the vast majority still chose to respond by snail mail. Only 251 churches responded by e-mail. Altogether, I got over 20% participation in the survey. I suppose I would have gotten more if I would have included return postage. However, with the cost of all the envelopes, labels, paper, postage, and printing just to get the survey out to 5000 churches, I had already spent more than I should have on the project.

I have been greatly encouraged by all the testimonies of so many faithful ministers who are diligently working to proclaim and live out the gospel in their communities of faith as well as in their communities of work outside the church. Recording the data and processing all this information was a long and tedious task. But the practical advice from the ministers in the trenches and the occasional stories of struggle and grace have made it all worth it. As I read the comments on the completed surveys I prayed for each church and minister.

# APPENDIX B

After analyzing the results from the first survey in the spring of 2017, I conducted another more detailed survey in the fall of 2017. The first survey was sent out to the 5,032 churches listed in the *2016 Directory of the Ministry*.[293] 1,258 ministers responded to the first survey. 432 of them indicated that they were bivocational ministers. My second survey was sent out to those 432 bivocational ministers. I kept the survey open until the end of the year and I received 194 responses. Here is the letter I sent out with the survey.

> Dear Bivocational Minister,
>
> I sincerely pray that your ministry is going well and that God is working in your life for His glory and the building up of His Kingdom. Thank you so much for participating in the "bivocational ministry survey" I sent out last spring. I have posted the initial results of the survey online at www.bivocationalpreacher.net/. The first stage of my research was mainly quantitative. I forgot to give people a cut off date so I am still getting some responses. However, I need to move on to the next stage in my research and

---

293    Judy Noll, *2016 Directory of the Ministry: A Yearbook of Christian Churches and Churches of Christ* (Springfield, IL: Specialized Christian Services, 2016).

I would like to tap into some of your insights and experiences as a bivocational minister.

As a bivocational minister myself, I know how important your time is. I drive a school bus for the Vancouver School District and in three more weeks, my summer break will be over. However, I really believe that your input will be very helpful not only to me but to hundreds of other bivocational ministers and ministry students. My goal is to write a book that will serve as a resource for bivocational ministers, churches, and ministry students. Will you please help me by completing the questionnaire I enclosed? You can return it to me either by snail mail or by email. I would prefer it in electronic form by email simply because it is easier to read and I can copy and paste quotes into my dissertation, but whatever works best for you is fine.

As you will see from some of the questions, I am especially interested in how the gospel or our response to the gospel can help us to have more effective and fulfilling ministries. If you have any questions, please feel free to contact me. If it is possible, please return this questionnaire by **Saturday, October 7, 2017**.

Here are the questions from the survey along with my analysis of the results.

## 1. What is your name?

I gave the participants three options concerning how I should report the comments they gave me.

- 151 said, "You can quote me and give me credit by name."
- 28 said, "You can quote me but please keep me anonymous."
- 6 said, "Please do not quote any of my answers in your dissertation."
- 9 said that they did not care, or they left it blank.

## 2. What is the name of the church where you serve?

I asked this question mainly so I could cross-reference the information from this survey with the previous survey as well as with the data listed in the

*Directory of the Ministry.* All the participants included the name of the church where they serve.

3. **Would you describe the community in which your church lives as rural, suburban, or urban?**
   - 130 said, "Rural."
   - 47 said, "Suburban."
   - 13 said, "Urban."
   - 4 said they were not sure, or they left this question blank.

4. **What kind of training and education have you gone through for your ministry in the church?**
   - 27 said they had a two-year associate degree from a Bible college or a Christian university.
   - 108 said that they had a bachelor's degree from a Bible college or a Christian university.
   - 32 said that they had a master's degree from a seminary or a Christian university.
   - 8 said that they had a doctorate in ministry.
   - 11 said that they had some other kind of formal training for ministry.
   - 8 said that they had no formal training in ministry.

5. **What kind of training and education have you gone through for your work outside the church?**
   - 31 said that they had a two-year associate degree for the work they do outside the church.
   - 16 said that they had a bachelor's degree for the work they do outside the church.
   - 12 said they had a master's degree for the work they do outside the church.
   - 6 said they have a doctorate for the work they do outside the church.
   - 57 said that they had some other kind of training for the work they do outside the church.

- 72 said that they had no formal training for the work they do outside the church.

6. **Do you believe God has called you to the church where you currently serve?**
   - 162 said, "Yes."
   - 9 said, "No."
   - 23 either left it blank or indicated that they were, "Not sure."

7. **Do you believe God has called you to the work you do outside the church?**
   - 108 said, "Yes."
   - 40 said, "No."
   - 46 either left it blank or indicated that they were, "Not sure."

8. **How effective do you believe your ministry has been?**
   - 2 said, "Not very effective."
   - 34 said, "Somewhat effective."
   - 85 said, "More effective than not."
   - 72 said, "Very effective."
   - 1 left this question blank.

9. **As a bivocational minister, how often do you have a sense of fulfillment and satisfaction?**
   - 2 said, "Almost never."
   - 23 said, "Sometimes."
   - 93 said, "Often."
   - 75 said, "Almost always."
   - 1 left this question blank.

10. **How can I pray for you and your ministry?**
    While this may seem like a question that is too personal for this kind of a survey, I have included the results here because it is important for us to know

how we can pray for our ministers. Please join me in praying for these faithful ministers in God's Kingdom. Several ministers listed more than just one of the following prayer requests.

- 64 are asking for prayers for effective evangelism and church growth.
- 54 are asking for prayers for church unity, discipleship, and spiritual growth.
- 48 asked for prayers for endurance, perseverance, or faithfulness.
- 30 asked for prayers for God's wisdom and guidance.
- 19 mentioned church leadership concerns.
- 11 left this question blank.
- 8 mentioned financial concerns either for themselves or the church.
- 6 mentioned time management concerns.
- 6 mentioned family concerns.
- 4 mentioned health concerns.
- 1 minister in Barstow, California mentioned that their church really needs a pianist.

Many of the ministers who answered this question spoke of their desire to stay faithful in ministry even when they are facing difficult situations, working hard, and not seeing the results they would like to. The following prayer request communicates the concerns of many bivocational ministers:

> Please pray that discouragement from not being able to do the quality of job I desire to do will not hinder my ministry. Pray that I will not grow weary of being so busy. Also, pray that I will not be tempted to give up out of discouragement.

Several bivocational ministers are senior citizens or close to retirement age. One of the common prayer requests in this demographic was for wisdom and guidance to know when and how to retire. Some of them know that they don't have the energy to keep doing all the things they are doing in ministry but for various reasons, they are having a hard time turning those responsibilities over to trained and capable members. Others are looking for an exit strategy that will help the congregation navigate the transition of leadership.

**11. How (if at all) has your work outside the church helped you to be more effective in your ministry?**

- 74 mentioned improved evangelistic efforts and opportunities.
- 71 mentioned a better understanding of the culture or a better understanding of people outside the church.
- 33 mentioned improved discipleship opportunities.
- 25 mentioned improved church leadership skills.
- 21 mentioned that there was less financial burden on the Church.
- 7 mentioned improved counseling skills and/or conflict resolution skills.
- 6 left this question blank or said, "Not sure."
- 4 said, "Not much" or "Not at all."

Several ministers shared observations of how their reputation as a pastor working in the "real world" raised their credibility both in the eyes of Christians and people in the community. This helped them to be more effective both in evangelism and discipleship. Thaddeus Hinkle shared the following response,

> First, my second vocation has allowed me to model, to my congregants, service and ministry in the world other than on Sunday morning, a model that I hope they can take into their own work. It allows me to teach that we all really have only ministry, no matter what our jobs happen to be.
>
> Second, because this is a rural church, my second vocation may be my more effective ministry. In urban churches, the congregants expect they will see their pastor only on Sunday. In rural churches, the congregants expect that they will see their pastor at the grocery store, at the ball games, etc. in addition to Sunday. Therefore, rural congregants look for a pastor who reaches them personally and look less to how he teaches and preaches. It could be said that, in rural churches, the sermon on Sunday is more a supplement and support of what congregants see and learn from us during the week.
>
> Third, my second vocation has opened doors to meet with and work with people who would not ordinarily come to church nor look for a pastor. Many people I serve or meet

in my second vocation are surprised when they learn I am a pastor. Many others who come to the church for the first time discover that they have already met the pastor of the church, which makes them a little more comfortable and assured. My second vocation allows me to demonstrate to people outside the church that I am the same during the week that I am on Sunday (or I better be!).

Fred Nelson noted that his bivocational ministry gives him more credibility as a genuine Christian leader who is not in the ministry for the money. Nelson responded,

Working outside the church makes me keenly aware of the need to budget my time. It also keeps me in semi-regular contact with unbelievers, and so reminds me to live and speak as salt and light. Others know that I am in ministry, but not in it for the money.

Jeff Blaine has observed that his role as a "blue collar" worker has made him more approachable in ministry both to Christians and those outside the church. Blaine writes,

People seem to gain a relational ease with a preacher that works a "blue collar" job and understands them in that regard; thus, people seem to be more receptive to a word spoken about Jesus and may even visit the church.

Mark Wright, who spent 20 years in "full-time" ministry before switching to a bivocational strategy, explained how his job in a non-Christian environment has helped him to be more effective in both evangelism and discipleship. Wright stated that

It keeps me in touch with the working class of Americans. I know what it is like to report to a job 5 days a week. Many pastors are in a bubble (working fulltime in the church with Christian staff, volunteers, and board) and forget what it is like to live and work in a non-Christian environment.

Mike Kirby, a preacher in Valley Falls, Kansas, has been bivocational on and off for over ten years not for financial reasons but because he sees the value of being in the community and helping people who are hurting. He writes,

> As an assistant funeral director (part-time), I am more aware of grief and loss. As a result, I can better sympathize and minister to people in those situations. I am better prepared to offer the hope of Christ to those who are grieving. I truly see the work I do as helping people. I don't get much income from it and I am a full-time minister at our church.

**12. How (if at all) has your ministry in the church helped you with your work outside the church?**

- 49 mentioned healthier relationships with people at work and/or a better work environment.
- 42 mentioned improved people skills.
- 37 mentioned evangelistic opportunities and/or results.
- 29 mentioned improved work quality.
- 28 mentioned opportunities to serve others spiritually.
- 22 left this question blank or said, "Not sure."
- 17 said, "Not much" or "Not at all."

One minister who also serves as an EMT made the following observations about how his ministry and his job as a first responder complement each other. He wrote,

> I am an EMT, coach, referee, Lion's Club member, Search and Rescue member, so I meet a variety of needs. As an EMT I often meet people at a time of need for both spiritual and physical support. I can "change hats" to minister to both needs. I also know more people in the community from ministering, coaching, EMT, etc.

Nate Powell is a minister and a school bus driver. Nate made the following observations about how his bivocational ministry has helped him. Powell writes,

> It connects me with many in the community that I wouldn't know otherwise. It keeps me more in touch with real-world

challenges that people face. It makes me a person that people look to in a crisis. It gives me opportunities to pray with people. And it makes me more patient and compassionate than others in my position.

13. **How (if at all) has your bivocational ministry been a blessing to the church (as a whole or individual members)?**
    - 79 wrote about how the church has less of a financial burden.
    - 56 said that more church members are willing to serve in some way.
    - 35 mentioned their improved relationships with church members.
    - 23 described how their improved leadership skills are helping the church.
    - 16 noted that the church is more evangelistic.
    - 7 said, "Not much" or "Not at all."
    - 6 left this question blank or said, "Not sure."

Dr. Jesse Carter Henderson serves as the minister of a small church in rural Kentucky. His Ph. D. is in education administration, but he also has an M. Div. from Cincinnati Bible Seminary. He described the financial blessing his bivocational ministry has been to the church and how it continues into his retirement years. Henderson wrote, "Because my wife and I are both retired from public education, our income and health provisions are cared for by the state, so we can serve the church for only business expenses."

Another minister stated that since he had to get a second job, he has noticed more members getting involved in various ministries. He writes,

After I started driving a school bus five years ago, I have seen a lot more people stepping up and volunteering to help out with things like teaching Sunday school, visiting shut-ins, serving communion, and helping out with special programs like VBS. I used to have to twist people's arms to get them involved. Now, almost every Sunday I can count on someone coming and asking if they can help out with something. And actually, when I look at the church in the book of Acts, that's the kind of church I see.

**14. How (if at all) has your bivocational ministry been a blessing to the community and people outside the church?**

- 67 wrote about improved relations between the church and the community.
- 63 described how they were serving the community more.
- 40 talked about more effective evangelism.
- 26 mentioned that more church members were serving in the community.
- 11 said, "Not much" or "Not at all."
- 8 left this question blank or said, "Not sure."

One minister said, "Through the years I have been able to minister to many people at work who have found their lives in crises."

Dr. Rob O'Lynn, a preacher in Kentucky, said this about his bivocational ministry: "It allows me to be seen as a more integrated member of the community. I am not here just to serve my congregation but the larger community."

Another minister described how his job outside the church has helped him to make connections with other organizations in the community which have developed into healthy partnerships with the church to bless the whole community. He writes, "We rent facilities to a local Zumba fitness group, we host a public high school baccalaureate, we host fundraisers for various organizations in the community, etc."

**15. How (if at all) has your bivocational ministry been a blessing to your family?**

- 87 wrote about the financial blessings to their family.
- 55 described how values are being effectively taught and exemplified to their children.
- 41 mentioned the support and/or unity that developed in their family.
- 16 said, "Not much" or "Not at all."
- 14 left this question blank or said, "Not sure."
- 4 mentioned the benefits of a more flexible schedule for their family.

One bivocational minister gave this response, "I guess the best thing for my family is that it has taught our children (who are now grown) to have a strong work ethic and to realize the importance of living life with purpose for the Lord."

Another bivocational minister noticed that the Biblical principles and values concerning his witness for Christ were being modeled to his family through his situation. He responded,

> Though at times it may be difficult to be a preacher's wife or a PK, they have come to realize that if a congregation cannot fully support the preacher, the preacher may need to have a secondary job, no matter how much he would rather be a full time, fully supported preacher. Outside jobs may be Monday through Friday but as Christians in a lost world, we are Christians witnesses and examples full time, 24/7!

Mark Wright made the observation that bivocational ministry may be a better option for older ministers who are empty-nesters. He wrote,

> My wife and I are empty-nesters. We work together both in the church and in the mortgage business. First of all, it is a blessing to work together and spend so much time together. But also it gives us more financial stability when we have different sources of income, and we do not depend entirely on the church for our income. This is a blessing. It also potentially allows the ministry family to be in a higher income bracket than most ministers. Note—I must confess that bivocational ministry would be more challenging to younger families with kids, because of the demands on your time. (But full-time ministry can also be a difficult situation for raising children).

**16. How (if at all) has your bivocational ministry been a blessing to you personally?**

- 56 testified to their sense of fulfillment in life.
- 34 described their character development.
- 31 described how they were refreshed by the change of pace and the variety of work.
- 26 wrote specifically about how their faith has grown.
- 25 mentioned their retirement and/or healthcare benefits.
- 22 pointed to the friendships they developed.

- 19 discussed their improved understanding of different kinds of people.
- 14 noted their improved skills and knowledge.
- 7 left this question blank or said, "Not sure."
- 5 said, "Not much" or "Not at all."

Richard Schimansky shared a powerful testimony of how God's grace is displayed in his bivocational ministry. He said,

> I am blessed to know that while I have to put time and energy into my secular job that might be better used in ministry work, that God makes a great increase through what I lack. Like the lad in John 6 that offered 2 fishes, Jesus does big things with our small offerings.

Drew Staudenmaier gave this perspective of how his bivocational ministry has been a blessing to him personally. He responded, "The biggest thing is that I'm not too caught up in either world of work or ministry. I don't get caught up in the drama of either place, and I can focus on each position individually when I need to."

Several bivocational ministers noted how the various physical activities they are involved in actually provide a refreshing break from the kind of work they typically do for the church. One preacher said, "In my odd jobs, I can work with my hands and forget about the struggles and trials at the church. It is a release from stress for me." Another minister said, "Contracting often became 'therapeutic' to me. A project gets finished and I can walk away. With the church, no one is ever finished."

Other bivocational ministers noted how all the interaction they have with people in the community is good for them and helpful for their spiritual growth. Don Smith, a professional horseshoer and storyteller, said, "I was well on my way to being a Christian Pharisee after college, but working with people not in vocational ministry, saved me."

**17. How (if at all) did the gospel influence your decision to be bivocational?**
- 81 identified the gospel as a factor in their decision to be bivocational.
- 44 mentioned the example of Paul as a major influence on their decision.
- 29 left this question blank or said, "Not sure."

- 23 said, "Not much" or "Not at all."
- 17 indicated that some principles of Scripture were a factor but not specifically the gospel.

Richard Schimansky gave this response,

> I know the Gospel must be preached...and so there must be a preacher. God happened to open a door for me to preach while I was still committed to a secular job. Had I not considered the Gospel so precious and urgent, I suppose I would not have gone to all the bother.

Another bivocational minister described how the gospel was his primary motivation for going into the ministry when he wrote,

> The Gospel gave me my first love – to work in the Kingdom of God. The message of being a servant is what made me willing to work other jobs so I can do my first love – working in the kingdom of God. If I didn't love Jesus, if I wasn't grateful for His gift of salvation, I would have stopped working in the church many years ago and switched to laboring in the world and making far more money with far less stress.

There were a few ministers who indicated that the congregation where they serve is in survival mode. These ministers believe that God has placed them there in a bivocational ministry because the gospel needs to be proclaimed in that community. They also believe that if they left for a full-time ministry somewhere else the congregation would close its doors. One minister said, "I chose to serve in a place that would have no minister if I didn't answer their call and work outside the church."

Some ministers and congregations have chosen to be bivocational even though the church is doing great financially and could afford to pay the minister a full-time wage. Jason Murray is a minister in Kentucky who also drives for a motor coach company. He made the following observations about how the gospel influenced his decision to be bivocational.

> Being bivocational gives me great independence and flexibility. My case is probably rare though, in that I don't

really need the second job. The church pays okay and my wife is a nurse. I would say the gospel has always made me willing to be bivocational since there is something incarnational about living in both the church and the marketplace.

## 18. How (if at all) does the gospel help you as a bivocational minister?

- 41 shared a general observation about how the gospel helps them, such as, "in many ways."
- 36 wrote about how the gospel helps them to love others and/or get along with people.
- 33 described how the gospel helps them to set priorities and/or stay focused.
- 18 described how the gospel helps them with their spiritual growth and character development.
- 18 left this question blank or said, "Not sure."
- 17 indicated that the gospel helps them to remain faithful.
- 16 mentioned evangelistic efforts.
- 6 said, "Not much" or "Not at all."
- 6 noted that the gospel makes their preaching and teaching meaningful or fulfilling.
- 3 said that the gospel helps them to pray more.

Some of the ministers who answered this question did not see the gospel as something that helped them as a bivocational minister any more than it would help them if they were a volunteer minister or a minister on full-time support. They made the observation that the gospel does help them, but they didn't actually identify how the gospel helps them. However, others were very conscious of how much they depend on the gospel as a powerful source of motivation and focus in their ministries. One bivocational minister wrote, "The Gospel is my reason for getting into other jobs and it is my reason for staying with ministry and other jobs to help supplement our income."

Dale Heimer explained how the gospel helps him with priorities and time management when he wrote, "It helps me establish my priorities. When planning a days/weeks work, opportunities to share the Gospel take priority."

Several ministers said that the gospel was the major influence in their decision to go into the ministry but the decision to be bivocational was more of a practical necessity. Lee Schroerlucke shared this testimony, "The Gospel influenced my response to God's call to ministry. The decision to be bivocational was more a matter of necessity and, of course, God's provision; maybe, this is what He had in mind all along."

John Frey said, "The Gospel of Jesus is my foundation. Without my hand firmly planted in Christ, I would not be able to function in this situation. Jesus is my strength, my confidence, my contentment."

The gospel is a message about peace, redemption, and the restoration of the broken relationship between us and God. Several ministers described how the gospel helped them with their people skills and their interaction with customers, coworkers, and supervisors. A minister who also works as a contractor noted how the gospel helps him when he has to deal with difficult people whether he is working at the church or at a construction site. He wrote, "God's grace gives me the perspective to endure difficult circumstances and respond graciously to difficult people." Jeff Gallup is a minister who also works as a special education assistant in a public school. He said, "The gospel gave me the principles for developing healthy relationships with the kids and staff I work with. As a result, I am able to share the love of Jesus with whoever I meet."

Another bivocational minister said that the gospel "refreshes my heart with humility, gratitude, and contentment. Without that work of the gospel on my heart, I wouldn't be able to do what I do in ministry."

**19. How (if at all) has your bivocational ministry provided opportunities for you to proclaim the gospel?**
- 11 left this question blank or said, "Not sure."
- 18 said, "Not much" or "Not at all."
- 29 indicated that being bivocational gave them some opportunities to proclaim the gospel.
- 136 indicated that being bivocational gave them many opportunities to proclaim the gospel.

Brian Thomason shared this testimony,

> I've been doing this for 11 years. On a construction site, people quickly figure out that I am not cussing and carrying

on like many of the stereotypical contractors. That opens up to questions, that often lead to spiritual conversations. Several people have come to church from those conversations to recommit their lives to Christ and others to accept Salvation for the first time.

Ian Farnsley shared the following response to this question, "I can't count the instances where I was able to say small things to encourage 'upward' thinking, to answer direct questions about Christ, and to pray with non/marginal believers. It's been awesome."

## 20. How (if at all) has your bivocational ministry provided opportunities for you to demonstrate or live out the gospel?

- 5 left this question blank or said, "Not sure."
- 7 said, "Not much" or "Not at all."
- 30 indicated that being bivocational gave them some opportunities to live out the gospel.
- 152 indicated that being bivocational gave them many opportunities to live out the gospel.

Drew Staudenmaier has noticed that the people he works with hold him accountable and look to him for leadership because they know he is a minister. He responded, "It holds me to a higher standard at work and I'm looked to as a leader in the workplace."

Another bivocational minister humbly acknowledged how his shortcomings have given him the opportunity to model and experience genuine repentance and forgiveness. He wrote,

At times, when I haven't held my tongue or if my body language has been less than God-like, I have apologized and asked for forgiveness for my actions. I have been humbled for by the forgiveness of those who seemingly do not profess any form of Christianity.

Fred Nelson testified to the demonstration of gospel perspective and gospel transformation as seen in a good work ethic and a joyful attitude. He responded to this question by saying,

Working diligently among lazy people has really demonstrated a stark difference, especially when others realize that I am a Christian and that my diligence is accompanied with a measure of joy and (most of the time) a lack of complaining.

21. **For young college students who are considering bivocational ministry, what advice would you give them?**
Only 3 participants left this question blank. The rest of the ministers gave encouraging comments and good practical advice for ministry students.

Jeff Blaine gives the following advice,

> Give it time. Don't seek out bivocational ministry as a necessity (because of debt or poor spending habits) but as an opportunity to walk with Jesus throughout your community. Be patient. Jesus will naturally share with you the best place for you and Him to be…together, and those around you will experience your relationship.

John Penn shared the observation that there are many churches that need bivocational ministers. He responded to this question with the following advice: "There are a large number of small churches that dot our countryside, many of which cannot (or even should not, for certain reasons) afford a full-time preacher."

Michael Robertson, a preacher and a school bus driver in West Virginia, gave similar advice when he wrote,

> Most of our churches do not pay a living wage. That is a fact. Try to cultivate skills that will enable you to be bivocational… In most of our congregations, you as a minister (and your family) will suffer financially unless you are bivocational or your wife has a good skill. In my understanding, bivocational ministers are the future of ministry in our churches with less than 150 in average attendance.

John Frey reminds ministry students that all the work they will be doing is a sacred opportunity to serve Jesus and influence people for Christ when he states that,

> It is important to see the image of God in every person with whom you will work. All labor whether in the church or outside of the congregation is a scared opportunity to serve the Lord Jesus. Your service to the Kingdom of God involves every area and aspect of your life.

Another bivocational minister encourages students to remember that, "Bivocational ministry is just as high a calling as any other service. It is a missionary type service that is often overlooked."

Dr. Richard Jenks works both as a counselor and a minister. He gave this practical advice, "It takes discipline and good time management skills to balance both jobs. It requires good financial planning—don't go into debt—live within your income." Several other bivocational ministers emphasized the need for good time management skills. One minister said that ministry students would benefit from some of the time management training available online from organizations like *Franklin Covey*.

There are a number of seminary and college professors who are bivocational ministers. They see their calling to teach and train people for ministry as complementary to their calling to preach and lead in a local congregation. Dr. Harley Ihm, a preacher at a church in Colorado, also serves as a professor at a Christian college. In his advice to ministry students, he notes the importance of seeking vocations that are truly in harmony with the students' gifts and calling. He writes, "Be sure that both vocations are where your talents lie. Be sure that it is a calling and don't choose something for the money and look for God to bless it."

**22. For the ministry departments in our Bible colleges and seminaries, what advice would you give them to help them better prepare students for bivocational ministry?**

9 participants left this question blank. There were a variety of ideas and views expressed by the ministers who answered this question.

Ian Farnsley offers this advice to schools preparing students for ministry,

> Full-time ministry is fading out in middle America. But I think there are a lot of great opportunities for the Kingdom

in it. Stop acting like being bivocational indicates failure. I never wanted to do this because I thought it meant I did not have a successful ministry. This was reinforced (at least in my mind) in college and Christian 'society.'

In light of the growing trend of bivocational ministry, Mark Wright gives the following advice to Bible colleges:

Bivocational ministry may very well be the wave of the future. Hire some professors with experience in bivocational ministry. Without compromising the mission of giving a foundation in Scripture to students, consider diversifying the curriculum to include other majors for work outside the church.

Several bivocational ministers offered advice that would encourage colleges and universities to offer training in vocations that would match up well with a ministry. Darrell Chase Jr. serves as a minister in Seattle and also works as a public school teacher. He encourages ministry students to,

Take the time to get trained or certified in a vocation outside of ministry. A basic wage job will dominate your time and may get in the way of ministry needs. Get into a profession that will allow for you to have time for both the vocation as well as the ministry, i.e. summers off…weekends and evenings off.

A few ministers said that there needs to be more practical training in Bible college that would prepare ministry students for the specific challenges. One bivocational minister shared the following advice,

I'd like to see more practical stuff, with hands-on training; not just how to preach a funeral or wedding, but how to love the people in those situations. Ministry students should learn about visitation for the sick, dealing with boards, and more of the nitty-gritty stuff that we face every day. And with no disrespect to any professor, being a weekend minister while teaching at a Bible college, is far different than living in a community, being part of that community, and dealing with folks who are not preachers in training.

Dr. Rob O'Lynn shared three excellent ideas in the advice he offered to Bible colleges and seminaries. O'Lynn writes,

(1) Hire qualified faculty who were bivocational.

(2) Remove the stigma that bivocational is lesser than full-time vocational ministry (we're still "full-time").

(3) Develop internship partnerships with congregations, church plants, and parachurch organizations where fundraising or bivocational ministry is preferred, expected, or common.

Several ministers said that they didn't receive any information about bivocational ministry when they were in Bible college. One minister who graduated from a well-known Bible college said that the professors at his school never talked about bivocational ministry. He learned about it by doing it. Warren Engel said, "Just to mention the idea would be more than what I got." Ronnie Gregory has been a bivocational preacher for over forty years. He said, "Bible colleges need to have actual classes on bivocational ministry taught by bivocational ministers. They need to build bivocational ministers up—don't put them down."

23. **For "full-time" ministers who, for the first time, need to switch over to bivocational ministry, what advice or encouragement would you give them?** Only 5 participants left this question blank. The rest of the ministers gave encouraging comments and good practical advice for their fellow workers in God's Kingdom.

Donald Ray Miller II shared this advice,

PRAY, it's not the end of the world, this does not mean you are an embarrassment or failure in the body of Christ because you have to become bivocational. Develop a great support system and remember to always take care of the family first. Keep a calendar of everything that is in planning. If they have a family, have a centralized calendar with all events on it. I have google calendar and I send my wife invites all the time so she will know if I have something going on. I also do this to make sure I'm not double booking myself.

With over 40 years of ministry experience, Dale Heimer gives the following advice to ministers who need to go out and get a second job:

Expect to spend more than the usual 40 hrs. per week. Be sure that the family is "on board" with this change. They will likely have less time with the bivocational minister unless he incorporates them into the work...which can be done. Don't be discouraged with the "full time" ministers that treat you as a "drop out" or less committed than they think they are. You may have to miss some "preacher's meetings" or conventions, but you can still stay "fresh" through study and interacting with folks in the congregation.

Glen Layfield from Scio, New York said, "They should select an integrated career that they love and one that they can use to build relationships."

Artie Carnes encouraged ministers to, "Do it! Get out there where your congregation is living life and see what they see."

Another minister writes,

It keeps me brushing elbows with the unchurched and helps me to get out of my "church bubble." I think it is healthy to go outside the church walls where no one knows your title. It gives you a better pulse on the real needs of your community. It is also good to not rely 100% on the church for your livelihood.

Alan Harris gave this encouragement, "The same priorities are in effect! God has allowed this for a reason and/or season. Seek what the Lord wants to teach you and embrace it. Don't be too proud to do anything for God."

**24. For churches that are considering bivocational ministry for the first time, what advice or encouragement would you give them?**

Only 4 participants left this question blank. The rest of the ministers gave encouraging comments and good practical advice for congregations that are considering a transition to bivocational ministry.

The following advice given by Thaddeus Hinkle will help congregations to focus on the partnership God has called them to in His grace. Hinkle writes, "If it helps, think of your pastor working in the 'real world' as advertisement for your church, as a gift you give your community on the church's behalf."

John Penn has been doing bivocational ministry for over forty years. When answering this question, he noted the need for congregations to help their preacher to protect the time and attention he needs to give to his family. Penn writes,

> It is a sacrifice of your time physically and mentally, which can take away from your family and activities you could have otherwise pursued. We wondered what effect this would have on our children, two boys, who grew up pretty much in our bivocational ministry (we did have a 4-year break between churches I served). However, both boys are solid Believers as are their wives, and we have and always have had a very good relationship with both, who are now in their 40's. Just as full-time ministry can ruin families, so can bivocational, but it does not need to!

Ron Hatley made the observation that congregations need to see bivocational ministry as an opportunity to get more members involved in ministry which actually makes a church healthier. He writes,

> Ministry needs to be a church-wide issue and not just something for the guy we hire. Prayer time, hospital calls, encouraging one another is everyone's job and duty. Bivocational ministry is actually a great thing because it forces more people into the ministry issues of the church.

Several ministers noted the importance of establishing clear expectations. One bivocational preacher gave the following advice to churches and church leaders who are transitioning into bivocational ministry.

> You need to discuss and agree on clear job expectations

for the bivocational minister. You also need to evaluate and adjust those expectations as time goes on. If both the minister and the church are new to bivocational ministry they may not realize what kind of expectations are realistic. Without clear communication and regular evaluations in this area, both the minister and the congregation are likely to get frustrated.

John Thybault noted that "It is best if the pastor does not need to work bivocationally because of financial necessity. It is freeing to be allowed to do this work because I want to!"

# APPENDIX C

In August of 2017, I conducted a survey of 34 Bible colleges and Christian universities listed in the *2017 Directory of the Ministry*[294]. I received 16 responses. I was a little surprised that less than half of these schools were willing to participate in this research project. I included a self-addressed stamped envelope with the survey, and I gave them plenty of time to respond. However, I get the impression that this is not a topic that many of the more expensive colleges and universities want to address. What student is going to be open to the idea of training for bivocational ministry when it puts them in debt to the tune of $50,000?

### Here are the colleges and universities
### listed in the *Directory of the Ministry.*

1. Cincinnati Christian University — http://ccuniversity.edu/
2. Emmanuel Christian Seminary — https://ecs.milligan.edu/
3. Hope International University — https://www.hiu.edu/
4. Lincoln Christian University — https://lincolnchristian.edu/
5. Johnson University — https://www.johnsonu.edu/Home.aspx
6. Master's International University of Divinity — https://ims.mdivs.edu/

---

294. Noll.

7. Summit Theological Seminary — — http://www.summit1.org/
8. Blueridge College of Evangelism — http://www.bce.edu/
9. Boise Bible College — http://www.boisebible.edu/
10. Carolina Christian College — https://carolina.edu/
11. Central Christian College of the Bible — https://www.cccb.edu/
12. Christian Institute of Biblical Studies — http://cibs-ky.com/
13. Christian Kingdom College — http://thechurchofchristsite.com/
14. Colegio Biblico — http://www.colegiobiblico.net/
15. College of the Scriptures — http://collegeofthescriptures.org/
16. Crossroads College — http://www.crossroadscollege.edu/
17. Dallas Christian College — http://www.dallas.edu/
18. Great Lakes Christian College — https://www.glcc.edu/
19. Grundy Bible Institute
20. Kentucky Christian University — https://www.kcu.edu/
21. Louisville Bible College — https://www.facebook.com/louisvillebiblecollege/
22. Manhattan Christian College — http://www.mccks.edu/
23. Mid-Atlantic Christian University — http://www.macuniversity.edu/
24. Mid-South Christian College — http://www.midsouthchristian.edu/
25. Midwestern School of Evangelism (no longer in operation)
26. Nebraska Christian College — https://www.nechristian.edu/
27. Northeast Ohio Bible College — http://www.neobc.org/
28. Northwest Christian University — https://www.nwcu.edu/
29. Northwest College of the Bible — http://ncbible.org/
30. Ozark Christian College — https://occ.edu/
31. Point University — https://point.edu/
32. St. Louis Christian College — https://stlchristian.edu/
33. Summit Christian College — https://www.summitcc.net/
34. William Jessup University — http://www.jessup.edu/

Here is the letter I sent to each school:

Dear President or Ministry Professor,
I am a ministry student at Western Seminary. I am currently working on a dissertation on "Effective Bivocational Ministry in the Churches of Christ and Christian Churches." I am studying

bivocational ministers because I want to find out why they are either successful or struggling in order to help ministers and ministry students to better prepare for effective bivocational ministry. I have completed a survey of all the churches listed in the Directory of the Ministry. The initial results of that survey have been posted at http://www.bivocationalpreacher.net/

As part of my research, I am also conducting a survey of all the colleges listed in the Directory of the Ministry. The more colleges that participate in this survey, the more helpful the results will be. I would greatly appreciate your willingness to support this research project through your participation. I will keep all your responses anonymous.

As a bivocational minister myself, I know how important your time is. However, I really believe that your input will be very helpful not only to me but to hundreds of other bivocational ministers and ministry students. One of my goals is to write a book that will serve as a resource for bivocational ministers and ministry students. Will you please help me by completing the enclosed questionnaire? You can return it to me either by snail mail or by email. I would prefer it in electronic form by email simply because I can copy and paste quotes into my dissertation, but whatever works best for you is fine.

I am especially interested in how the gospel or our response to the gospel can help us to have more effective and fulfilling ministries. If you have any suggestions or questions about this project, please feel free to contact me. If it is possible, please return this questionnaire by Tuesday, October 31, 2017.

Here are the survey questions with the results from those schools that participated in the survey.

1. **What percentage of the ministry professors in this school are also serving as ministers or elders in a local congregation?**
   - 3 schools: 100%
   - 1 school: 90%

- 1 school: 85%
- 1 school: 75%
- 1 school: 66%
- 2 schools: 60%
- 1 school: 50%
- 1 school: 40%
- 1 school: 30%
- 1 school: 22%
- 1 school: 20%
- 1 school: 11%
- 1 school: "unknown"

**2. Does the school offer a course on bivocational ministry?**
- 1 school said, "yes."
- 15 schools said, "no."

**3. Does the school offer any ministry courses that include a section on bivocational ministry?**
- 10 schools said, "yes."
- 6 schools said, "no."

**4. The ministry professors here believe that the school needs to have a course on bivocational ministry.**
- 1 said, "Strongly Agree."
- 6 said, "Mildly Agree."
- 8 said, "Mildly Disagree."
- 0 said, "Strongly Disagree."
- 1 said, "It has not been discussed."

One participant added that there was in the past an interest in this, but it is not strong at this point.

Another school noted that they had a degree program in "Marketplace Ministry" that was geared to biovocationals. It was discontinued because the churches that hired the graduates from that program complained about the students not having adequate preparation.

While another school added, "It is a reality and students enter ministry knowing this."

5. **The ministry professors here see bivocational ministry as an effective biblical model that ministry students today should consider.**
   - 2 said, "Strongly Agree."
   - 12 said, "Mildly Agree."
   - 1 said, "Neutral."
   - 1 said, "Mildly Disagree."
   - 0 said, "Strongly Disagree."

6. **The ministry professors here see bivocational ministry as a growing reality for which ministry students need to prepare.**
   - 5 said, "Strongly Agree."
   - 7 said, "Mildly Agree."
   - 3 said, "Mildly Disagree."
   - 0 said, "Strongly Disagree."
   - 1 said that they haven't discussed it.

   One school also said, "Students are counseled on balancing multiple income sources and family."

   Another school added, "This is especially true for getting students into countries otherwise closed to them."

7. **The ministry professors here present bivocational ministry as a less effective option that should be avoided if possible.**
   - 1 said, "Strongly Agree."
   - 0 said, "Mildly Agree."
   - 8 said, "Mildly Disagree."
   - 6 said, "Strongly Disagree."
   - 1 did not answer this question.

8. **The ministry professors here present full-time ministry as the preferable goal that ministry students should prepare for and pursue.**
   - 6 said, "Strongly Agree."

- 7 said, "Mildly Agree."
- 1 said, "Mildly Disagree."
- 2 said, "Strongly Disagree."

One school also noted, "We inform students that it is rare to find a full-time ministry position."

9. **The ministry professors here intentionally present the gospel as an essential key for effective ministries.**
   - All 16 said, "Strongly Agree."

10. **The ministry professors here intentionally teach that gospel proclamation and demonstration are essential not only for evangelism but also for effective pastoral leadership.**
    - All 16 said, "Strongly Agree."

# APPENDIX D

The Testimony of Another Bivocational Minister

by **Jeff Adams**

My experience has been mostly full of abundant blessings as Christ has used me over the years in bivocational ministries. For over 35 years I've served in various states, working secular jobs, while successfully ministering with local churches. I've milked cows, worked as a mechanic, ran my own business, written for a local newspaper, led a private school, and even driven a school bus. Currently, I serve as an interim preacher, while I work full-time as a chaplain (religious coordinator) for Washington State Department of Corrections. I sincerely appreciate Mike Kennedy's wisdom on bivocational ministry and would like to share with you some words of caution from my own personal experience.

First, caution is advised for the individual, considering bivocational ministry.

While the opportunities of specialized ministries in secular jobs are truly remarkable, it is possible the good minister could neglect his flock and his family. If you're like me and don't require much sleep, you can get a lot done, holding a couple of full-time jobs or a full-time and a couple of part-time ones. I've enjoyed letting Christ shine through me in my secular jobs as I aim for and achieve excellence as I strive to do all things in a way to please the Lord (Colossians 3:23). I've led countless people to the Lord and back to the Lord by being the best I can be in the workplace, while developing great relationships.

However, at times I did neglect my family. Early on I learned I have to put family time on my calendar, and I have to set things up so that during family time, I don't let "church work" or secular jobs interfere. If you don't put those safeguards in place while you attempt to juggle multiple things, you too could neglect your family.

I'm thankful God permitted me to learn early in life how I needed to prioritize my family.

While I certainly have made more than my fair share of errors along the way in the ministries to which God called me, I don't think I neglected the churches I've served. Even some of my staunchest critics have noted how readily available I am and always have been to the church body. Even so, I can see how it could happen, and have seen it happen in the lives of others.

When one is juggling another job while serving in a paid leadership role in a church, it is not hard to see how hours can consume. Many of my years in ministry have been filled with 20 to 40 or more hours per week with secular jobs, and well over 40, serving the churches. If you simply do the math, you will learn there is only so much time, and you must manage it well in order to not neglect the church.

Let's say you work 60 hours, total, in a week for two jobs. There are only 168 hours in a week. If you take 8 hours for sleep a night, that only leaves 52 hours or an average of 7.42 per day for prayer, personal Bible study, commuting, shopping, managing bills, phone calls, messages, emails, eating, getting ready, running errands, and spending time with friends and family. It is my belief as a successful minister, you must have quality and quantity with your family as you manage meeting the needs of the church you serve. It would be easy to neglect the church you serve or your family, while juggling two or more jobs.

The author of this book is a prime example of how it can be done well. He is a preacher, professor, and a bus driver. Meanwhile, he does short-term missions, spends time with family, and even enjoys motorcycle rides! On top of all that he earned his doctorate and wrote a book – all while doing bivocational ministry with excellence. His demonstrated faith in his bivocational ministries is stellar. In my opinion we can learn much from him and from others like him.

Not only should we not be so quick to judge and criticize bivocational ministers, I believe in most cases we should esteem them, and learn from them. Over the years I've met some of the most dedicated, proven, and effective ministers who are bivocational. Rhyan Smith is a successful, proven lead pastor, a successful real estate broker, and owner of a very well-known local coffee shop business. George Faull is another example of a very esteemed bivocational minister who has demonstrated well how to successfully lead a seminary, a church, and a business, simultaneously. In my opinion successful bivocational ministers are a rare breed and only a few in the ministry are cut out to do it. If you happen to know one, I encourage you to observe, esteem, and learn from him. These individuals remind me of the likes of Alexander Campbell, who seemed to do everything with such excellence, even while responsible for many things (leading leaders of churches, leading a college, running a farm, running a publication business, and leading a movement). In most cases it is only right to esteem our bivocational ministers. Few can do what they do.

The other word of caution is to the churches, served by bivocational ministers. It's very easy to become overly critical and judgmental of such servants. I know. I made that mistake, myself.

Many years ago, a minister who greatly impacted my life, Don Raiford, informed me he had begun driving a school bus, while preaching at a small church in Oklahoma. Immediately, my mind went to thoughts like this, "What has happened to this great preacher – that he now has to drive a school bus to make ends meet, while preaching?" I was deeply saddened even as he shared with me how great a ministry opportunity it was for him. For years I thought so negatively about that, and I shouldn't have.

Since that time, I've learned of many ministers and youth ministers, who drove school buses and thrived in both positions. I, personally, drove a school bus for more than eight years, and developed strong relationships. Many were drawn to a personal walk with Jesus as a direct result.

I now believe school bus driving is one of the many jobs which fits perfectly with ministry positions. In our district most routes end before office hours begin, and you only spend about two hours each afternoon driving, and then you're back at ministry. Plus, you're actively demonstrating genuine Christianity in a workplace environment which often desperately needs it, and you're positively impacting school children on a daily basis. How cool is that?

Anyone who knows me knows I am one of the least negative, judgmental, critical people you'll meet. Knowing an eternal optimist like me judged a very respected mentor certainly means there's a good chance others could do the same. I caution you not to be judgmental toward bivocational ministers.

Usually, we judge bivocational ministers who work what we deem to be "beneath them." Our pride kicks in and we simply don't like others knowing our minister is doing that other job. We think it makes us or our church look bad. However, we don't think this if the minister happens to be a seminary professor, is a professional writer, or something else which appears "bragworthy." I've never heard someone suggest their minister is neglecting the church because he spends too much time, teaching at the Bible college.

I've watched well-meaning Christians wreak havoc in their churches as they criticize ministers who work other jobs. While confirming the ministers never neglect their churches or families, they still criticize, fabricating possible scenarios where "there could come a time when we need him, and his other job will keep him from being available." In my 35+ years of mostly bivocational ministry, that never happened – not once. But there were people who speculated it could happen, and they criticized and undermined, discouraged, and divided.

There is a reason Paul's two letters to the Thessalonian church warn against idleness. Idleness breeds sin. I've discovered often the people who struggle with judging and criticizing others are the ones who aren't actively leading others to Christ or closer to Christ. They don't realize how counterproductive they are, and seem unaware of their greater need to self-evaluate, rather than judge others. Idleness, lack of leadership, and lack of focus can lead small groups in churches to become catalysts for gossip, malice, slander, and other forms of divisive and destructive behaviors. The collateral damage can spread far and wide, running off families, individuals, and even ministers.

Ministers and churches have been destroyed because well-intentioned Christians are judgmental and critical of their bivocational leaders. While we should be commending these dedicated servants of the Lord for sacrificing so much and setting such good examples, we do the devil's bidding by undermining their ministries.

Most children of bivocational ministers will say things like, "My dad is the hardest and most sacrificial worker I know." I've heard it a lot. Imagine what it feels like to them to hear their parent they respect so much for their impeccable work ethic being criticized for possibly "not working hard enough for the church." This is not okay.

If you are blessed with an outstanding bivocational minister, build him up, rather than tear him down (2 Corinthians 13:10; 1 Thessalonians 5:11).

In case you haven't noticed, we are losing ministers faster than we are training new ones. We are closing more churches than we are opening new ones. If there was ever a time when we must encourage our ministers, it is now. Bivocational ministry is not a sign the church can't afford a good minister (I actually had one of my own extended family members say this about me – yet they had continually said they esteemed me much as a minister.). To me bivocational ministry is a sign somebody is following a clear New Testament pattern. It is a sign someone is taking seriously their calling. It is a sign of commendable dedication.

So, be careful not to neglect your ministry or family, and be careful not to judge bivocational ministers.

Jeff Adams currently serves as Interim Pastor with Central Kitsap Christian Church in Bremerton, Washington, while working full-time as a Religious Coordinator (Chaplain) for the Washington State Department of Corrections. He continues to counsel, blog, podcast, and write a weekly column for the Nisqually Valley News (since 2007). He has been married to his wife, Stephanie over 32 years, and all their children are grown. He is an active Lions Club member, weightlifter, outdoorsman, and a frequent world-traveler (including short-term missions). He is a graduate of Ozark Christian College and Northwest College of the Bible, and has held ministries in Missouri, Arkansas, Texas, Indiana, and Washington.

# BIBLIOGRAPHY

Allen, C. Leonard. *The Cruciform Church: Becoming a Cross Shaped People in a Secular World.* Abilene, TX: Abilene Christian University Press, 1990.

Alton, Larry. "How Millennials Are Reshaping What's Important In Corporate Culture." *Forbes.* Last modified June 20, 2017. Accessed May 18, 2018. https://www.forbes.com/sites/larryalton/2017/06/20/how-millennials-are-reshaping-whats-important-in-corporate-culture/.

Anderson, Leith, and Jill Fox. *The Volunteer Church: Mobilizing Your Congregation for Growth and Effectiveness.* Grand Rapids, MI: Zondervan, 2015.

Ash, Anthony Lee. *The College Press NIV Commentary: Philippians, Colossians, and Philemon.* Joplin, MO: College Press, 1995.

Bauer, Walter, and F. Wilbur Gingrich. *A Greek-English Lexicon of the New Testament and Other Early Christian Literature.* Edited by William F. Arndt and Frederick W. Danker. 2nd edition. Chicago, IL: The University Of Chicago Press, 1979.

Beck, John A. *The Baker Illustrated Guide to Everyday Life in Bible Times.* Grand Rapids, MI: Baker Books, 2013.

Bercot, David W., ed. *A Dictionary of Early Christian Beliefs: A Reference Guide to More Than 700 Topics Discussed by the Early Church Fathers.* Peabody, MA: Hendrickson Pub, 1998.

Bickers, Dennis. *The Art and Practice of Bivocational Ministry: A Pastor's Guide.* Kansas City, MO: Beacon Hill Press, 2013.

————. *The Bivocational Pastor: Two Jobs, One Ministry.* Kansas City, MO: Beacon Hill Press of Kansas City, 2004.

Bickers, Dennis W. *The Tentmaking Pastor: The Joy of Bivocational Ministry.* Grand Rapids, MI: Baker Books, 2000.

————. *The Work of the Bivocational Minister.* Valley Forge, PA: Judson Press, 2007.

Black, Doug. *Marathon: A Manual For Bivocational Ministry.* Philadelphia, PA: CreateSpace Independent Publishing Platform, 2014.

Bonhoeffer, Dietrich. *The Cost of Discipleship.* New York, NY: Touchstone, 1995.

Bromiley, Geoffrey W. *The International Standard Bible Encyclopedia Vol. Four: Q-Z*. Grand Rapids, MI: Eerdmans Pub Co, 1995.

Bruce, F. F. *The Book of the Acts*. Grand Rapids, MI: Eerdmans, 1988.

Bruce, F.F. *Paul: Apostle of the Heart Set Free*. Grand Rapids, MI: Eerdmans, 1994.

Campbell, Alexander. *Christian Baptist*. Joplin, MO: College Pr Pub Co, 1983.

Carson, D. A. *The Cross and Christian Ministry: Leadership Lessons from 1 Corinthians*. Grand Rapids, MI: Baker Books, 2004.

Chambers, Arron. *Eats with Sinners: Reaching Hungry People Like Jesus Did*. Cincinnati, OH: Standard Publishing, 2009.

Chambers, Mary. *Church Is Stranger Than Fiction*. Downers Grove, IL: InterVarsity Press, 1990.

Chapman, Gary. *The 5 Love Languages: The Secret to Love That Lasts*. Chicago, IL: Northfield Publishing, 2015.

Chouinard, Larry. *The College Press NIV Commentary: Matthew*. Joplin, MO: College Press, 1997.

Clapp, Steve, Ron Finney, and Angela Zimmerman. *Preaching, Planning & Plumbing: The Implications of Bivocational Ministry for the Church and for You : Discovering God's Call to Service and Joy*. Fort Wayne, IN: Christian Community, 1999.

———. *Preaching, Planning & Plumbing: The Implications of Bivocational Ministry for the Church and for You : Discovering God's Call to Service and Joy*. Fort Wayne, Ind. (6404 S. Calhoun Street, Fort Wayne, Ind. 46807): Christian Community, 1999.

Cohn, D'Vera, and Jeffrey S. Passel. "A Record 64 Million Americans Live in Multigenerational Households." *Pew Research Center*, April 5, 2018. Accessed May 18, 2018. http://www.pewresearch.org/fact-tank/2018/04/05/a-record-64-million-americans-live-in-multigenerational-households/.

Cole, Neil. *Organic Church: Growing Faith Where Life Happens*. San Francisco, CA: Jossey-Bass, 2005.

Cottrell, Jack. *Set Free! What the Bible Says About Grace*. Joplin, MO: College Press, 2009.

———. *Studies in First Peter: 35 Lessons for Personal or Group Study*. Mason, OH: Christian Restoration Association, 2017.

———. *The College Press NIV Commentary Romans Vol 2: Chapters 9-16*. Joplin, MO: College Press, 1996.

———. *The Faith Once for All: Bible Doctrine for Today*. Joplin, MO: College Press, 2002.

———. *Tough Questions Biblical Answers/Part 1*. Joplin, MO: College Press, 1985.

Covey, Stephen R. *The 7 Habits of Highly Effective People: Powerful Lessons in Personal Change*. Anniversary edition. New York: Simon & Schuster, 2013.

Crane, Charles Arthur. *A Practical Guide to Soul Winning*. Joplin, MO: College Press Publishing Company, 1987.

Crouch, Andy. *Culture Making: Recovering Our Creative Calling*. Downers Grove, IL: IVP Books, 2013.

Danby, Herbert. *Tractate Sanhedrin, Mishnah and Tosefta: The Judicial Procedure of the Jews*. Forgotten Books, 2008.

Deloitte. "2018 Deloitte Millennial Survey: Millennials Disappointed in Business, Unprepared for Industry 4.0." *Deloitte*. Last modified 2018. Accessed May 18, 2018. https://www2.deloitte.com/global/en/pages/about-deloitte/articles/millennialsurvey.html.

Dever, Mark. *The Church: The Gospel Made Visible*. Nashville, TN: B&H Academic, 2012.

Dorr, Luther M. *The Bivocational Pastor*. Nashville, Tenn: B&H Publishing Group, 1988.

———. *The Bivocational Pastor*. Nashville, TN: B&H Publishing Group, 1988.

Dorsett, Terry W. *Developing Leadership Teams in the Bivocational Church*. Bloomington, Ind.: Crossbooks, 2010.

———. *Developing Leadership Teams in the Bivocational Church*. Bloomington, IN: Crossbooks, 2010.

Edersheim, Alfred. *Sketches of Jewish Social Life: Updated Edition*. Peabody, MA: Hendrickson Publishers, 1994.

Edington, Mark D. W. *Bivocational: Returning to the Roots of Ministry*. New York, NY: Church Publishing, 2018.

Elliott, John Y. *Our Pastor Has an Outside Job: New Strength for the Church Through Dual Role Ministry*. Valley Forge, PA: Judson Pr, 1980.

Estep, Jim, Gary Johnson, and David Roadcup. *Enjoy His People*. Joplin, MO: College Press Publishing Company, Inc., 2011.

———. *Lead His Church*. Joplin, MO: College Press Publishing Company, Inc., 2010.

Estep, Jim, David Roadcup, and Gary Johnson. *Answer His Call*. Joplin, MO: College Press Publishing Company, Inc., 2009.

Ferguson, Everett, ed. *Encyclopedia of Early Christianity, Second Edition*. New York, NY: Routledge, 1990.

Fisher, David C. *21st Century Pastor*. Grand Rapids, MI: Zondervan, 1996.

Flann, Rick, and Chris Pope. *Youth Ministry Bi-Vocational Survival Guide*. Bloomington, IN: WestBowPress, 2016.

Fleenor, Rob, and Mark S. Ziese. *The College Press NIV Commentary: Judges & Ruth*. Joplin, MO: College Press, 2008.

Friedeman, Matt. *Cutting Edge of the Kingdom: The Necessity of Dynamic Bi-Vocational Ministry*. 1 edition. CreateSpace Independent Publishing Platform, 2018.

Friesen, Garry. *Decision Making & the Will Of God*. Portland, OR: Multnomah, 1982.

Fry, Richard. "Millennials Are the Largest Generation in the U.S. Labor Force." *Pew Research Center*, April 11, 2018. Accessed May 18, 2018. http://www.pewresearch.org/fact-tank/2018/04/11/millennials-largest-generation-us-labor-force/.

Fulenwider, Ray. *The Servant-Driven Church: Releasing Every Member for Ministry*. Joplin, Mo: College Press Publishing Company, 1998.

Garland, David E. *Baker Exegetical Commentary on the New Testament: 1 Corinthians*. Grand Rapids, MI: Baker Academic, 2003.

Gilder, Ray. *Uniquely Bivocational-Understanding the Life of a Pastor Who Has a Second Job: For Bivocational Pastors and Their Churches*. Forest, VA: Salt & Light Publishing, 2013.

Gonzalez, Justo L. *The Story of Christianity, Volume 1: The Early Church to the Dawn of the Reformation*. San Francisco, CA: Harper & Row, 1984.

Gower, Ralph. *The New Manners & Customs of Bible Times*. Chicago, IL: Moody Publishers, 2005.

Greene, James. *The Dual Career Minister*. Cary, NC: Baptist State Convention of North Carolina, 1989.

Gross, Ashley, and Jon Marcus. "High-Paying Trade Jobs Sit Empty, While High School Grads Line Up For University." *NPR.Org*. Last modified April 25, 2018. Accessed April 26, 2018. https://www.npr.org/sections/ed/2018/04/25/605092520/high-paying-trade-jobs-sit-empty-while-high-school-grads-line-up-for-university.

Guinness, Os. *The Call: Finding and Fulfilling the Central Purpose of Your Life*. Nashville, TN: Thomas Nelson, 2003.

Haemig, Mary Jane. *The Annotated Luther, Volume 4: Pastoral Writings*. Minneapolis, MN: Fortress Press, 2016.

Halter, Hugh. *Bivo: A Modern-Day Guide for Bi-Vocational Saints*. Littleton, CO: Missio Publishing, 2013.

Halter, Hugh, and Matt Smay. *AND: The Gathered and Scattered Church*. Grand Rapids, MI: Zondervan, 2010.

Harris, Alex, and Brett Harris. *Do Hard Things: A Teenage Rebellion Against Low Expectations*. Colorado Springs, CO: Multnomah, 2008.

Harrison, R. K. *Old Testament Times: A Social, Political, and Cultural Context*. Grand Rapids, MI: Baker Books, 2005.

Herndon, Lamar. *Constructing Blue Collar Leaders in a White Collar World: A Biblical Perspective on Helping Bi-Vocational Church Leaders Become 21st Century Global Leaders.* Legacy Book Publishing, 2015.

Highland, James W. *Serving as a Bivocational Pastor.* Newburgh, IN: Newburgh Press, 2013.

————. *Serving as a Bivocational Pastor.* Newburgh Press, 2013.

Hughes, R. Kent. *Philippians, Colossians, and Philemon: The Fellowship of the Gospel and The Supremacy of Christ.* Wheaton, IL: Crossway, 2013.

Jackson, Dr George B. *Ordination Training for Bivocational Clergy.* San Bernardino, CA: CreateSpace Independent Publishing Platform, 2017.

Keller, Timothy. *Every Good Endeavor: Connecting Your Work to God's Work.* New York, NY: Penguin Books, 2014.

Keller, Timothy, Michael Horton, and Dane Calvin Ortlund. *Shaped by the Gospel: Doing Balanced, Gospel-Centered Ministry in Your City.* Grand Rapids, MI: Zondervan, 2016.

Keller, Timothy, and Kathy Keller. *The Meaning of Marriage: Facing the Complexities of Commitment with the Wisdom of God.* New York, NY: Penguin Books, 2013.

Kennedy, Michael. "Bivocational Ministry for the Sake of the Gospel: A Study of Effective Bivocational Ministry among the Churches of Christ and Christian Churches." DMin. Dissertation, Western Seminary, 2018.

Kinnaman, David, Dale Brown, and Brown. *The State of Pastors: How Today's Faith Leaders Are Navigating Life and Leadership in an Age of Complexity.* Ventura, CA: Barna Group, 2017.

Kinnaman, David, and Ralph Enlow. *What's Next for Biblical Higher Education.* Ventura, CA: Barna Group, 2017.

Kinnaman, David, and Christopher Kopka. *The Generosity Gap: How Christians' Perceptions and Practices of Giving Are Changing—and What It Means for the Church.* Ventura, CA: Barna Group, 2017.

Kinnaman, David, Jason Malec, and Roy Peterson. *The Bible in America: The Changing Landscape of Bible Perceptions and Engagement.* Ventura, CA: Barna Group, 2016.

Kittel, Gerhard, and Gerhard Friedrich, eds. *Theological Dictionary of the New Testament: Vol. VII.* Grand Rapids, MI: Eerdmans Pub Co, 1979.

Knowles, Victor, ed. *Repent or Perish: Selected Sermons & Essays of Archie Word.* Joplin, MO: College Press, 1994.

Lai, Patrick. *Tentmaking: The Life and Work of Business as Missions.* Downers Grove, IL: IVP Books, 2006.

LaRochelle, Robert. *Part-Time Pastor, Full-Time Church.* Cleveland, OH: Pilgrim Press, 2010.

Lewis, C.S. *The Screwtape Letters*. New York, NY: HarperOne, 2015.

Lincoln, Dr Andrew T. *Word Biblical Commentary: Ephesians*. Grand Rapids, MI: Zondervan, 2014.

London Jr., H.B., ed. *Refresh, Renew, Revive: How to Encourage Your Spirit, Strengthen Your Family, and Energize Your Ministry*. Colorado Springs, CO: Focus on the Family Publishing, 1996.

Long, Jesse C. *The College Press NIV Commentary: 1 & 2 Kings*. Joplin, MO: College Press, 2002.

Love, Bill R. *The Core Gospel*. Abilene, TX: ACU Press, 1992.

Lowery, James. *Bi-Vocationals: Men And Women Who Enrich the Human Ecology And the World Surrounding*. West Conshohocken, PA: Infinity Publishing, 2006.

Lowery, James L. *Case Histories of Tentmakers*. Wilton, CT: Morehouse-Barlow Co. , Inc., 1976.

Luther, Martin. *Three Treatises*. Philadelphia, PA: Fortress Press, 1990.

McCarty, Doran C., ed. *Meeting the Challenge of Bivocational Ministry*. Nashville, TN: Seminary Extension of the Southern Baptist Seminaries, 1996.

Miller, Paul E. *A Loving Life: In a World of Broken Relationships*. Wheaton, IL: Crossway, 2014.

———. *The J-Curve: Dying and Rising with Jesus in Everyday Life*. Wheaton, IL: Crossway, 2019.

Moore, Mark. *The College Press NIV Commentary: Acts*. Joplin, MO: College Press, 2011.

———. *The Chronological Life of Christ*. Joplin, MO: College Press, 2007.

Morris, Leon L. *1 Corinthians*. Downers Grove, IL: IVP Academic, 2008.

Muller, Richard A. *Dictionary of Latin and Greek Theological Terms: Drawn Principally from Protestant Scholastic Theology*. 1st edition. Grand Rapids, MI: Baker Book House, 2006.

Murch, James D. *Christians Only: A History of the Restoration Movement*. Cincinnati, OH: Standard Publishing, 1962.

Nelson, Tom. *Work Matters: Connecting Sunday Worship to Monday Work*. Wheaton, IL: Crossway, 2011.

Nerger, Steve. *Bivocational Church Planters*. 10th edition. Church Planter Resource Library, 2007.

Noll, Judy. *2013 Directory of the Ministry: A Yearbook of Christian Churches and Churches of Christ*. Springfield, IL: Specialized Christian Services, 2013.

———. *2017 Directory of the Ministry: A Yearbook of Christian Churches and Churches of Christ*. Springfield, IL: Specialized Christian Services, 2017.

North, James B. *A History of the Church from Pentecost to Present*. Joplin, MO: College Press Publishing Company, Inc., 1991.

———. *Union in Truth: An Interpretive History of the Restoration Movement*. Cincinnati, OH: Standard Publishing, 1994.

Osbeck, Kenneth W. *101 Hymn Stories*. Grand Rapids, MI: Kregel Publications, 1982.

Oster, Richard E. *The College Press NIV Commentary: 1 Corinthians*. Joplin, MO: College Press Publishing Company, Inc., 1995.

Picardo, Rosario. *Ministry Makeover: Recovering a Theology for Bi-Vocational Service in the Church*. Wipf & Stock, 2015.

Rainer, Thom. "One Key Reason Most Churches Do Not Exceed 350 in Average Attendance." *ThomRainer.Com*. Last modified March 25, 2015. Accessed May 28, 2017. http://thomrainer. com/2015/03/one-key-reason-churches-exceed-350-average-attendance/.

Rainer, Thom S. "Eight Characteristics of the New Bivocational Pastor." *ThomRainer.Com*, January 18, 2016. Accessed June 17, 2016. http://thomrainer.com/2016/01/eight-characteristics-of-the-new-bivocational-pastor/.

Rainer, Thom S., and Eric Geiger. *Simple Church: Returning to God's Process for Making Disciples*. Nashville, TN: B&H Books, 2011.

Randall, Robert L. *The Time of Your Life: Self/Time Management for Pastors*. Nashville, TN: Abingdon Press, 1994.

Roadcup, David, Gary Johnson, and Jim Estep. *Reflect: His Character*. Joplin, MO: College Press Publishing Company, Inc., 2009.

Robinson, Haddon, and Craig Brian Larson, eds. *The Art and Craft of Biblical Preaching: A Comprehensive Resource for Today's Communicators*. Grand Rapids, MI: Zondervan, 2005.

Rushford, Jerry. "The Wondrous Cross of Christ." *Heartlands Church*. Last modified 2011. Accessed June 14, 2018. http://www.heartlandschurch.org/sermons/2011/9/11/the-wondrous-cross-of-christ.

Russell, Bob. *After 50 Years of Ministry: 7 Things I'd Do Differently and 7 Things I'd Do the Same*. Chicago, IL: Moody Publishers, 2016.

Russell, Bob, and Rusty Russell. *When God Builds a Church: 10 Principles for Growing a Dynamic Church*. West Monroe, LA: Howard Books, 2000.

Ryken, Leland. *Redeeming the Time: A Christian Approach to Work and Leisure*. Grand Rapids, MI: Baker Books, 1995.

Schuler, Jon. "Antioch." *Antioch Church*. Accessed May 28, 2018. http://antiochspokane.com/.

Searcy, Dr Nelson, and Richard Jarman. *The Renegade Pastor's Guide to Time Management*. Boca Raton, FL: Church Leader Insights, 2017.

Seibert, Warren. *The Calling of a Part-Time Pastor*. Bloomington, IN: WestBowPress, 2016.

Shelley, Bruce. *Church History in Plain Language: Fourth Edition*. Nashville, TN: Thomas Nelson, 2012.

Sherman, Amy L., Steven Garber, and Reggie McNeal. *Kingdom Calling: Vocational Stewardship for the Common Good.* Downers Grove, IL: IVP Books, 2011.

Simson, Wolfgang, and George Barna. *The House Church Book: Rediscover the Dynamic, Organic, Relational, Viral Community Jesus Started.* Carol Stream, IL: BarnaBooks, 2009.

Sinek, Simon. *How Great Leaders Inspire Action,* 2009. Accessed June 14, 2018. https://www.ted.com/talks/simon_sinek_how_great_leaders_inspire_action.

———. *Start with Why: How Great Leaders Inspire Everyone to Take Action.* New York, NY: Portfolio, 2011.

Smith, Gordon T. *Courage and Calling: Embracing Your God-Given Potential.* Revised and Expanded edition. Downers Grove, IL: IVP Books, 2011.

Steinbron, Melvin. *The Lay Driven Church: How to Impower the People in Your Church to Share the Tasks of Ministry.* Ventura, CA: Regal Books, 1997.

Stevens, R. Paul. *The Other Six Days: Vocation, Work, and Ministry in Biblical Perspective.* Grand Rapids, MI: Eerdmans, 2000.

Stone, Roxanne. "Meet Those Who 'Love Jesus but Not the Church.'" *Barna Group.* Accessed May 28, 2018. https://www.barna.com/research/meet-love-jesus-not-church/.

Swenson, Vernon. *What Can Be Done?: Indigenous Bi-Vocational Ministry and Ministry Education by Extension.* 1st edition. Lima, Ohio: Fairway Press, 1991.

Temple, Helen. *Put in the Sickle: Stories of Bivocational and Home Mission Pastors in the United States.* Kansas City, MO: Beacon Hill, 1981.

Thiselton, Anthony C. *The First Epistle to the Corinthians.* Grand Rapids, MI: Eerdmans, 2013.

———. *The New International Greek Testament Commentary: The First Epistle to the Corinthians.* Grand Rapids, MI: Eerdmans, 2013.

Tracy, Brian. *Eat That Frog!: 21 Great Ways to Stop Procrastinating and Get More Done in Less Time.* Oakland, CA: Berrett-Koehler Publishers, 2017.

Tripp, Paul David. *Dangerous Calling: Confronting the Unique Challenges of Pastoral Ministry.* Wheaton, IL: Crossway, 2015.

Veith Jr, Gene Edward. *God at Work: Your Christian Vocation in All of Life.* Wheaton, IL: Crossway, 2011.

Verbrugge, Verlyn, ed. *New International Dictionary of New Testament Theology: Abridged Edition.* Abridged edition. Grand Rapids, Mich: Zondervan, 2003.

Walker, Williston. *A History of the Christian Church.* New York, NY: Simon Schuster Trade, 1970.

Walton, John H., ed. *Zondervan Illustrated Bible Backgrounds Commentary Vol 1: Genesis, Exodus, Leviticus, Numbers, Deuteronomy.* Grand Rapids, MI: Zondervan, 2009.

————, ed. *Zondervan Illustrated Bible Backgrounds Commentary Vol 3: 1 & 2 Kings, 1 & 2 Chronicles, Ezra, Nehemiah, Esther*. Grand Rapids, MI: Zondervan, 2009.

Warren, Rick. *The Purpose-Driven Church: Growth Without Compromising Your Message And Mission The Purpose-Driven*. Grand Rapids, MI: Zondervan, 1995.

Westrom, Tim, and Becca Westrom. *Help for the Bivocational Pastor: Thriving in Your Multifaceted Calling*. San Bernardino, CA: CreateSpace Independent Publishing Platform, 2017.

Wheeler, David R. "Higher Calling, Lower Wages: The Vanishing of the Middle-Class Clergy." *The Atlantic*. Last modified July 22, 2014. Accessed June 12, 2018. https://www.theatlantic. com/business/archive/2014/07/higher-calling-lower-wages-the-collapse-of-the-middle-class-clergy/374786/.

Winter, Mr Bruce W. *After Paul Left Corinth: The Influence of Secular Ethics and Social Change*. Grand Rapids, MI: Wm. B. Eerdmans Publishing Co., 2001.

Witherington, Ben. *Conflict and Community in Corinth: A Socio-Rhetorical Commentary on 1 and 2 Corinthians*. Grand Rapids, MI: Eerdmans, 1995.

Witherington III, Ben. *A Week in the Life of Corinth*. Downers Grove, IL: IVP Academic, 2012.

"Definition of VOCATION." Accessed March 3, 2018. https://www.merriam-webster.com/ dictionary/vocation.

"Vocation - Definition of Vocation in English | Oxford Dictionaries." *Oxford Dictionaries | English*. Accessed August 21, 2017. https://en.oxforddictionaries.com/definition/vocation.